D1274637

JANE FONDA'S WAR

Also by Mary Hershberger

Traveling to Vietnam:
American Peace Activists and the War

JANE FONDA'S WAR

A Political Biography of an Antiwar Icon

MARY HERSHBERGER

THE NEW PRESS

NEW YORK
LONDON

Published in the United States by The New Press, New York, 2005
Distributed by W. W. Norton & Company, Inc., New York

LIBRARY OF CONGRESS CATALOGING-IN-PUBLICATION DATA

Hershberger, Mary.
Jane Fonda's war : a political biography of an antiwar icon / Mary Hershberger.
p. cm.
Includes bibliographical references and index.
ISBN 1-56584-988-4 (hc.)
1. Fonda, Jane, 1937– 2. Political activists—United States—Biography.
3. Motion picture actors and actresses—United States—Biography.
4. Vietnamese Conflict, 1961–1975—Protest movements—United States.
5. Peace movements—United States. I. Title.

E840.8.F66H47 2005
959.704'31—dc22
[B] 2005045139

The New Press was established in 1990 as a not-for-profit alternative to the large, commercial publishing houses currently dominating the book publishing industry. The New Press operates in the public interest rather than for private gain, and is committed to publishing, in innovative ways, works of educational, cultural, and community value that are often deemed insufficiently profitable.

www.thenewpress.com

Composition by Westchester Book Composition

Printed in the United States of America

2 4 6 8 10 9 7 5 3 1

For Erica

CONTENTS

ACKNOWLEDGMENTS

I GREW INTERESTED in the controversy over Jane Fonda's antiwar activism when researching the activities of hundreds of Americans who traveled to Hanoi, North Vietnam, during the war years. They carried mail for the American prisoners of war in Hanoi and brought back information about the conduct of the war. Jane Fonda's 1972 visit to Hanoi was only one of these journeys that many Americans made. When Fonda returned from North Vietnam, some government figures and others singled her out and created a drumbeat of accusations against her that were never leveled against other antiwar activists. I became intrigued by an apparent gulf between these accusations and what Fonda had done. This book is the result of my efforts to find out what Fonda actually did as an antiwar activist and to discover how the allegations about her first emerged and then mushroomed into charges of treason—and worse.

To the greatest extent possible, I have relied on documents from this period rather than on memories that time can alter. I want to thank the researchers who helped me in this project, including archivists at the State Historical Society of Wisconsin, the Healy Library at the University of Massachusetts, the Ohio State University, and the Vanderbilt Television News Archives. Ruth Hubbard graciously granted me access to George Wald's papers, and Suzanne McCormick was helpful with other archival material. Reverend Calvin Van Kirk Hoyt provided documents relating to Jane Fonda's visit to his church in 1972. I also thank Walter and Jeanne Wilber for sharing their experiences, along with Edison Miller, Edwin Hawley, and other former prisoners of war. I want to thank Jerry Lembcke for his insights and for materials on the 1988 events in Waterbury, Connecticut. John Dean generously pointed me to relevant materials from the Nixon presidential papers, and Elvin Kraybill provided assistance with a key contact.

I owe special thanks to Robbie Lieberman and Charles Chatfield. I am grateful for the thoughtful comments of Carol Richardson, Susan Warrener Smith, Ruth Deacon, Madeleine Trichel, and Deborah Ling. I owe much to the staff at The New Press, including my editor, Marc Favreau, and Sarah Fan. Above all, I want to thank Dave, Jessica, and Erica Kraybill for their help and encouragement while this book was being written.

JANE FONDA'S WAR

1

BECOMING AN ACTIVIST

ACCORDING TO A RECENT Annenberg Survey, most Americans over the age of fifty associate Jane Fonda's name with the Vietnam War.[1] This is no accident of history. Rather, it is the political outcome of a decades-long effort to come to terms with the United States' defeat in Southeast Asia. The public memory of Jane Fonda's opposition to the war in Vietnam has become entangled with that defeat. Her name is evoked as a cautionary tale for celebrities and ordinary people alike that they, too, will face unremitting censure for speaking out against war. The Fonda-Vietnam connection has come to encapsulate a number of arguments about antiwar activism generally: that American citizens should never, ever travel to a country that the United States is waging a war against, that citizens who oppose a war also oppose the troops fighting that war, and that opposition to war is tantamount to treason. In short, Jane Fonda's name has become intimately bound up with a myth intended to intimidate democratic opposition to U.S. military ventures.

Defeat in Vietnam stripped the United States of a usable narrative of the war's origins, its course, and its conclusion. The preferred tale of triumph was replaced by grim photos of suffering civilians and sardonic quotations about "winning hearts and minds" in Vietnam. With the end of the war, explanations for national defeat emerged from different quarters. The most potent alleged that defeat came from within, that the nation lost the war because it was betrayed by antiwar activists, craven politicians, and, ultimately, a fearful public that lacked "will." In this narrative of betrayal from within, the antiwar figure of Jane Fonda was pressed into service to represent the alleged disloyalty of a wide swath of the American public. As a popular and attractive young actress who had once been a sex symbol within the walls of the military barracks but who rejected that role and became an antiwar activist—even traveling to the "enemy" territory—Jane Fonda became the perfect target for those who found defeat in Vietnam inexplicable and humiliating.

The narrative of internal betrayal generated its own supporting cast of stories, and these stories were not long in coming after the Vietnam War came to an end. These included charges that Washington had callously left American prisoners of war behind; that the antiwar movement was unpatriotic and had waged a vendetta against the troops; that antiwar activists had crudely spit on returning veterans; that Americans had given up too soon.[2] The stories about Jane Fonda grew to incorporate pieces of all these allegations. Fonda allegedly hated GIs, called on them to desert, and blamed them for atrocities. When she visited Vietnam in 1972, according to this narrative, she deliberately "betrayed" and taunted American prisoners of war (POWs) who were subsequently tortured by Vietnamese officers. One version of the stories asserts that American POWs in Hanoi spit on her in disdain. Another charges that POWs were killed because of her.

The stories about Fonda provided a convenient peg on which to hang all of the unresolved contradictions of defeat in Vietnam. The allegations about Fonda, first promulgated and encouraged by the Nixon White House, the FBI, and the Pentagon in the early 1970s, developed fully only in the late 1980s after "internal betrayal" as a cause of defeat in Vietnam was etched in the political culture by movies about the war and the POWs.[3] The Fonda myth has only grown with the passing of time. In the 1990s, the ease of posting anonymous tales on the Internet boosted the number and variety of allegations about Fonda. Stickers showing a drawing of Fonda's face continue to be sold by right-wing groups expressly for placing them in urinals, where it was not unusual to find them on military bases.[4]

The allegations that Fonda betrayed her country and caused harm to American POWs in Hanoi are false. In the early 1970s, Fonda did become a well-known opponent of the war in Vietnam, especially of its heavy reliance on massive civilian bombing.[5] She was a skillful organizer who helped establish the Indochina Peace Campaign and raised funds for Vietnam Veterans Against the War and its activities, including the 1971 Winter Soldier Investigation. She also became a tireless activist on behalf of rights for American GIs. In 1972, she traveled to Hanoi, the capital of North Vietnam, to film life in the war zone and to investigate United States' bombing of Vietnam's dikes. Finally, Fonda used her celebrity status to educate Americans about the war and to urge them to oppose it. Even after her controversial trip to Vietnam in 1972, she remained a sought-after speaker who drew tens of thousands of listeners at churches, universities, GI coffeehouses, and public rallies.

Many Americans deeply respected Jane Fonda's courage and commitment. Indeed, in 1973, after she went to Hanoi, the Gallup poll first listed her as one of the most admired women in America, a position that she held for years.[6] Yet by the late 1980s and following, Fonda's image was deeply dented by claims that she had committed treason, that she had caused American pilots in Hanoi to be tortured and even killed. These claims tapped into powerful emotions left over from the Vietnam War era and eroded public awareness of Fonda's actual antiwar work.

This book is an effort to document Fonda's antiwar work, to account for how and why she became an opponent of the war in Vietnam, and to describe her activities as an antiwar activist. It is also an effort to understand the context in which the false allegations about Fonda arose and how they have changed over time.

The story of Jane Fonda and the war in Vietnam is more complex than the simple images imposed by the myths of war. Fonda was, in fact, not living in the United States as the war in Vietnam intensified during the 1960s. She lived in Paris from 1963 to 1969, a period when the U.S. military presence and bombing in Vietnam reached its height and public debate over the war sharpened. In Paris, she made several films, including the science-fiction sex fantasy *Barbarella,* married filmmaker Roger Vadim, and at first paid scant attention to the war. There was good reason not to. Fonda, born in 1937, had grown up during the Cold War era of McCarthyism and its politics of anticommunism. Her father, well-known actor Henry Fonda, had friends who were blacklisted in Hollywood for their liberal political ideas. Jane Fonda responded to the red-baiting of the McCarthy era by becoming politically cynical, not even reading the newspapers because, as she put it, "Why bother? What could I possibly do to change anything?" She followed the footsteps of her father into the theatrical and film world and viewed her filmmaking as strictly entertainment.[7]

But as she lived in Paris during the 1960s, Fonda looked back across the Atlantic to see a United States that was changing. The civil rights movement and the antiwar movement were remaking America. Ordinary citizens were learning tactics of organized protest, they were holding massive public rallies for civil rights, and they were marching in the streets and defying unjust laws, risking their own comfort and security. French newsreels began to broadcast pictures of American crowds carrying signs against the war in Vietnam. "All over French television," Fonda said, "one would see tens of thousands of American people in the streets protesting the war. And I remember how astonished I was to see how changed things had gotten. And it was the people in the streets of America who forced me to begin to think about Vietnam."[8]

The people in the antiwar crowds that Fonda saw on French newsreels included many women whose presence Fonda noted as a marker of how much had changed in the United States. "I watched women leading marches," she said later. "I watched women getting beaten up. I watched women walking up to the bayonets that were surrounding the Pentagon and they were not afraid. It was the soldiers who were afraid. I will never forget that experience. It completely changed me."[9]

In Paris, Fonda began to read books about Vietnam and pay closer attention to the news. She read Jonathan Schell's *Village of Ben Suc* and Fred Branfman's *Voices from the Plain of Jars.* Schell's book described the wanton destruction of a village under the control of an officer who assured Schell that the "Asian mind is completely different from what we know as the Western mind." Fred Branfman described the horrific bombing that he witnessed in Laos that turned a once-thriving area into a moonscape of bomb craters. Other books that influenced her thinking on Vietnam included Howard Zinn's *Vietnam: The Logic of Withdrawal,* Frances FitzGerald's *Fire in the Lake,* about Vietnamese history and culture, and David Halberstam's *Best and the Brightest,* on the personalities and the political culture of the government leaders in the United States who had begun the war. Periodicals like *Christian Century, The Nation, Ramparts,* the *Village Voice,* and *Liberation* carried regular reports and commentary on the war. Fonda got a subscription to *Ramparts,* a magazine written for Catholic laity, and began to read it, including one of its first articles on Vietnam called "All for Vietnam," written by antiwar activist Tom Hayden, whom she later married.[10]

While Fonda was in Paris rethinking the war in Vietnam, opinion polls showed that over half of all Americans now believed the war was a mistake. GIs were deserting the Army in record numbers. Tens of thousands of draft and GI deserters went to Canada, but there were over five hundred in Sweden and at least fifty in Paris, where they spoke at public rallies about the relentless bombing in Vietnam and the massacres there. The American GIs in

Paris had political asylum but little else, and sympathetic supporters opened a small GI office to raise money and help them with lodging and food. Fonda contributed money and material aid to the GI office in Paris and talked with the GIs who passed through. She developed a deep respect for the courage of the antiwar GIs.

As American casualties climbed into the thousands between 1965 and 1969, opposition to sending more American "boys" to Vietnam had grown wide and deep. Republican Congressman George H. W. Bush sent his constituents a newsletter in 1967, saying "I frankly am lukewarm on sending more American boys to Viet Nam. I want more involvement by Asians."[11] In 1969, in response to rising opposition to GI deaths, President Nixon implemented "Vietnamization," a program of slow withdrawal of American troops who were replaced by young Vietnamese men to fill the ranks of a newly-trained Vietnamese army. The French had tried this same tactic in the 1950s before leaving Vietnam in defeat: withdrawing French troops and replacing them with French-trained Vietnamese ones to fight the Vietnamese independence forces. Now, struggling for an elusive victory, the Americans followed the French example in hoping that Vietnamese deaths would replace the increasingly unpopular American ones.[12]

Fonda studied the course of the war in Vietnam for over two years before speaking out publicly against it. When she became pregnant with her first child in 1968, she felt she had an additional reason to work against the violence of war. In early 1969, she left Paris and flew to California with her infant daughter to make the film *They Shoot Horses, Don't They?* Her marriage to Roger Vadim was breaking up, and when the filming was over she decided to stay in the United States.

In November of that year, Fonda heard news of the massacre in My Lai, where American GIs had killed over three hundred villagers eighteen months earlier. Some Vietnamese said, bitterly, that the massacre was an "ordinary" one and expressed surprise that Americans saw it as unusual, but American newspapers printed graphic photos of My Lai and drew a public outcry that startled Pentagon and White House officials. "You can understand a little bit of this," Secretary of Defense Melvin Laird said to National Security Advisor Henry Kissinger of the massacre, "but you shouldn't kill that many." Laird said that he would like to "sweep it under the rug," but the pictures of "the atrocity thing" wouldn't allow that. "There are so many kids lying there," Laird said of the photos.[13]

Fonda had already developed a firm opposition to the war in Vietnam, an opposition strengthened by meeting young American GIs in Paris and by joining their support network there. Now, back in California, Fonda learned about a similar network of supporters: GI coffeehouses in the United States that had become an important part of the energetic antiwar movement within the army. At a party one night in Los Angeles, Fonda heard someone talking about these GI coffeehouses and she asked him for more information. The person turned out to be Fred Gardner, a veteran and antiwar activist who had started the first GI coffeehouse near Fort Jackson, South Carolina, in 1968.

The coffeehouse movement originated in informal gatherings by antiwar enlisted men in Fort Jackson, an Army base in South Carolina that had sent thousands of young men to Vietnam. When the base commander at Fort Jackson refused to allow Gardner and other GIs to hold meetings where criticism of the war was expressed, they called for a prayer service in the base chapel with the express aim of praying for an end to the war. Over thirty GIs gathered inside the chapel as Fort Jackson military police ringed it. When two GIs dropped to their knees and began to pray, the military police moved in and arrested them. Charges against the two, Robert Tatar and Steven Kline, were dropped, but the commander still refused to allow them to meet on the base, so Fred Gardner opened a meeting place for GIs outside Fort Jackson and called it the "UFO Coffeehouse." GIs liked the UFO, and by late 1969, there were over twenty other GI coffeehouses near military bases across the nation.[14]

The coffeehouses were run by veterans and civilians who offered GIs a friendly environment, food, nonalcoholic beverages, entertainment, and antiwar literature. They published GI newspapers and provided counseling on GI rights. Some draftees were deeply alienated by their abrupt loss of the ordinary rights of free speech and association in the military and the coffeehouses offered them a safe place where they could live, for a time at least, as if these rights were restored.[15]

The Army tried to shut down the coffeehouses, even though they were located on private property. In the case of the Shelter Half, a coffeehouse in the city of Tacoma, Washington, the army charged that it was "a source of dissident counseling and literature and other activities inimical to good morale, order, and discipline within the Armed Forces" and ordered its local staff to appear before the Army's Disciplinary Control Board. The staff argued that they were supporting the troops and used the resulting national publicity to solicit funds to pay their legal bills.[16] The Shelter Half coffeehouse stayed open. The courts usually prohibited the Army from closing down the off-base coffeehouses, but the legal harassment created a constant financial struggle. There were other ways of closing them down, too. One coffeehouse, the Covered Wagon in Mountain Home, Idaho, was burned to the ground the day after someone broke into it and wrote the words "This is just a warning" on the wall.[17]

Fonda traveled around the country to visit these coffeehouses, getting to know the people who ran them and talking to the GIs who came there. Her visits were informal and low-key, but as word of her interest spread, she began to receive invitations from coffeehouses across the nation, asking her to come and speak with GIs at informal meetings. Fonda also began her long support of the antiwar movement by making significant contributions to the United States Servicemen's Fund, which provided start-up and some operating funds for the coffeehouses.

By mid-1970, Fonda was virtually a full-time supporter of the GI and antiwar movement. She attended antiwar events at churches, on university campuses, and at GI coffeehouses from Seattle to Miami, from Plainfield, Vermont, to San Antonio, Texas, and in small towns across the nation. The meetings on campuses were informal and often held in student lounges, with students filling the armchairs and sitting on the floor. Fonda usually sat on the floor with them, joining antiwar activists, teachers, and veterans who were experienced in public speaking and in talking to students. After a brief talk by one or more of the speakers, the meeting typically turned into an open discussion, with people from the audience asking questions or speaking about their experiences. Often young Vietnam veterans, now students, were present, and the audience solicited their experiences as having a validity that no expert or celebrity could match: the veterans were the real celebrities at these events.[18]

Fonda kept a low profile in the antiwar movement at first. She did not speak at public rallies, and her appearances at GI coffeehouses or on college campuses were informal conversations. But all that changed when President Nixon summoned the news cameras to the White House on April 30, 1970, and announced to a shocked nation that he had ordered the bombing and a ground invasion of Cambodia. That the U.S. military was bombing Cambodia did not especially surprise Fonda. She had already heard details of the secret bombing from eyewitnesses like Vietnam veteran Donald Duncan, who wrote articles about his war experiences in Southeast Asia for *Ramparts* and was a well-known speaker in the antiwar movement.

Donald Duncan had been a master sergeant in the Special Forces, better known then as Green Berets. After ten years in the

Army, Duncan, once a fierce anticommunist, turned down a commission to rank of captain in 1965, left the Army, and published an indictment of the war in *Ramparts*. In mid-1966, when Washington officials were denying that the United States was bombing Cambodia, he joined a fact-finding delegation to Cambodia called Americans Want to Know. The group was organized by Women Strike for Peace, which had been sending American delegations to Southeast Asia and Hanoi since 1965 and had begun to carry mail for American POWs in Hanoi and their families. In Cambodia, Duncan's delegation itself barely escaped being bombed by weapons that Duncan, as a military officer, identified as "trademark U.S.A.: American bombs, American rockets, American napalm."[19]

When Americans Want to Know returned to the United States in August 1966 with photographs and other documented evidence that the U.S. military was bombing Cambodia, reporters pressed State Department officials about their bombing denials. Within days, a State Department official grudgingly acknowledged that American planes were bombing Cambodia, but he said it was merely an error; the military thought they were bombing Vietnam, but they had just discovered that their maps in Saigon were "wrong." It was all an innocent mistake, the spokesman said with a straight face.[20]

The secret bombing of Cambodia continued, but when Nixon announced a full-blown ground invasion of that country in 1970, opposition came swiftly—from within his own administration. Two hundred and fifty State Department officials sent a letter of protest to Secretary of State William Rogers. Two of Henry Kissinger's principal aides, Roger Morris and Anthony Lake, resigned over the invasion.[21] The day after Nixon's announcement, the Senate Armed Forces Committee voted to repeal the 1964 Gulf of Tonkin Resolution, which had authorized the invasion of Vietnam. The full Senate voted to repeal the resolution the next month, and the full House did so by year's end. The invasion of Cambodia prompted the Massachusetts Legislature to pass a law that prohibited young men from Massachusetts from being sent to combat zones outside the United States for more than sixty days without a congressional declaration of war.[22]

The invasion of Cambodia shocked the nation. Students at hundreds of universities across the country went on strike in protest. Young men and women walked out of their classes and held rallies against the war, where they encouraged draftees to resist the draft that might send them to Cambodia. Their protest rankled the president. He had not expected the largest student strike that the United States had ever known to follow his invasion, and he went on the offensive. He couldn't publicly attack Kissinger's aides who had resigned, or the two hundred and fifty State Department employees who sent the letter of protest, or the Senate Armed Forces Committee, or the entire Massachusetts Legislature. But he could attack the students.

On the afternoon of May 1, Nixon went to the Pentagon to talk to employees there about the invasion of Cambodia. He told his audience what he thought of those students who objected to his war. "You see these bums, you know, blowing up the campuses," he said, warming to his subject. "Listen, the boys that are on the college campuses today are the luckiest people in the world, going to the greatest universities, and here they are burning up the books, storming around about this issue. You name it—get rid of the war, there will be another one."[23] The next day, Nixon held a meeting with his aides and told them to "stand tough." No matter how many people took to the streets to protest the invasion, he told them, they should not give an inch. He told them what words to use in the future: war words, traitor words. They should say that those protesting the war were "giving aid and comfort to the enemy." They should draw the line "hard and deep" and use accusing words like "treason," he said. "Use that word," he urged, "don't worry about divisiveness. Having drawn the sword, don't take it out—stick it in hard . . . hit 'em in the gut."[24]

The president's inflammatory references to students as "bums" emboldened supporters of the war to take steps they may otherwise not have taken. One of these steps was taken by Ohio governor James Rhodes, who called the National Guard to the campus at the University of Kent State in Kent, Ohio. The guardsmen carried loaded guns with bayonets fixed. They may have felt threatened, but the milling students they fired into on May 4 were not threatening them. Four people in the crowd were killed, thirteen were wounded, and one was paralyzed. Not a single guardsman was injured. The White House only added to the national tension when it issued a cold impersonal statement saying that "when dissent turns to violence it invites tragedy."[25] Nor did it help when the president said several days later at a press conference that "perhaps bums is too kind a word." It was left to the grieving father of one of the slain students at Kent State to put a human face on the war that had killed his son. "My child was not a bum," he tearfully told a reporter in a remark aimed not at the guardsmen, nor even at Governor Rhodes, but straight at the White House.[26]

Fonda was at the University of New Mexico in Albuquerque when the nation reeled under the Cambodia invasion and the killings at Kent State. She was scheduled to meet with students in a lounge in the student union in the informal setting that she always used. But student leaders at the university came to Fonda and told her that they had called an emergency meeting because of the invasion of Cambodia, and they expected a lot of students to attend. They asked Fonda to speak at that meeting, where they planned to call for a campus-wide student strike in solidarity with other striking campuses. For the first time, Fonda agreed to speak at a public rally. That evening, over seven hundred students packed into the room where Fonda spoke. Behind her, some students had scrawled in huge letters the word "Strike" on the blackboard. On the podium before her was a sign that said simply "Vietnam."

When Fonda spoke against the war in public for the first time, she developed a method that came to characterize her speeches against the war. She began by talking to the crowd of students in Albuquerque about recent war reporting from Vietnam. Then she talked about the gap between conventional news and news from alternative sources. For example, she told the students that, although the president and the media presented this recent invasion of Cambodia as something new, American planes had been secretly bombing Cambodia for years. Americans who had gone to Cambodia, she said, had seen the results of that bombing in the past. Military pilots confirmed that they were still assigned those bombing raids. And then she talked to the students about the GIs in the war and how a lot of them did not support the war; indeed, many of them opposed it. They needed support, she said. She said that the students could work for peace in Vietnam by supporting GI rights. Armed Forces Day was coming up, she told them, and that would be a good day to organize support for antiwar GIs. And then she talked about the rage that many people felt at the moment and how important it was that their actions remain nonviolent. "Let the violence stay with those who are really violent—the police and the administration," she said. She ended by telling them not to write off conventional politics and to "write letters every two weeks to the president and congressional representatives."[27]

After Fonda finished her brief remarks, over one hundred students decided to march to University President Ferrel Heady's nearby home and demand that he shut down the university to protest the invasion of Cambodia and the killings at Kent State. They asked that President Heady send a telegram to President Nixon protesting the invasion of Cambodia and the bombing of Vietnam. They asked that the Reserve Officer Training Corps be removed from the Albuquerque campus and that the National Guard not be called in. In memory of the slain students at Kent State University, they called their group "They Shoot Students, Don't They?" paraphrasing the title of Fonda's most recent film, for which she had received an Academy Award nomination and which had played in Albuquerque earlier that month.[28]

University president Heady did send a telegram to President Nixon protesting the Cambodian invasion, and the students did call a university-wide strike. The campus remained calm. But the governor of New Mexico, David Cargo, ordered the National Guard to break up the student strike. On May 8, a National Guard unit came to the University of New Mexico with bayonets fixed on their rifles. They moved menacingly toward students who were standing outside Union Hall. Bill Norlander, a television news cameraman, was standing on the porch with some of the students when one of the guardsmen reached out and stabbed him with his bayonet. Norlander tried to escape, but three guardsmen closed in on him, jabbing him with their bayonets and shoving him backward. He jumped off the porch, leaving behind him a trail of blood. Students fled the campus with guardsmen pursuing them. The guardsmen bayoneted nine others, including a student on crutches.[29]

Similar events occurred on other campuses as antiwar organizers called for a massive protest rally in Washington on May 9, 1970. They asked Fonda to welcome the crowd, and she agreed to do it. Early that morning, over 100,000 people poured into the city, gathering in grief and anger at the war in Vietnam, the killings at Kent State, and the invasion of Cambodia. To begin her welcoming remarks, Fonda took her cue from the president. He had called the student war protesters "bums," handing Fonda a usable reference. "Greetings, fellow bums," she called out to the cheering throng and then she spoke briefly about the war. Her remarks set the tone for speakers that day who were, as one reporter put it, "all against violence, more passionately so than any from the Capital's authorities or President Nixon himself."[30] And the crowd roared in approval when several hundred people marched into sight under banners that read "Federal Employees for Peace" and "Federal Bums Against the War."[31]

After the May 9 rally in D.C. Fonda returned to her tour of coffeehouses and universities a changed person. She no longer shied away from public speaking and her language about the war and about the administration became more personal. When she visited a coffeehouse near Fort Hood, Texas, right after the D.C. rally, she took some leaflets, went boldly to the east gate of the base, and began to hand out the materials, knowing full well that the military claimed the right to control all printed materials on the base and had arrested GIs who handed out antiwar literature. Her leaflets were not profane, violent, or obscene. But they did have a clear perspective:

> Last week at Kent State University, four students involved in a peaceful demonstration were shot and killed. Another died of bayonet wounds. These deaths and the thousands of injuries caused by police violence are a direct result of the government's repression of the antiwar movement so it may continue its dirty war uninterrupted. We demand an end to the use of police, national guard and federal troops to suppress popular movements.[32]

A military police officer, Lieutenant John T. Hoffman, arrived immediately and told Fonda that she was under arrest for "breaking Fort Hood regulations," presumably regulations against antiwar speech. Hoffman ordered Fonda into his military police car and took her to the provost marshal's office, where she was detained and given a letter warning her that she would be fined five hundred dollars and given six months imprisonment if she returned to the base.

As soon as the provost marshal released her, Fonda went to the nearby GI coffeehouse, the Oleo Strut, run by Vietnam War veterans and former Fort Hood soldiers David Kline and Rod Hawkins. News of her arrest drew reporters to the Oleo Strut and Fonda spoke to them bluntly. "I'm not here as a movie star—as a publicity stunt," she told them. "I am a person who is fighting against the war and for GI rights. I went on Fort Hood because GIs aren't allowed to distribute literature there." When the reporters began to ask her about the violence at Kent State, Fonda turned their attention in an unexpected direction. "It is easier to shoot students when our national leaders brand them as bums and buffoons," she said. "I think Nixon is as guilty of pulling those triggers as the National Guard."[33]

The language that Fonda used in her speeches often responded directly to the rhetoric of the administration. She took phrases from the president's and vice president's speeches and turned them upside down. For example, Richard Nixon and his vice president Spiro Agnew had run on a campaign of "law and order," and Agnew habitually couched his incendiary blasts against liberals and antiwar activists in the same language. After a mob violently attacked peaceful antiwar marchers in New York City and after the attacks on students on college campuses, Fonda began to hold the vice president to his own standard by calling on the courts to indict him for "crossing state lines to incite riots." She referred to Agnew as "the nation's most unguided missile." She also reached inside the president's rhetoric about national "honor" requiring the war's continuation to suggest a more personal motivation. "Nixon's worried about being the first president to lose a war," she told many crowds. "He might be the first president to lose his army."[34]

As she began to speak in public, Fonda gained a reputation for strong antiwar speeches that, combined with her generosity in funding antiwar causes and her ability to draw large crowds, made her an ideal speaker and fund-raiser for antiwar groups on campuses and in the community. She didn't insist on being the main attraction and she was willing to speak at small events. She could keep an exhausting schedule. She was soon constantly booked at universities, churches, GI coffeehouses, community colleges, and public rallies.

As a popular entertainment figure, her appeal cut across political categories: she helped connect the antiwar movement to the cultural mainstream. The people who turned out to hear Fonda speak were also turning out to see her latest film, *They Shoot Horses, Don't They?* In the film, directed by Sydney Pollack, Fonda played a young woman, Gloria, whose tough spirit was ground down by the brutality of a Depression-era dance marathon that offered a purse of fifteen hundred dollars to the couple that remained standing on the dance floor after all others collapsed. Based on a 1935 book of the same title by Horace McCoy, the film is a tale of greed and callousness, in which the public exhibition of the destitute helps the comfortable audience feel both pity and entertainment as they buy tickets to gawk at the impoverished and exhausted dancers, comforted with the assurance that part of their ticket payment would go to the hungry winners. "The audience wants to see a little misery so they can feel a little better about themselves," the organizer tells Gloria. "That's the American way," he adds.

They Shoot Horses is one of the most troubling pictures of the Vietnam War era and it bears remarkable resemblance to war. The marathon dancers are told that they can survive their ordeal by dancing to "victory." They are as regimented as soldiers, taking brief respites from their grueling work in barracks-like rooms. The bodies of the downed dancers lie like fallen soldiers on the battlefield, with doctors and nurses on the sidelines ready to patch them up and send them back to the dance floor, where they wear the glassy-eyed stare of the shell-shocked soldier. Audiences in 1970 were not indifferent to this stark symbolism. *They Shoot Horses* played to large audiences across the country and on university and college campuses in the early months and summer of 1970. Fonda's strong performance in the film, in which her character rejected a system of suffering and exploitation, was the political image of Fonda that her audiences brought with them when they came to hear her speak about the war in Vietnam. The film established Fonda as a person to whom politics mattered before she first spoke out publicly on the war.[35]

In her coffeehouse visits, Fonda often heard GIs speak with frustration about the straitened life that conscription had imposed on them, including their rights to free speech. Barred from expressing their own values and beliefs, subjected to military codes that often appeared arbitrary and punitive, some GIs grew restive in the military and felt that society offered them little support while the Army relied on threats of courts-martial to keep their politics in line. Fonda said that listening to the GIs in the coffeehouses provided her with ample evidence that "opponents to the war are not simply those who are deserting or burning their draft cards or filing for conscientious objector status. The military is filled with men who are against the war."[36]

GIs were in a difficult position in 1970. The draft that dragooned them into the military was ending as Vietnamization shifted the cost of the war onto young Vietnamese men. These GIs were the last crop of draftees in a war that some of their families, friends, and role models opposed. The respected Dr. Benjamin Spock was openly urging young men to resist the draft. Boxer Muhammad Ali, heavyweight champion of the world, refused to participate in the Vietnam War. For that refusal, the World Boxing Association stripped Ali of his title and boxing license—

barring him from boxing during his prime years. Ali bore his penalty like a badge of honor. Even conservative members of Congress began to publicly distance themselves from the war that seemed to roll on because President Nixon did not want to be, as he put, "the first president to lose a war." GI complaints multiplied, but the military brass, facing the transition to an all-volunteer army, was unsure of the end results of that transition and preferred to ignore complaints by GIs, who would rotate out in a year anyway.

Within the military, soldiers protested political restrictions, sometimes at personal cost. Indeed, only relentless protest, which led to courts-martial for some and dishonorable discharges for others, brought them the right to attend off-base antiwar events. For example, when Lieutenant Henry Howe attended an off-base protest rally at Texas Western College in 1965, he was arrested and court-martialed merely for being present at the public rally.[37] But by 1970, so many GIs attended antiwar events off base that it would have been too costly to arrest them all.

Some GIs went further in claiming constitutional rights to free speech in the military. In 1966, three soldiers in the Second Armored Division at Fort Hood, Texas, called a news conference and said that they would perform all their assigned military duties in the United States, but would refuse to obey their Vietnam travel orders.[38] Military police arrested them—at the antiwar rally where they were scheduled to speak—and put them in the stockade. The three soldiers appealed to the courts. Their attorney argued that Congress had not declared war and the three could not constitutionally be required to go to Vietnam. He pointed to a 1952 case in which President Truman seized steel mills when their workers went on strike. Truman said that the national emergency of the Korean War gave him the power to seize the mills, but the Supreme Court disagreed, ruling that the seizure was unconstitutional because Congress had not declared war in Korea. The attorney for the Fort Hood Three argued that if the president could not take over a steel industry without a congressional declaration of war, then he could not take over the lives of citizens without a congressional declaration of war. It made a good argument, but the judge cut off the attorney and dismissed the case. He said that it was not the function of the courts "to challenge the validity, the wisdom or the propriety of the Commander in Chief of our armed forces abroad."[39]

With the Army holding the threat of courts-martial over GIs for activities that were protected in civilian life, soldiers chafed under the restrictions of enlisted life. Some were detained and arrested for distributing pamphlets that contained nothing more than the Bill of Rights or congressional petitions; some were even arrested for flashing the "V" peace sign. The military even claimed rights over their mail. In May 1969, someone at the Pentagon wrote a memo called "Guidance on Dissent" that ordered Army commanders in Vietnam to confiscate personal mail "suspected" of carrying "antiwar or other dissident publications sent to soldiers there." The directive was supposed to be secretly implemented but someone leaked a copy to a reporter who wrote a news story about it. The United States Postal Service protested that no government agency could seize mail without a court order and pointed out that no such order had been given. Pentagon officials offered no defense of their illegal seizure of mail, saying only that the leak of the memo raised concerns that Army communication "might have been compromised."[40]

As she heard more and more complaints about these policies from GIs at coffeehouses and on military bases, Fonda decided to do something concrete. The problem, as she saw it, was that GIs had little voice and no independent representation when they faced harassment from officers or had a conflict with military regulations. She set out to give them representation and a voice. Because the American judicial system had abandoned constitutional oversight of military laws, she turned to elected representatives in Congress. Fonda believed that the military might be responsive if members of Congress took an interest in specific GI cases.

In June 1970, between her speaking engagements, Fonda went to Congress with two colleagues, Donald Duncan, the former Green Beret, and Mark Lane, an attorney who had written *Rush to Judgement,* a rebuttal to the Warren Commission's report on the Kennedy assassination. On Capitol Hill, they talked to Senator Charles Goodell, chair of the Senate Subcommittee on Veteran Affairs. Fonda proposed that they set up an independent office in Washington that would act as a clearinghouse for GI allegations of mistreatment. She said that she would raise funds for the office, which would be called the GI Office. Senator Goodell offered his support as did three other senators: Marlow Cook from Kentucky, Alan Cranston from California, and J. William Fulbright from Arkansas.

The GI Office opened on August 8, 1970, with a mandate to "represent servicemen and women whose rights have been violated by the military." The office was managed by Donald Duncan and Marilyn Moorhead, who worked with the United States Servicemen's Fund. Duncan and Moorhead said that it was "a tragic irony that men and women in uniform, sworn to uphold and defend the Constitution—give their lives for it, if necessary—are the last to derive any benefit or protection guaranteed by it."[41] Over the next months, Fonda raised over $50,000 for the GI Office.

Until the draft was completely phased out in 1972, the GI Office sent investigators to army bases around the country to meet with GIs and collect information about allegations of mistreatment and harassment. Attorneys in the GI Office documented charges and wrote reports for representatives on Capitol Hill, who referred the charges to congressional committees, including the Senate Armed Forces Committee, which could press the military for better treatment of GIs and improved procedures.

Fonda tracked the GI Office work closely and continued to raise money for its operations.

Fonda's support for enlisted men's rights was popular with many GIs, who wanted greater freedom within the armed forces. Indeed, opposition to the war within the army was the principal impetus for discarding the draft system. GIs who returned from Vietnam, often tired and disillusioned, sometimes found their greatest welcome home within the antiwar movement, where they discovered people who were knowledgeable about Vietnam and who supported them.[42]

In mid-June 1970, Fonda began filming *Klute* in New York City. She organized her life so that she could work on the set and, using the telephone, carry on without interruption the fund-raising and schedule-planning that her antiwar commitments required. During the day, she worked on the movie set. Evenings found her speaking at antiwar events and holding fund-raisers in the New York City area. Whenever she could, especially on weekends, she flew to speaking engagements around the country. Alan Pakula, the film's director, said he was initially concerned that Fonda's mind would not be on the film because of her time-consuming antiwar work. Fonda would be making endless phone calls on the set, he said, when he would come to her to say that the crew was ready for her scene. She would stand quietly and concentrate for a short time and then be completely ready, Pakula said. When the scene was finished, she would return to her phone, finishing her dozens of calls for the day.[43]

In the summer of 1970, after helping to set up the GI Office, Fonda agreed to work with Vietnam Veterans Against the War (VVAW). That organization was made up of thousands of Vietnam Veterans who planned antiwar actions and rallies. The group was formed in 1967 in New York City when some veterans, just home from Vietnam, found themselves together at a planning meeting for the national Spring Mobilization Against the War. The veterans had participated in antiwar rallies, but they wanted an organization of people who shared directly their experiences of Vietnam. Now, in 1970, the veterans who ran VVAW wanted to increase their visibility, but the usual route for growth was closed to them because the Veterans Administration refused to give them its lists of discharged veterans, lists it routinely gave to the American Legion and Veterans of Foreign Wars. So VVAW needed to create its own publicity in order to reach out to its natural constituency.

They found a good ally in Fonda. She was willing to speak at every coffeehouse in the country, to go on military bases even in the face of arrest, and she was fast becoming a sought-after speaker at community events and at universities. Most importantly, she had national visibility. When Al Hubbard, executive secretary of VVAW, asked Fonda to help them in the summer of 1970, she agreed; it was a natural extension of the work she had been doing with GIs for months. Fonda earned the respect of the veterans and other antiwar activists because she didn't coast on her name recognition, didn't ask for any favors, and shouldered even the most mundane organizing activities—stuffing envelopes, for example, or answering the office telephone. "That lady was out there working in coffeehouses without telling anybody who she was," Jan Barry, a founder of VVAW, said admiringly.[44]

Fonda knew that she was under FBI surveillance and that working with VVAW would increase that surveillance. In fact, FBI agents had immediately noticed VVAW in 1967 when the group placed an ad in the *New York Times* that read: "We are veterans of the Viet-Nam War. We believe that this 'conflict' in which our country is now engaged is wrong, unjustifiable, and contrary to the principle of self-determination on which this nation was founded."[45] Secretary of Defense Robert McNamara saw the veterans' ad and was furious. McNamara picked up his phone and called J. Edgar Hoover at the FBI and told him that he wanted every single signer of the ad investigated. He wanted the files on those people sent to him. Hoover was pleased to comply. He put the FBI on the case and personally delivered the veterans' files to McNamara. After that, the Army joined the FBI in investigating and infiltrating VVAW, which the FBI called "possibly the first antiwar group formed by veterans of an American war still being waged." They went after it with the same zeal with which they hounded civil rights activists.[46]

Over the course of 1970, Fonda used every national talk-show appearance she could arrange to talk to viewers about VVAW. At the VVAW national office that summer and fall, they began to notice that every time Fonda was on a national talk show, their membership rose noticeably. Beyond numbers, Fonda's media appearances brought in committed activists. For example, Ed Damato first heard about Vietnam Veterans Against the War when Fonda was a guest on the *Dick Cavett Show*. Damato joined the group and later became a national coordinator and then its president. Scott Camil, who had been a forward observer with the First Marine Division in Vietnam, went to hear Fonda speak at the University of Florida in Gainesville "to see what a movie actress looked like." But when he heard Fonda, he decided to join VVAW. He went on to become its Southeast Coordinator and one of its most effective organizers.[47]

It was Fonda's work on behalf of the rights of GIs to free speech and association that drew her into the antiwar movement. She supported GI coffeehouses by holding fund-raisers, traveling frequently to a variety of them across the nation, and publicizing their presence near army bases. Her work on behalf of GI rights led her to organize, and raise funds for, the GI Office, based in Washington, D.C., which offered enlisted men legal representation and support in Congress. Because of Fonda's solid reputation as a fund-raiser and organizer, VVAW asked her to help them publicize their work and activities. By the end of 1970, Jane Fonda was known above all for supporting GIs and veterans who were working to end the war.

2

GI JANE: WINTER SOLDIER AND *FREE THE ARMY*

Jane Fonda's activism was marked by consistent support for antiwar GIs and veterans. She supported GIs in the Army who were pressing for greater rights, even the right to openly criticize the war and organize to end it. She respected the courage of the veterans who had been to Vietnam and returned to urge Americans to call for an immediate end to the bombing and a negotiated settlement. She objected to the Pentagon's shifting all responsibility for atrocities to lower-level GIs and officers while giving medals to those in the Pentagon who planned the policies of body counts and free-fire zones that rendered atrocities inevitable. She worked tirelessly to raise money for coffeehouses, for the GI Office, and for activities that antiwar veterans planned. Her commitment to these led her to play a major role in two important antiwar campaigns, one planned by veterans and the other in support of GIs in the Army.

The first of these was the Winter Soldier Investigation into war crimes, organized by VVAW. The idea was spurred by the news of the massacre of hundreds of villagers in the hamlet of My Lai in Vietnam in March 1968, where a platoon of American soldiers, under the command of First Lieutenant William Calley, herded villagers together and systematically killed almost all of them.[1] When the news of the massacre finally emerged eighteen months later, military officials called it an isolated incident and placed the responsibility for it on low-ranking officers and GIs. Many in the antiwar movement were offended by this approach. They believed that ultimate responsibility for atrocities rested with those who planned and implemented the tactics of war. The Nuremburg

Trials following World War II had seemed to establish individual soldiers' duty to refuse carrying out orders that would kill civilians. And yet, the conventional tactics in Vietnam inevitably killed thousands of civilians. What was their duty, GIs asked, when they operated in areas where ordinary people lived, and military tactics required them to force these people off their land, engage in massive bombardment, and define success by "body counts," which assumed that all dead Vietnamese had been enemies? "My Lai was not a criminal incident in an otherwise 'just' war," the editors of the *Christian Century* wrote. "It simply represents the ultimate logic of a criminal war."[2]

The first effort to hold a public war-crimes investigation came in January 1970, only weeks after the news of My Lai broke. Four GIs at Fort Gordon, Georgia, printed leaflets calling for a GI-sponsored War Crimes Commission that would provide a public forum for Vietnam War veterans to testify about atrocities that they had seen or heard about in Vietnam. The four GIs said they wanted Americans to understand that My Lai "wasn't an isolated incident." They said they planned to send the information they gathered to members of Congress and to members of the Bertrand Russell War Crimes Tribunal held in Stockholm in 1967.[3]

These four GIs—Terrance Kline, Charles Horner, Timothy Johnson, and Lawrence Czaplyski—had been meeting with other soldiers at the home of Ellis Rece, a professor of religion at Paine College in Augusta, Georgia. The Army's Criminal Investigation Division sent undercover agents to the Rece home to find out what Ellis Rece told the GIs who came by the dozens to his house. One of the agents came posing as a photographer. "This seemed a little foolish," Mrs. Rece told a reporter. "We are completely open and have been from the beginning." The same day that the GIs posted their leaflets calling for the War Crimes Commission, military police arrested them and put them in the stockade. They were charged with spreading "disloyalty and disaffection among the troops and impairing the loyalty, morale, and discipline of the United States."[4]

At the same time that these GIs were being charged at Fort Gordon, other groups began to organize Citizens Commissions to look into war crimes in Vietnam. The first commission was held in Annapolis, Maryland, in February 1970. Veterans for Peace in Baltimore, helped by Tod Ensign and Jeremy Rifkin, sponsored it. People in Springfield, Massachusetts, convened another commission and David Bressem, a former helicopter pilot in Vietnam who testified there, said that, on one occasion, crews on several helicopters killed at least 33 civilians in a "turkey shoot." Within hours of Bressem's testimony, the Pentagon sent criminal investigators to his home. They asked him to tell them the names of the men still in uniform so that they could single out those individuals and prosecute them. Bressem told them that singling out individuals for prosecution only obscured the body-count tactic, planned in Pentagon, that encouraged the massacres in Vietnam. He said that the officials who planned those tactics should be singled out for trial, not the lower-level young men.[5]

Over the next few months, local groups organized similar Citizens Commissions in Richmond, Virginia; Buffalo, New York; New York City; Minneapolis; Los Angeles; Cincinnati; Boston; and Portland, Oregon. At that point, VVAW began to plan a national investigative hearing that would allow veterans to testify in a context that would link these atrocities to military policies.

VVAW called their hearings the "Winter Soldier Investigation." The name came from Thomas Paine's *Crisis* in which he wrote: "These are the times that try men's souls. The summer soldier and the sunshine patriot will, in this crisis, shrink from the service of his country; but he that stands by it now, deserves the love and thanks of men and women." These veterans of Vietnam saw themselves, too, as winter soldiers. They asked Jane Fonda to help organize and raise funds for the Winter Soldier Investigation, and

Fonda found herself on the road in the fall of 1970 raising most of the money for the investigation, speaking at over fifty colleges and universities in addition to scores of churches, coffeehouses, and public rallies across the United States. Fonda's fund-raising efforts included concerts that she called "Acting in Concert for Peace" with singers Graham Nash, David Crosby, and Phil Ochs. She enlisted Dick Gregory, Donald Sutherland, and Barbara Dane to entertain and perform at fund-raisers with her. She helped to organize mailings and to write VVAW newsletter articles on the Winter Soldier Investigation.

She even moved to Detroit in late 1970 to help oversee the local and national details of organizing the event. She worked to win endorsements of the investigation from the local United Auto Workers, from attorneys working in Detroit, from Michigan Secretary of State Richard Austin, and from Business Executives Move for Peace. For the veterans who were coming to Detroit to testify, she arranged housing through the Detroit Metropolitan Council of Churches, whose members opened their homes to the veterans and their supporters. "It's important that the public realize that American atrocities in Vietnam are an everyday occurrence," said John Forsyth, director of Detroit's Metropolitan Council of Churches, as he announced his support of the Investigation.[6]

The Winter Soldier Investigation took place between January 31 and February 2, 1971, at the midtown Howard Johnson Hotel in Detroit, Michigan. Vietnam Veterans Against the War said that they wanted "to establish, once and for all, that war crimes stem from conscious military policies—not isolated misconduct of GIs." They had sponsored this War Crimes inquiry "for the express purpose of ending the 'scape-goating' of individuals and fixing the blame where it belongs—on the Johnsons, Nixons, Westmorelands, Abramses." Their flyer said:

> Individual soldiers should not be made scapegoats for policies designed at the highest levels of government. Instead, responsibility for War Crimes should be placed where it truly belongs, upon the U.S. Government. B-52 pattern raids against undefended villages and populated areas, free-fire zones, forcible removal of civilian populations, defoliation and crop destruction, and "search and destroy" missions have been sanctioned as official tactical policies of the U.S. Government. "Search and destroy," "free-fire zones," strategic hamlets, etc. are all policies designed by the military brass, National Security Council, and major universities and corporate institutions, and passed down through the chain of command for conversion into Standard Operational Procedures in the field. Many of the over two million GIs who have served in Vietnam have been forced to employ military tactics which violate the Rules of Land Warfare, the Geneva Conventions and Accords, and the Nuremberg Charter.[7]

William Crandell, a rifle platoon leader in Vietnam who helped organize the hearings, said that the veterans needed "to tell our country that these horrible acts were not simply aberrations or psychotic episodes, but the inevitable outcomes of the direction soldiers in Vietnam had been given. The nightmares we had participated in during our tours in Vietnam were following us home and spilling into the streets." Crandell said the veterans wanted to bring their "brothers and sisters in uniform home alive and untainted by further involvement in such deeds."[8]

To that end, the hundred and five veterans who testified at the Winter Soldier Investigation appeared on panels arranged by unit so they could corroborate one another's reports. They came from the 1st Marine Division, the 3rd Marine Division, the 1st Air Cavalry Division, the 101st Airborne Division, the 82nd Airborne

Division, the 173rd Airborne Brigade, the 5th Special Forces, the 25th Infantry Division, the 1st Infantry Division, the 4th Infantry Division, the 9th Infantry Division, the Americal Division, and from smaller units. At the hearings, veterans and civilian experts who had been to Vietnam testified about how the use of established tactics such as "harassment and interdiction" and "free-fire zones" made killing civilians inevitable. One soldier with the 9th Infantry Division told the panel about the tactics he and his fellow GIs routinely used, tactics that, he said, came down from the battalion commander:

> We used to shell villages at times, like five or six rounds every thirty minutes or so all through the night. On the perimeter of the village, people had a curfew and were supposed to be in. But if some mama-san got up during the middle of the night and had to move her bowels, she was ducking flak, too. We had free-fire zones; we had "mad minutes," just about throughout the 9th Division. You know about mad minutes. A mad minute—everybody gets on line, everybody in the company, and you play Machine Gun Murphy. You're told to fire a magazine through your weapon and you just pepper the countryside. Usually you do this about six o'clock at night because you get colors off the tracers. I don't know why.[9]

For three days, testimony poured out from former sergeants, privates, corporals, captains, and majors. Much of what they talked about was gruesomely familiar to Americans who had followed the accounts of the massacre at My Lai. Dr. David Galacia, a former major and Army psychiatrist in Vietnam, said of his year in Vietnam that "when you get there, you arrive with your ethics, your values. After a while you get the impression that standard operating procedure for the day is, anything goes there.

If you're involved in an atrocity, other people have done it too, and you have something in common. Three days after you're there you're a part of it, or in for a year of bedlam."[10]

Army helicopter pilot and former captain E. P. Sachs said he watched bound prisoners thrown from his landed ship to the ground. It was cruel, he said, and he knew he could have stopped it. But, he went on, the captain on the ground said nothing, and a lieutenant said nothing, "and that's probably the greatest regret and personal moral anguish I'll ever have to bear." Kenneth Campbell, who had been a Marine corporal in Vietnam, said, "We're passing the buck and a certain number of the cents of that dollar belong to us. But the people who make the policy should be the first to burn."[11]

Two women testified at the Winter Soldier Investigation. One was Dr. Marjorie Nelson, who worked at the American Friends Service Committee's rehabilitation center and was captured by the Viet Cong and held prisoner for six weeks following the Tet Offensive in 1968. Nelson was released because "she had come to Vietnam to help, not to harm," her captors told her.[12] The other was Virginia Warner, mother of Marine Lieutenant James Warner, who was shot down over North Vietnam in 1967 and was a POW in Hanoi. Warner said she wanted the Nixon administration to cease using the POW issue as a way of building public support for the war. "I would like to put up a billboard reading, 'President Nixon, End the War So the Prisoners of War Can Come Home,'" she said. "The last thing I want is any more bombings of the North. I am not proud that my son helped bomb Vietnam and I don't want any more Vietnamese killed, or my son or any other POW killed by American bombs." She felt alone in Middle America, she said. She knew that she would be called a radical and a communist, but, she said, "I am not. I am an American, and I love my country. I don't want it torn apart any longer by this senseless war. . . . I would like to go up to each of them [the Vietnamese people] and hold their hands in mine and say to them that I am sorry about the bombing of their country, and I am terribly sorry that Jim was part of it. It is not much, but what more can I say?"[13]

The Winter Soldier testimony revealed some aspects of the war that the White House had tried to hide. These revelations included the secret war in Laos, when two Marines testified about their secret assignments there in 1969 to carry out search-and-destroy missions.[14] The Winter Soldier Investigation also introduced the first public testimony in the United States on the dangers of Agent Orange, which the Pentagon was still insisting was perfectly safe when Dr. Bert Pfeiffer of the University of Montana presented evidence of its toxic effects on humans.[15]

The testifying veterans brought with them their service records and unit citations to prove they had been in the Army, Navy, or Marines, and had served in Vietnam. But the press, more accustomed to covering the war by relying on briefings from the Pentagon, at first covered the hearings in Detroit with obvious skepticism. The Detroit *Free Press* began by referring to "alleged" veterans recounting "alleged" atrocities. (The veterans responded by referring to the "alleged" war in Vietnam.) Then the skeptical *Free Press* checked the credentials of every veteran who testified at the Winter Soldier Investigation and found that all the veterans were exactly who they said they were. To its credit, the no-longer-skeptical *Free Press* also reported that, as a result of its own investigation into the veterans' credentials, it found "additional witnesses, two ex-Marines who have no connection with the Winter Soldier Investigation, who confirmed that several Marine companies participated in a search-and-destroy operation inside Laos in February and early March 1969."[16] The *New York Times* allotted one column deep inside the paper to the hearings. The reporter who covered it observed that nothing was particularly newsworthy—much of what the veterans said had been reported before.[17]

When Donald Duncan closed the Winter Soldier Investigation on the third day, he told the assembled crowd that "no president could have sent us, soldiers and others, to Vietnam had there not been some sort of cooperation or concurrence, passive or active, on the part of a large segment of this country. How that consent was come by is rather irrelevant. The fact is they had it. Whether it was because we were bent by the media, bent by propaganda, or whatever, the point is now the blinders must be removed."[18]

VVAW followed the Winter Soldier Investigation with a march to Arlington National Cemetery on April 18, 1971. With them marched a delegation of Gold Star mothers carrying wreaths. Federal officials at the cemetery refused to let the veterans and mothers lay their wreaths. When they returned to Capitol Hill, some sympathetic senators arranged for the veterans to testify before the Senate Armed Forces Committee.[19] Lieutenant John Kerry, one of the leaders in VVAW at the time, told the nation that he and his friends had come to the Capitol

> on one last mission—to search out and destroy the last vestige of this barbaric war, to pacify our own hearts, to conquer the hate and the fear that have driven this country these last ten years and more, so when thirty years from now our brothers go down the street without a leg, without an arm, or a face, and small boys ask why, we will be able to say "Vietnam" and not mean a desert, not a filthy obscene memory, but mean instead the place where America finally turned and where soldiers like us helped it in the turning.[20]

On Capitol Hill, Republican Senator Mark Hatfield from Oregon had the complete testimony of the Winter Soldier Investigation read into the *Congressional Record*. Hatfield cited what he called "the institutionalized racist attitudes of the military in their training of the men who are sent to Vietnam—training which has indoctrinated them to think of all Vietnamese as 'gooks' and subhuman." Beyond that, Hatfield said, the testimony showed that the atrocities carried out "were the consequence of reasonable and known policies adopted by our military commanders and that the knowledge of incidents resulting from these policies was widely shared. Several of the allegations made in this testimony would place the United States in violation of the Geneva Convention and other international agreements relating to the conduct of war which have been ratified by our Government."[21]

In March 1971, after the Winter Soldier Investigation was over, Fonda had hoped to travel to Hanoi to carry letters to the POWs there through the mail service that Women Strike for Peace offered to them and their families at home. Fonda had to cancel that trip after a new assault on Laos and North Vietnam that the Pentagon called "Dewey Canyon II." Because the assault threatened Vietnam's commercial air corridors, Hanoi canceled all visas for international visitors and Fonda put her planned visit to North Vietnam on hold.[22]

Instead of going to Hanoi in March 1971, Fonda again took to the lecture circuit that spring, traveling nonstop to college and university campuses all over the country. The national media had virtually shut out the Winter Soldier hearings, but at every place she spoke, Fonda told the thousands of people who came to hear her about them. The reason that the veterans stood up and told their stories in Detroit, Fonda said to her audiences:

> is because they thought the time had come for the American people to know what is being done in our names; that it is time for the American people to know that the My Lai massacre happens daily in Vietnam. It is not an isolated incident and it is not the result of individual soldiers going crazy, freaking out on dope, or going criminally insane. It is

> the result of the policy formulated in our government, by our leaders, by the CIA, by the Pentagon, by the Joint Chiefs of Staff. These things happen, perhaps on a lesser level, but they happen daily in South Vietnam. . . . They [the veterans] told about how, from the time they set foot on the bases in this country and jammed their bayonets into the dummies, they had to repeat constantly "the only good gook is a dead gook" and how they are told that these people are sub-human, that they are not to be respected and consequently it is easier to torture them and easier to kill them. They are told there are ways to attach field radios to male genitals and crank them up so that they are electrocuted until they talk. There was a panel in which a young man said that the last thing that they were told before they were sent to Vietnam—that their officer stood up with a rabbit, held it up by its feet, took a knife and ripped open its belly, took out its guts and threw it out to the men in the audience and said, "Off you go to Vietnam." One by one for three days these men talked about cutting off ears, cutting off heads, cutting off hands—they talked about the rape of the women, they talked about the torture. . . . The people that were there—and most of them had come very skeptical as I was the first time I heard these stories four years ago—went away ashen and said, "We never would have believed it—we never would have believed it."

"I don't mean to imply that every soldier who was there participated or even witnessed these kinds of things," she added, "but it is happening a lot and most men who are in combat on the ground at least heard about it."[23]

As much as, or more than, any other activist, Fonda played a key role in spreading the findings of the Winter Soldier Investigation to a wider audience and in keeping before the public the fact that many veterans of Vietnam were deeply troubled by the conduct of the war there and wanted to tell their fellow Americans about the things they had experienced in Vietnam. Fonda told her audiences about tactics that the veterans described and which the media seldom referred to or bothered to explain: free-fire zones, Operation Rolling Thunder, the Phoenix Program, strategic hamlets. Her speeches gave the war a context that the administration and the media obscured or ignored. She urged her audiences to consider the perspective of the Vietnamese, to try to understand why people in a country far away would resist American air power and force. Fonda's audiences heard her discuss topics they seldom read about in the newspapers or heard on the evening news and that was why many of them came out to hear her. In his study of television coverage of the war in Vietnam, Daniel Hallin found that "television painted an almost perfectly one-dimensional image of the North Vietnamese and the Vietcong as cruel, ruthless, and fanatical—clearly beyond the bounds of legitimate controversy." Beyond that, the American media barely covered news from North Vietnam even though it was available. European media presented a fuller picture of Vietnam and of the war by presenting at least a part of the Vietnamese perspective as well as the American one.[24]

At her public talks, Fonda sometimes would run a film of recent television news with its bland recitation of Pentagon news releases (or, more likely, very little war news at all) until the audience would interrupt the newsreel with catcalls and boos. Given all of the trivial news the media covered, Fonda would point out that it was "sad and important" that most people didn't know that the Winter Soldier Investigation even took place. When they had asked the networks and newspapers why the investigations hadn't been covered, Fonda said they were told, "We've done our duty. We've reported the My Lai trials and from time to time we show photographs of prisoners of war being thrown out of helicopters; we've done our job." Fonda said the media really did believe "they had done their job." "What they didn't understand," she said, "is that by reporting it from time to time and by reporting the My Lai massacre trials the way the administration would like them to, [the media] is avoiding the real issue, which is that these things are not isolated incidents. They are the result of our policies in Vietnam. This is something that is very hard for us to admit. It is very hard for us to come to terms with, but it is essential that we do so, because these things are being done in our name."[25]

By 1970, dissatisfaction in the armed forces had reached an all-time high. The draft still brewed resentment. Daily casualties ground down morale. Enlistees and conscripts alike chafed under the hierarchical structure and restricted rights in the military. Discontent in the ranks rose so high that on June 7, 1971, months after Fonda began telling her audience about these things, the *Armed Forces Journal* printed a long article by Colonel Robert D. Heinl Jr. called "The Collapse of the Armed Forces."

Heinl's article is an astonishing recitation of what he called "social turbulence, pandemic drug addiction, race war, sedition, civilian scapegoatism, draftee recalcitrance and malevolence, barracks theft and common crime" pervading the armed forces in Vietnam. He went much further than Jane Fonda did in painting an entirely bleak picture of the state of the military in Vietnam. Heinl began by saying that no active duty senior officer dared share his assessments openly but mid-level officers in all services shared "virtually unanimous support" for his conclusions:

> Morale, discipline and battleworthiness of the U.S. Armed Forces are, with a few salient exceptions, lower and worse than at any time in this century and possibly in the history of the United States. By every conceivable indicator, our army that now remains in Vietnam is in a state approaching collapse, with individual units avoiding or having refused

> combat, murdering their officers and non-commissioned officer, drug-ridden, and dispirited where not near mutinous.[26]

Combat refusal was common and considered "safe" enough by the troops, Heinl said, "that a rifle company from the famed 1st Air Cavalry Division flatly refused—on CBS-TV—to advance down a dangerous trail." Instead of combat, he said, "symbolic antiwar fasts (such as the one at Pleiku where an entire medical unit, led by its officers, refused Thanksgiving turkey), peace symbols, 'V' signs not for victory but for peace, booing and cursing of officers and even of hapless entertainers such as Bob Hope, are unhappily commonplace."

Discipline was practically gone, Heinl lamented; obedience was occasional at best. He noted grimly that Admiral Zumwalt had called the desertion rate "a personnel crisis that borders on disaster" and had taken to wearing sideburns to enhance the Navy's appeal to young men. The Pentagon had reported 109 fragging cases in 1970, and Heinl added that "bounties, raised by common subscription in amounts running anywhere from $50 to $1,000, have been widely reported put on the head of leaders who the Privates and SP4s want to rub out."

Heinl saw no recourse in the court system. GIs wanted to wear peace symbols on their uniforms. When they appealed to the courts over the military brass, they won the right to wear those symbols, he said. Things had gone so far that a group of active-duty officers had formed the Concerned Officers Movement and filed a lawsuit against Defense Secretary Melvin Laird, asking for an injunction to halt the Defense Department's "retaliation" against them.

Heinl agreed with Fonda that antiwar GIs had forced big changes. They were publishing over 140 underground newspapers now, he said; they had organized fourteen GI antiwar organizations that were brazen enough to operate openly. There was a network of lawyers, many of them veterans, who supported their dissent; there were nearly thirty coffeehouses run by GIs that offered what Heinl called "disruptive counsels." Heinl cited churches as a major source of help to dissident GIs. Churches offered space to dissenters to meet. They even provided political refuge to GIs, and they were joined by what Heinl called "a community of turbulent priests and clergymen."

To this general list of aiders and abettors, Heinl singled out two people: Jane Fonda and Congressman Ron Dellums. Fonda he scored for her endless work at GI coffeehouses. At least, said the colonel, Fonda could be banned from military bases, but that was the most the Army had succeeded in neutralizing her.

Even while Heinl was denouncing Fonda's work, she was already developing a new idea to show public support for the dissident GIs. Many GIs had expressed their dissatisfaction to Fonda with what they called racist and sexist entertainment on their bases. Standard fare was Bob Hope's comic repertoire combined with a few singers, a Miss America or Miss USA, and other female sex symbols. When Hope took his first trip to Vietnam in Christmas of 1965, in his comic routine, he assumed that the war was a good one and would soon be over. The troops "roared," *Newsweek* reported, "when he called the United States bombing raids of North Vietnam 'the best slum clearance project they [the Vietnamese] ever had.' "[27] But as the war soured, so did the GIs, and by 1969, Hope's reception among the troops in Saigon was noticeably tepid. Hope began to joke that he himself was a hawk who had "now turned chicken." GIs kept complaining, but they cheered Hope again when he tried out new jokes, telling the GIs that instead of taking marijuana away from the soldiers, "we ought to give it to the negotiators in Paris."[28]

Fonda regarded the GI's dissatisfaction as an opportunity to launch a revue that would both give voice to the antiwar sentiments within the military and also serve as an outlet for unhappy

GIs. She envisioned a revue that would be entertaining and funny while treating the war as a serious issue, and that would provide opportunities for the GIs to talk to the performers afterward. She called the proposed revue *Free the Army,* and she enlisted other actors, writers, and musicians to plan the programs and perform with the troupe. These included actors Donald Sutherland, Elliott Gould, Gary Goodrow, Peter Boyle, comedian Dick Gregory, folksingers Holly Near, Len Chandler, Barbara Dane, the rock group Swamp Dogg, and Johnny Rivers, among others. Writers Jules Feiffer, Barbara Garson, and Herb Gardner wrote many of the scripts. Troupe members came and went as their schedules allowed, but Fonda remained a constant member. "A lot of us who have different points of view about the war and what's happening in this country have decided the time has come to speak to the forgotten soldiers. They are the majority of the soldiers and they want peace and freedom," Fonda said. "They need our support."[29]

Free the Army debuted near Fort Bragg at the Haymarket Coffee House on March 13, 1971. Fonda chose Fort Bragg because it was under the command of Lieutenant General John Tolson, one of the architects of the army's "new look" effort to boost morale. The "new look" meant longer hair, mustaches, and "go-go girls" in on-base service clubs. Fonda wondered if the "new look" could include *Free the Army.* When she asked Tolson for permission to perform on base, he asked her to send him the script. Fonda sent it to him and Tolson read it. He wrote back that *Free the Army* couldn't appear on base—it would be "detrimental to discipline and morale," he said.[30] Moreover, allowing Fonda on Fort Bragg, where she had recently been "banned" for distributing antiwar leaflets, could have been embarrassing. When GIs at Fort Bragg heard that Tolson had refused to allow *Free the Army* on base, they drew up a petition to Congress protesting Tolson's decision and within days, nearly two thousand GIs at Fort Bragg had signed it.[31] With that publicity, Tolson changed his stated reason for banning the show. He now told reporters he had rejected the *Free the Army* script because it was "not so much antiwar as poorly done."[32]

Deprived of Fort Bragg's facilities, Fonda asked to use the public auditorium in Fayetteville, which seated four thousand. Officials there, too, turned down her request to rent their public facility. When Fonda appealed to the courts, Federal Judge Algernon Butler upheld the city's refusal. So *Free the Army* went to the Haymarket Coffee House, which seated only five hundred. It was standing room only for all three shows that weekend. Opening night was an uncertain event, with the military brass clearly disapproving and the GIs unsure what to expect. But then Dick Gregory bounced on stage, and the GIs laughed as he told them to vote as a bloc to raise the draft age to seventy-five and "send all them older cats to Vietnam with John Wayne leading 'em." And when folksinger Barbara Dane began to sing "Insubordination," the GIs clapped softly to the rhythm and sang along: "I don't want nobody *over* me, I don't want nobody *under* me. . . ."

During the performance, actor Donald Sutherland read from Father Daniel Berrigan's "The Trial of the Catonsville Nine," about war resisters who, in 1968, had poured homemade napalm, made from a recipe in the Special Forces Handbook, over draft records in Catonsville, Maryland. At their trial for draft card destruction, defendant and Jesuit priest Daniel Berrigan had made a statement, which Sutherland now read to the GIs at the Haymarket Coffee House: "Our apologies, good friends, for the fracture of good order, the burning of paper instead of children, the angering of the orderlies in the front parlor of the charnel house. We could not, so help us God, do otherwise."[33] While Sutherland was reading, the hall turned deadly silent, but when he finished, the GIs burst into applause for the Catonsville Nine.

One of the crowd favorites of *Free the Army* was a skit in which Jane Fonda, as Pat Nixon, rushed into a room to talk to Richard Nixon, acted by Gary Goodrow:

Fonda (*agitated*): Mr. President. . . .

Goodrow: What is it, Pat?

Fonda: Mr. President, there is a massive demonstration going on outside.

Goodrow: There is a massive demonstration every day, Pat.

Fonda: But this one is *completely* out of control.

Goodrow: What are they asking for today?

Fonda: Free Angela Davis and all political prisoners, out of Vietnam now, and draft all federal employees.

Goodrow: All right. We have people to take care of that, Pat. Let them do their job, you do yours, and I'll do mine.

Fonda (*hysterically*): Richard, I don't think you *understand!* They're about to storm the White House!

Goodrow: I'd better call the Army.

Fonda: You *can't,* Richard!

Goodrow: Why not?

Fonda: It *is* the Army!

The cheer that followed Fonda's last line was "more than a cheer," one reporter wrote. It sounded to him like "a roar, a visceral reflex that burst from five hundred throats in the same instance."[34]

The songs, skits, comic routines, and readings that made up *Free the Army* were a biting blend of political satire and irreverent humor, with stand-up comics challenging Pentagon planners of the war to thunderous laughter and applause, actors reading somberly from Father Daniel Berrigan's essays or Dalton Trumbo's *Johnny Got His Gun,* and Holly Near and others singing songs about the absurdity of war and sometimes adding folk songs from Vietnam. It *was* a subversive show; it challenged the military hierarchy and the concept of war itself. It provided a voice and emotional rapport for antiwar GIs who felt pent up in the military. Her troupe was not saying anything new, Fonda said, but they were "underlining what the soldiers already know. *They* know that the war is insane. They know what GIs have to contend with better than we do. We're simply saying, 'We know what you're up against and we support you.' "[35]

The show was as informal as the military was rigid. Barred from the well-equipped base facilities freely given to Bob Hope's troupe, *Free the Army* had to contend with sparse facilities off base: the sound systems didn't always perform well, and lighting was often makeshift. But the troupe was accessible and friendly. Many of the GIs stayed around afterward and talked about their own military experiences. These were some of the best times for the troupe members. Folksinger Len Chandler said that he hadn't "felt that kind of solidarity since the early days of the civil-rights movement. These guys were dying to talk about what bothered them, to get things off their chest. They weren't star-stuck in any way; it was just a chance to open up and know that someone cared."[36]

"Vietnam is a good radicalizer," said a GI after one show. "I was super-straight until I came into the service. Spent four years in the Marine Corps. I *enlisted!* Man, if I had it to do over, I would have gone to Canada." Another told the cast angrily, "Yes, we're Vietnam returnees, 173rd Airborne Brigade. Only reason a lot of them put up with this s— is they don't know their rights. I'd say 90 percent of the returnees feel this way. Man, we are mad. You know 45 percent of our outfit is in the stockade right now." From its opening night, *Free the Army* looked like a hit. "They'll pack them in wherever they go," said Captain Fred Blitzer, an officer in the audience at the Haymarket Coffee House.

Some GIs became furious when they talked about what they had seen in combat. "I got a buddy who had both his legs blown off a year and a half ago—in Cambodia," one of them said angrily.

"You get it? *In Cambodia,*" he emphasized, since the White House had denied having troops in Cambodia at that time. One slight young man showed pictures that he carried around with him to a few reporters after the show in Fayetteville. One photo was of a Vietnamese woman with her side and head mostly blown away, her trousers yanked down to expose her genitals. "I took this picture," said the young man, clearly upset. "I've seen a lot worse than this. They told me the young woman was just running across a field. You think I should show this to Jane? I think she should see it. She's a woman. She should know about this."[37]

During the performances of *Free the Army,* Fort Bragg military authorities tightened security all around the base. They put fifty jeeps and army trucks on alert behind the base barracks. They blocked off all access points to the stockade, where nearly half of the 173rd Airborne Brigade was incarcerated that weekend. GIs told reporters that more than the usual number of soldiers had been sent off on weekend duty when *Free the Army* came to town.[38]

In March 1971, just after Fonda set out on the *Free the Army* tour, she was nominated for an Oscar for her performance in *Klute.* In April, she went to the Academy Awards in Los Angeles and won the Oscar. Then she went back to her *Free the Army* shows where FBI agents sat in the audience and wrote reports on them. Their reports affirmed what the news media was reporting—audiences loved *Free the Army.* One FBI report noted that "throughout the political and military-oriented entertainment there was continuous, spontaneous and interrupting applause. The audience was captivated."[39]

Occasionally, GIs invited *Free the Army* members into base cafeterias to eat and talk together. Base officials tried to prevent these gestures. For example, at Mountain Home Air Force Base in Idaho, Jane Fonda, Donald Sutherland, and a few other troupe members accompanied about 150 airmen to the cafeteria. As they were sitting down with their trays, an Air Force officer suddenly ordered all personnel on duty back to their desks. The remaining GIs regrouped around the tables, an undercover FBI agent now among them. But no sooner had the GIs gathered than two security officers strode into the cafeteria and announced that a bomb threat had been received. Everybody had to leave. The cafeteria meeting was over.[40]

Fonda tried to play down the contrast between her show and Bob Hope's. She did point out that Hope was freely given all the hospitality that bases could offer: the military paid for the transportation and lodging of Hope's troupe, arranged all the details, and gave the performer VIP treatment. Even though *Free the Army* was popular among GIs, enlisted men were only allowed to hear entertainers like Hope on their bases. "It's been disconcerting for many of us in Hollywood," Fonda said once, "to see that Bob Hope, Martha Raye and other companies of their political ilk have cornered the market and are the only entertainers allowed to speak to soldiers in this country and Vietnam."[41]

The media often drew contrasts between Fonda's show and Bob Hope's revue. "The Troops Get an Alternative to Bob Hope," was a typical headline. One reporter wrote that when *Free the Army* came to town, it was "an alternative to the Bob Hope show which even the Pentagon had to admit was panned by the GIs." The reporter added that for Fonda's troupe, "the young soldiers swarmed to the coffeehouse." Another reporter noted that the themes of *Free the Army* were "distinctly counter to the Hope theme . . . instead of the curvaceous Gold-diggers drawing whoops and whistles with a precisely choreographed routine, there was Miss Dane in gray, woolen shift singing a Vietcong morale song in her folk singer's contralto."[42]

Free the Army toured coffeehouses and public halls near military bases for the rest of 1971. In November and December, Fonda took the troupe to the Pacific. She asked for permission for *Free the Army* to perform at United States air bases in South Vietnam and Thailand, but the Pentagon turned down the request, so Fonda raised money to take the troupe to coffeehouses, makeshift auditoriums, and public halls near military bases in Hawaii, the Philippines, and Okinawa, Japan. Even there, without the benefit of publicity that the troupe's appearances garnered in the mainland United States, the crowds were large and appreciative. In Honolulu, for example, over four thousand people, most of them military, turned out to hear the show at the Civic Center. The crowds often stood, clapping in time and singing along.[43]

In 1972, *Free the Army* was adapted into a film called *F.T.A.* The film showed skits and music from the show and devoted much of its time to interactions between the troupe and its audiences so that viewers saw and heard GIs speaking about the war and its impact on their moral and political thinking after the shows. *F.T.A* never saw wide distribution because its distributor, a small company called American International Pictures, pulled the film without explanation shortly after it opened.

In one of those strange twists of history, Bob Hope tried to go to Hanoi while Fonda was performing in the Pacific in late 1971. Hope was a close friend of President Nixon, who enlisted him in an effort to get Hanoi to release the American POWs before the war was over. Hanoi's consistent position was that it would begin discussions on prisoner releases either when the United States set a date for withdrawal from Vietnam, or signed a peace treaty. Hanoi also made the American prisoner release contingent on the guaranteed release of the thousands of political prisoners held by the American-backed government in Saigon. The Nixon White House refused to enter into any such talks, instead trying other, often unlikely, stratagems, one of which involved Bob Hope.

In December 1971, Bob Hope traveled to the Vietnamese embassy in Vientiane, Laos, and asked officials there for a visa to Hanoi. Hope told the press about his plan before even speaking to Vietnamese officials. "I think I could make them a financial proposition," he told the press when he announced his trip. He would go to Hanoi and offer to pay ten million dollars for the release of the American POWs, he said. He was also going to offer to put on his GI revue show in Hanoi—free of charge. The Vietnamese officials in Vientiane were polite but firm. Hope's jokes about the American bombing raids being the best slum clearance project that the Vietnamese ever had had not gone over well in Hanoi. They wouldn't give him a visa to go to Hanoi now, Vietnamese officials told the comic, but they would be happy to see his act after the war was over. And they added that the POW issue was a political problem that needed to be solved at the negotiation table, not by Bob Hope's wallet. As news of Hope's failed mission emerged and the comic boarded his plane to leave Laos, the Pentagon announced vast new air strikes over North Vietnam.[44]

Fonda's *Free the Army* eventually played to an estimated 64,000 soldiers. "When you think that we have hundreds of thousands of men stationed along 'our defensive perimeter,' as Kissinger likes to describe it, the show doesn't look like a big deal," Fonda observed once. "It's a fact that a majority of military personnel never saw the show. But a vocal, enthusiastic minority did turn out to see us and rap with us after performances. It's the active minority that brings about historical change. You've got to remember that it wasn't easy to see *Free the Army.* The shows were kept off base. Guys had to travel at their own expense and risk getting hassled and harassed. The CID (Criminal Investigation Division) was always around taking snapshots. It cost something to turn out for our show."[45]

And Fonda was aware that *Free the Army* might cost her

something. A reporter asked her if, since she was touring the country, raising the hackles of the military, she worried about jeopardizing her film career. Fonda admitted it was a possibility, but a risk she was willing to take. Her political work was that important to her. If it prevented from working in Hollywood again? "I would work elsewhere," she said. "That's all."[46]

3

SPYING ON FONDA

THE FBI WAS SHADOWING Jane Fonda by May 1970, "to determine the extent of [her] affiliation with the Black Panther Party." Other FBI references suggest that the bureau targeted Fonda because it hoped to charge her with sedition or conspiracy and it planned to use, as evidence, secretly taped conversations she had with American GIs at coffeehouses. To accomplish this, the FBI sent agents and informants to Fonda's meetings, where they taped her speeches and pored over the transcripts for language that was either "seditious," violence-inciting, or obscene. When these efforts proved futile, the FBI tried to damage Fonda's reputation by having her arrested under a ruse that included false allegations of illegal drug use and assault. One FBI agent, with J. Edgar Hoover's enthusiastic assent, tried to plant a false story about her in a Hollywood gossip column. Agents went to Fonda's bank and, without a warrant, obtained secret access to all her banking transactions. They telephoned her home under false pretenses to find out her schedule, and they followed her daughter to her kindergarten and investigated the school. The FBI slapped "anarchist" and "subversive" labels on her files, which they passed on to the White House, where officials, including President Nixon, read them avidly.

Special Agent Richard Wallace Held in Los Angeles opened the first FBI investigation on Fonda. He had help from Washington, where his father, Richard G. Held, was FBI Associate Director and deeply immersed in the FBI's war against the American Indian movement and the Black Panthers. Richard G. Held helped organize the FBI assault on American Indian activists on South Dakota's

Pine Ridge and Rosebud Sioux reservations. He managed the cover-up of the murders of Black Panther Party leaders Fred Hampton and Mark Clark in 1969, and he helped send Panther leader Geronimo Pratt to jail on trumped-up murder charges.

The "extent of Jane Fonda's affiliation with the Black Panther Party" involved Fonda's 1970 fund-raising for bail money for Black Panthers who were imprisoned, often, as it turned out, without evidence. Fonda had helped raise money for the Black Panthers' breakfast program for inner-city children, and she worked with the National Committee of Artists to Free Angela Davis, a radical African American whom the Justice Department had charged with kidnapping. Davis was later acquitted of these charges by a jury.[1]

At the same time that Held opened the first FBI file on Fonda, he was involved in efforts to ruin actress Jean Seberg, who had also contributed bail money to the Black Panthers. Held placed a wiretap on Seberg's phone and learned that she was pregnant. He then prepared a false story about her to plant in the media. Held's story claimed that Seberg, married to novelist Romain Gary, was involved with a Black Panther, who was the baby's father.

Held sent his proposed media story on Seberg to FBI Director J. Edgar Hoover and requested approval to carry out his scheme, saying that it "could cause her [Seberg] embarrassment and serve to cheapen her image with the general public." He added that "usual precautions would be taken by the Los Angeles Division to preclude identification of the Bureau as the source of the letter if approval is granted."[2] J. Edgar Hoover enthusiastically approved Held's plan, noting that "Jean Seberg has been a financial supporter of the BPP [Black Panther Party] and should be neutralized." Hoover paid attention to detail; he told Held to wait to unfold his scheme for several months until Seberg's pregnancy became obvious. Held heeded the order and then sent his letter to Hollywood gossip columnist Joyce Haber under a false name, purporting to be a friend of Seberg's. Held's letter said that Seberg had confided to the letter-writer that the father of her baby was a leader of the Black Panther Party.

Gossip columnist Joyce Haber took the bait and printed the item in her *Los Angeles Times* column. She didn't name Jean Seberg, calling her "Miss A," but she printed unique details of Seberg's life and career that made the identity of "Miss A" obvious. Haber's column reported that around Hollywood, "Topic A is the baby Miss A is expecting." Haber added that "Papa's said to be a rather prominent Black Panther."[3] Newspapers and magazines around the country picked up the story, and an emotionally fragile Seberg attempted suicide. Doctors tried to save her baby's life by performing a cesarean section, but the baby lived only two days. At her child's funeral, a pale but defiant Seberg insisted on holding up her baby in her arms for the press to see that it was white.[4]

While busy destroying Seberg's reputation, Held was working on a parallel scheme to defame Jane Fonda. Under the name of "Morris," he prepared a letter for Army Archerd, a gossip columnist for Hollywood's *Daily Variety*. In the letter, "Morris" said that he had attended a Black Panther Party fund-raiser where Fonda (whom he called "Vadim's Joan of Arc,") was present. "Dear Army," Held's "Morris" letter began,

> I saw your article about Jane Fonda in the "Daily Variety" last Thursday and happened to be present for Vadim's "Joan of Arc's" performance for the Black Panthers Saturday night. I hadn't been confronted with this Panther phenomena before but we were searched upon entering Embassy Auditorium, encouraged in revival-like fashion to contribute to defend jailed Panther leaders and buy guns for "the coming revolution," and led by Jane and one of the Panther chaps in a "we will kill Richard Nixon and any

> other M—— F—— who stands in our way" refrain (which was shocking to say the least!) I think Jane has gotten in over her head as the whole atmosphere had the 1930s Munich beer-hall aura. I also think my curiosity about the Panthers has been satisfied. Regards, Morris.

J. Edgar Hoover encouraged this correspondence as well. He wrote back to Held that Fonda's reputation needed to be damaged, and this letter might accomplish that. He reminded Held to ensure that the letter to Archerd could not be traced back to the FBI. If the letter succeeded, Hoover added, it would have the desired effect and "detract from [Fonda's] status with the general public."[5]

While Richard Wallace Held was planning this attack on Fonda, Jean Seberg's baby died, an event that must have given Held at least a moment's pause. When the plot was revealed years later, Army Archerd said that he did not recall receiving the letter, which he never published. But Held used his power as an FBI agent to devise other schemes to discredit Fonda, hampered only by the fact that she offered so little opportunity for defamation. Fonda didn't use profanity (Held's fevered letter to Archerd notwithstanding); was not much of a marijuana user and didn't use other illegal drugs; was focused, direct, and even-tempered in her public speeches; and was a popular speaker who attracted audiences across the political spectrum.

Held and Hoover wanted to charge Fonda with sedition under the Espionage Act of 1917. The Act calls for the imprisonment of anyone who "incite[s] insubordination, disloyalty, mutiny, or refusal of duty in the military or naval forces of the United States, or . . . shall willfully utter, print, write, or publish any disloyal, profane, scurrilous, or abusive language about the form of government of the United States." The act goes on to say that "whoever shall by word or act support or favor the cause of any country with which the United States is at war or by word or act oppose the cause of the United States therein, shall be punished by a fine of not more than $10,000 or imprisonment for not more than twenty years, or both." The act even penalizes those who would "suggest" doing such things.[6] The Espionage Act had proved useful to the FBI over the years. It was passed in the heat of World War I and it criminalized a range of speech whose definition was subject to the whim of federal prosecutors. The act was used to imprison nearly nine hundred people opposed to the United States going to war in Europe in 1917. Its most famous catch was Socialist Party leader Eugene Debs, who was arrested for a speech he made in 1918 in Dayton, Ohio, in which he charged that the war profited primarily the wealthy and that the U.S. government was run by the well-heeled at the expense of the poor. "Wars throughout history have been waged for conquest and plunder," Debs said, "and that is war in a nutshell. The master class has always declared the wars; the subject class has always fought the battles. . . ."

For his public speech, Debs was charged with "uttering words intended to cause insubordination and disloyalty within the American forces of the United States, to incite resistance to the war, and to promote the cause of Germany." A federal judge sentenced him to ten years in prison and stripped him of his American citizenship. In the blind heat of war, the Supreme Court upheld his conviction. "I have been accused of obstructing the war," Debs said in court. "I admit it. Gentlemen, I abhor war. I would oppose war if I stood alone." His statement when he was sentenced ranks among the great classics in courts of law:

> Your Honor, years ago I recognized my kinship with all living beings, and I made up my mind that I was not one bit better than the meanest on earth. I said then, and I say now, that while there is a lower class, I am in it, and while

> there is a criminal element, I am of it, and while there is a soul in prison, I am not free. I listened to all that was said in this court in support and justification of this prosecution, but my mind remains unchanged. I look upon the Espionage Law as a despotic enactment in flagrant conflict with democratic principles and with the spirit of free institutions.[7]

The Espionage Act that sent Debs to jail runs roughshod over basic civil liberties of free speech, and not a single case of its use against free speech can be cited with pride. Still, it was with this law that Hoover and Held hoped to ruin Fonda's reputation, and they began by recruiting informants among the GIs who attended her informal coffeehouse meetings.

The FBI files from Fonda's April 21, 1970, visit to the Inscape Coffeehouse at Fort Carson, Colorado, provide a glimpse into the direction of its early investigation. Fonda had gone to Fort Carson to support GIs on the base who had organized a "sick strike" against the war as a way of circumnavigating the prohibition of all political speech or action. Fonda went to the Inscape and spent several hours there on the evening of April 21. Several weeks later, the FBI contacted the Special Processing Detachment at Fort Carson and asked it to provide the names of people who had attended the coffeehouse the evening that Fonda was there. The Special Processing Detachment office provided the FBI with nine names. Agents questioned these people at length about whether Fonda had urged GIs to desert, whether she had spoken favorably of violence, or whether her message could be interpreted as urging them to disobey Army regulations. They asked whether her talk seemed to "undermine" the United States government. Of the nine informants, two vaguely agreed with the FBI agent that Fonda had told GIs to desert, but neither one could remember any specific statements that she had made to that effect.[8]

The other informants claimed that Fonda had not urged GIs to desert the Army. The closest she had come to such a suggestion, one informant said, was her comment that "it might be better to receive a dishonorable discharge than to have to serve in Vietnam." The other informants said that Fonda had expressly urged GIs not to desert, that she had said that deserting "would not help the cause for peace." She had talked about the possibility of filing for conscientious objector status, some of them said, and had told them where they could get legal help if they wanted to explore that option. Fonda had said nothing about violence or disobedience to Army regulations, another informant said, and added that he was certain nothing she said "could be construed to be undermining to the U.S. government."[9]

Other informants said that Fonda really didn't do a lot of talking at the meeting but rather "a lot of listening." One GI said that the base's military chaplain had objected to Fonda's comments about the war in Vietnam benefitting wealthy and powerful interests at the expense of GI lives. Wasn't she rich, too? the chaplain asked. Couldn't she just go back to Beverly Hills whenever she wanted? She was wealthy, Fonda told the chaplain, but she could not face herself in the morning unless she tried to do her part along with everyone else.[10]

Many of the GIs at the meeting appeared to concur with Fonda's views. When Fonda told the base chaplain that, despite her wealth, she was trying to do her part, the GIs cheered. At another moment, Fonda said it seemed ironic that soldiers supposedly fighting for democracy themselves lacked it while in the military, "trained by a system that is most"—and here Fonda paused, groping briefly for the right word, when a GI offered the word "fascist." A reporter at the meeting said that when the GI spoke up, cheers from the other GIs drowned out Fonda's reply.[11]

The FBI files on Fonda reveal a politically driven investigation, replete with error. Informants at the same meeting sometimes gave starkly contrasting reports of what Fonda said. Agents also enjoyed considerable freedom to guide the answers. They asked informants for direct quotations from meetings weeks after the fact and suggested particular responses. Names in the files are misspelled, leading to the possibility of false identification. The name of one of Fonda's friends, Elizabeth Vailland, for example, is always misspelled as Elizabeth Voight, and references to Sydney Peck, a well-known figure in the antiwar movement by then, consistently turns up in Fonda's FBI files as Sydney Rick. Many of the people that the FBI talked to defended Fonda as entirely civil, focused on the issue of the war, and helpful to her audience. But a few told the agents what they wanted to hear: one agent wrote that his unnamed "source" said Fonda "claimed to be a Marxist." Another agent wrote that Fonda had used unspecified "profane" language. These entries are rare, but eagerly noted with an asterisk or some notation in the margin, indicating keen interest on the FBI's part.

After monitoring Fonda's Fort Carson visit, the FBI office set up a continuous "sedition" investigation with the sole purpose of bringing treason charges against her. The reason given for opening a sedition case was based on a statement that Fonda had once made, that "it would be more honorable to get a dishonorable discharge than to go to Vietnam and kill people."[12] This proved the most seditious statement that the FBI could produce.

Beyond their sedition scheme, the agents shadowing Fonda also hoped to link her to communism. Their questions to informants encouraged them to expand on any evidence in that direction. The places where Fonda spoke were sometimes characterized as having links with communism. For example, a June 12, 1970, FBI entry notes that the agent "observed" Fonda at a fund-raiser for the Alcatraz Indian Center. The fund-raiser was held at the First Unitarian Church in Los Angeles, which, the agent noted, had been "utilized for meetings by Communist Party members and sympathizers over a period of years. Speakers and lecturers at the church," the agent wrote in his report on Fonda's talk, "frequently espouse Communist causes or follow the Communist Party line. This same infiltration extends to adjuncts of the Church such as the Unitarian Public Forum and the Fellowship for Social Justice." The agent did note that "membership in the First Unitarian Church does not, of itself, connote membership in or sympathy with the Communist Party."[13]

Toward the end of 1970, the FBI officially labeled Fonda "a Marxist." The agent who penned those words in her file wrote that she had "privately" claimed to be a Marxist. He provided no source or evidence for the assertion, but being so labeled was necessary to move her to Category I, the highest "watch" category. Fonda was now considered a person who was "potentially dangerous or has been identified as member or participant in communist movement or has been under active investigation as member of other group or organization inimical to the United States." Under the guise of protecting the president, the Secret Service claimed the right to spy on any person labeled a "Marxist," so Fonda's new designation brought her under Secret Service surveillance. Moreover, designating Fonda a Marxist meant that whenever she traveled internationally, the FBI could order American embassies and consulates to spy on her.[14]

Under these circumstances, the FBI's surveillance of Fonda was joined by surveillance from the United States Army, the Secret Service, and the CIA. These agencies put wiretaps on Fonda's phone, opened her mail, copied her financial transactions, and sent undercover informants to her meetings. One agent got the address of the kindergarten that Fonda's daughter attended and set out to find if it taught "an anti-law enforcement attitude." The witch hunt had its entertaining moments. One agent reported that Fonda's talk at a church *was* revolutionary, but he added that her many revolutionary quotes "came from U.S. historical figures."[15]

After Fonda addressed the antiwar rally in Washington, D.C., on May 9, White House aide Charles Colson directed the FBI to send its reports on her to the White House. Colson passed these reports around to the president, his aides, his speech writers, and Henry Kissinger and his aides. One government official quipped that "what [Soviet General Secretary] Brezhnev and Jane Fonda said got about the same treatment."[16]

Around the time that the FBI's campaign against Fonda was moving into high gear, she began to receive death threats. The first one came to her father's residence in New York City in late October 1970, in a letter postmarked Everett, Washington. Henry Fonda was in Los Angeles when the letter came, so his housekeeper in New York forwarded the message to him there. He opened the envelope to find a short message composed of letters made by a plastic labeler pasted to a light blue sheet of paper. The letters, complete with obvious misspellings, were arranged to read:

> YOUR DAUGHTER HAS BEEN TRIED FOR TREASON FOR BEING A TRAITOR. HER DATE OF EXECUTION WILL BE DEC 197 TO PROTECT HER & SAVE HERE PAY 50,000 CASH. NO FBI NO COP'S OR BOTH OF YOU GETI HAVE MONEY WITH YOU PLACE ADD IN PERSONAL COL.. SEATTLE P.I. NOV. 1 70 TO READ JOHN LOVES MARY WITH PHONE NO TO CAL INSTRUCTIONS WILL BE GIV L IF NO ADDSENTANCE WILL BE COMPLETED COME YOUR SELVE.

The letter was signed "THE SILENT ONES." Henry Fonda immediately took the letter to the FBI office in Los Angeles, the same office which, unbeknownst to him, was directing the FBI campaign against his daughter. Officers there advised him to place an ad in the Seattle paper as directed. They even offered to place the ad themselves and have their Seattle office set up a telephone number to take any response. The FBI files reveal no effort to find the sender of the letter. The agents later told Henry Fonda that a male caller had called the phone number in the ad they placed, but he had hung up when the operator asked for his name. At that point, the FBI dropped the investigation completely.[17]

The same day the Los Angeles office told Henry Fonda they had taken a phone call about the death threat, Jane Fonda flew from a speaking engagement in Canada to the Cleveland airport, straight into a trap the FBI had laid for her. The agency had asked U.S. Customs agents in the Cleveland airport to detain Fonda and search her and her luggage. When she arrived at the airport in the early morning hours, customs agents abruptly ordered her to a small room. Fonda complied, going with them and showing them her luggage. Without a warrant, the agents took away her luggage, rifled through it, and seized and copied her notebook filled with addresses of personal friends, acquaintances, and activists. They found several bottles of vitamins and prescribed medications. With no reason to suspect the pills were anything but what the bottles indicated, the agents confiscated them.[18]

Because she had her period, Fonda had planned to use the bathroom immediately upon landing in Cleveland. But the federal agents refused to let her into the airport bathroom, claiming they wanted a "matron" to search her body first. The matron was nowhere to be found and so the agents ordered Fonda to wait. By this time, two local Cleveland police officers had joined the scene. For several hours, the customs agents refused to give Fonda permission to use the bathroom. Finally, she got up and began walking toward the restroom. Several agents bodily blocked her. Fonda tried to push them aside. Robert Pieper, a Cleveland police officer who had no reason to be in the customs area, promptly slapped handcuffs on her and arrested her "for assaulting an officer." Speaking to reporters later, he also claimed that she had called him a "pig," a charge uncorroborated by any witnesses, even those standing beside him, and one that Fonda denied. "I pushed him to try to get to the bathroom," she said.[19]

Fonda was now arrested for "suspected narcotics possession" and "assaulting a police officer." It proved easy for the FBI to trumpet these false accusations to the entire nation. Television and print journalism that evening reported everything federal agents told them: that Jane Fonda had been arrested for smuggling "suspected narcotics" and "kicking and slapping a policeman."[20] Some of the officers at the scene appeared overanxious to advance the plot. One of them told reporters that Fonda was "dirty and filthy" when she arrived at the airport, an assessment not borne out by photographs of her arrest. She was "wearing blue jeans," the officer added, as if that were incriminating. Reporters, who were not eyewitnesses, passed along the "dirty and filthy" quote to their readers and viewers as fact.[21]

Hauled off to prison, Fonda was put in a cell with a young woman who identified herself as Barbara Kahn, eighteen years old. Kahn said she had been arrested for "carrying an unauthorized red flag" at a march against a United Hard Hats of America parade the previous summer. At her arrest, she told Fonda, she had also been charged with "assaulting a police officer" just as Fonda had been and for that she was now serving a sentence of six months, apparently in the Cuyahoga County Jail. She showed Fonda bruises that she said had come from the guards beating her.

After spending the night in jail, Fonda was taken, in handcuffs, to Federal Court. By that time, the customs office had dropped the "suspected narcotics" language, but in a new effort to justify Fonda's arrest, customs officials said they now planned to file charges against her of "introducing prescription pills into the country." The judge ordered Fonda released on bond. But as she was leaving the courthouse, she was immediately rearrested on the charges of assaulting Pieper at the Cleveland airport the night before and ordered to appear in court again the following day. In addition, Pieper filed a $100,000 civil suit against Fonda for "assault and battery."

After wading through the collection of law enforcement officials and lawyers outside the courtroom the next day, Fonda entered a plea of innocent to the assault charge that Officer Pieper had levied against her. When she left the courthouse, she went to the county prosecutor's office to talk to prosecutor John Corrigan about Barbara Kahn, her young cell mate who claimed to have been sentenced to six months in jail for assaulting a police officer. Fonda told Corrigan about Kahn's bruises and asked that she be given better treatment in jail. Corrigan responded that Kahn was no longer in prison, that she had been moved to a psychiatric hospital and couldn't be contacted.[22]

After her sleepless night in jail, her release at noon, her subsequent rearrest on the "assault" charge, and then her release on bond, Fonda kept her commitment to speak at Central Michigan University that evening. She spoke briefly of her arrest the day before but placed it in perspective. "I kept thinking," she told the students, "that if I were nobody, if nobody knew I was in jail, the police could do anything they wanted with me, but some of the best people in this country are in jail and I feel proud to be with them. If this can happen to me," Fonda said, "you can imagine what happens to less visible people who are trying to do something in this country."[23]

All of the charges against Fonda unraveled completely, but not before turning into a comedy of errors. As the charges were proven transparently false, officials in Cleveland cooled their collaboration with the FBI. Richard Matuszak, the federal customs agent who had arrested Fonda, stopped talking to the press. Reporters went to Matuszak's superiors in Cleveland, who bluntly said that the orders to arrest Fonda had come from U.S. Customs officials in Washington, D.C., and it was the Washington office's responsibility to justify the arrest. They did volunteer the information that officials in D.C. had put Fonda on a "special attention" list and had told them to check Fonda carefully whenever she left or entered the country.[24]

The federal charges of "smuggling" pills from Canada were dropped six months later at the request of U.S. attorney Frederick Coleman, who acknowledged that Fonda was carrying only vitamins and prescribed medications in her luggage, exactly as she had stated, and not illegal drugs, as federal agents had alleged. Municipal judge Edward Feighan dismissed the charges against Fonda of assaulting Pieper because the affidavit bringing the charges did not mention Pieper's name. Additionally, the judge noted, Pieper lacked jurisdiction to arrest Fonda in the customs area of the Cleveland airport. At first, prosecutor Everett Chandler said that the omission of Pieper's name from the affidavit was "just a slight technicality" and he promised to refile the charges."[25] But when the second police officer who was with Pieper that night at the Cleveland airport, and who would have been a key witness in court, said publicly that he thought Pieper's assault charge was "somewhat of a joke," Chandler said that he "didn't have sufficient evidence to convict her" and asked the judge to dismiss the case. Pieper's civil suit likewise was withdrawn.[26]

Richard Wallace Held and his FBI superiors never expected to keep Fonda in the Cleveland jail for long. Their successful efforts to arrest her on false pretenses and create negative stories in the national media emboldened them. They now used false pretenses to get their hands on Fonda's bank account. They did not seek a warrant. FBI agents simply went to Henry J. Rohlf, vice president of the Morgan Guaranty Trust Company of New York, and asked him to authorize handing over all of Fonda's personal bank transactions because it was "a matter of national security." Rohlf, in turn, told his bank officers to hand over to the FBI whatever they wanted without informing Fonda. Likewise, officers at the City National Bank of Los Angeles readily, and also without a warrant, handed over to the FBI all of Fonda's bank records there. From December 1970, and for years afterward, Fonda's bank officers turned over to the FBI every banking transaction that she made—donations to the National Council of Churches, the GI Office, United States Servicemen's Fund, Asian-Americans for Peace, the People's Coalition for Peace and Justice, Entertainment Industry for Peace and Justice.[27]

Several days after her arrest at the Cleveland airport, Fonda told a crowd of over 3,000 at Notre Dame University that "the harassment and intimidation that is going on in this country is a serious thing. This is supposed to be a free country but that, in fact, is not the case." She urged the students to look more closely at the campus environment. "There should be no more ROTC on campus," she said. "There should be no recruiters of death coming on campus. There should be no war research on campus." A heckler got up and claimed that he had come from a communist country, which he did not identify, and that there he had seen political executions and hundreds thrown in prison. "Is that what you want?" he asked Fonda. "I don't think that what other countries have done means we should condone what we are doing," she said to loud applause. She praised the students for their antiwar efforts:

> You must never forget that it wasn't the McGoverns and the Hatfields and the Fulbrights that forced Nixon to withdraw his troops last June from Cambodia; it was the students of America who, for the first time [applause from the audience] that's right, you went on strike, and for the first time in the history of this country you closed down the schools and that's what made Nixon withdraw his troops from Cambodia. He never expected that kind of response, that

> was a people's victory and it must never be forgotten. It was the students of America that forced Nixon to rush to the Lincoln Memorial. Students coming from all over the country because they were really concerned, because they wanted to carry on a dialogue with our leaders."[28]

"We are withdrawing out troops," Fonda told the students, "and thank God there are fewer American lives being lost. But is that all that it takes to pacify the American conscience? The time may very well be at hand when we don't have to send troops anywhere. They will just have to press a button and an entire country will be wiped out. And will the American people say 'right on,' our hands are clean because our men aren't being killed? We cannot allow that to happen."[29]

Fonda sometimes called herself a socialist or an internationalist who believed that "we must remove our military presence from abroad so that those countries can determine for themselves what kind of political and economic government structure they want to live under. We must guarantee them non-intervention and non-exploitation." She told her audiences that "the peace movement must join hands with the oppressed minorities. The respectable white liberals must forsake safety for the sake of truth. Marx said that shame is the only revolutionary sentiment. Can't we use that shame to bring true democracy and power to people?"

Fonda encouraged her audiences to rethink the conventional definition of violence. "What is violence?" she asked her audience sometimes. "Who are the people who are killing black people in their sleep? Who are the people that are killing hundreds of thousands of people in Vietnam? Who are the people that threw the bombs in Birmingham, Alabama, that killed four black children? Violence is making a black man or any man live in a house where his children are eaten by rats. Violence is stripping a man and woman of their dignity. Violence is when a young boy or girl grows up in the streets of America under the constant threat of racist police brutality."[30]

Richard Wallace Held and J. Edgar Hoover stayed on Fonda's trail. Held soon had his hands on Fonda's notebook of personal addresses and phone numbers that customs agents at the Cleveland airport had illegally copied and handed over to the FBI as directed. Held wrote in his files that the notebook contained information on "many revolutionary and leftist groups." It may have looked that way to Held, but Jane Fonda's notebook reads like an honor roll of civil rights activists and antiwar groups: Ossie Davis, Clergy and Laymen Concerned About Vietnam, Dick Gregory, William Sloan Coffin, Edwin Reischauer, Senator Charles Goodell, Gloria Steinem, the Vietnam Moratorium, James Earl Jones, Nelson Algren, Cyrus Eaton.

After the Winter Soldier Investigation in 1971, FBI director J. Edgar Hoover ordered that surveillance of Fonda be stepped up. He ordered the FBI to designate Fonda a "Key Activist." She was a "well-known supporter of anti-Vietnam war activities," he wrote to his agents, and he ordered them to find out and follow Fonda's complete travel plans and to "consider possible counterintelligence techniques which might be discreetly utilized to neutralize subject's effectiveness." Hoover repeated his customary warning that all "actions" against Fonda must avoid "embarrassment to the Bureau" and he ordered Assistant Attorney General Robert Mardian to "determine if any violation of the Sedition Law has been made."[31] FBI instructions emphasized that the FBI "is interested in following Fonda's progress throughout the country from the standpoint of a possible violation of Sedition Law."[32]

The FBI campaign against Fonda in the 1970s proved helpful to an emerging campaign by right-wing media agitators against what they began to call "the liberal media." At the time, these individuals and their furious accusations reached limited markets, and often were not taken seriously by mainstream media. Over the next decades, their influence and impact widened and deepened and became a powerful factor in moving media rhetoric and public policy to the far right.

Soon after Fonda began her tour to raise money for the Winter Soldier Investigation, attorney Morris Leibman, an outspoken anti-communist public figure in Chicago, informed William Sullivan, third in rank at the FBI, that he was going to appear on a Chicago television program as a counterpoint to Jane Fonda. Upon receiving this information, William C. Sullivan wrote to Hoover's right-hand man, Clyde Tolson, commending Leibman for the service that he had long provided the bureau. Sullivan said that Leibman had been on the FBI's "Special Correspondents" list for years. Sullivan noted that the FBI's special correspondents were helpful to the agency because they could be counted on to be "strong and faithful supporters of the Director and the Bureau." He praised Leibman for his television performance in Chicago against Fonda, saying that he had stood up against Fonda's "usual line of diatribe" by "exposing Fonda for the phony that she is and setting the record straight as a spokesman for the truth and the principles on which our democracy was founded."

J. Edgar Hoover sent a warm letter to Leibman for his service to the FBI on the TV show opposite Fonda. Marlin Johnson, the former special agent in charge of the Chicago office, also sent a congratulatory letter to Leibman, telling him that "it is most difficult to enter into a debate with an individual like Jane Fonda, who believes in freedom of speech for herself and her crowd but not for others. She is a very dangerous woman. I thought you did a truly magnificent job in raising the lack of credibility of her statements and posing questions to her that showed her up for what she really is."[33]

At the same time that Leibman was in touch with the FBI regarding his work to undermine Fonda, Jesse Helms was pioneering the use of television to create a right-wing drumbeat. Helms, who went on to become a U.S. senator, was then the executive vice president and vice chairman of the Board of Directors of the Capitol Broadcast Company, which owned TV Channel 5 in Raleigh and Durham, North Carolina. Helms was best known in North Carolina for his regular commentaries on Channel 5 in which he let loose a stream of vitriol against desegregation, liberalism, racial equality, and communism, which he considered entwined. Helms was, political scientist Larry Sabato once said, "an angry white male before most of his compatriots were."[34]

One of Helms's most blistering TV commentaries was aimed at Jane Fonda. It came after she spoke at Duke University on December 11, 1970, to raise awareness of the upcoming Winter Soldier Investigation. Nothing in Helms's commentary indicates that he attended her talk at Duke or had ever heard her speak, but he seized the occasion of Jane Fonda's visit to deliver a commentary that captured perfectly the technique that he had begun to hone: a heated blend of vicious and false attacks on the media and on an individual selected for being too "liberal" or "left-wing."

Helms ignored what Fonda had to say about the upcoming investigation in Detroit and about Vietnam. Instead, he called her a "self-declared 24-carat, revolving left-winger" and "an outrageous bore" who was "crude and shallow" and an "intellectual vacuum." He claimed that students had flocked to the auditorium at Duke University to hear Fonda "mock and revile her country." It was *because* of this, he said, that the "left-wing" media "glorified" her. It proved, he said, that "the liberal news media refuse to tell the whole truth about what's going on." Instead, he said, Fonda was "constantly publicized and glorified" by the "left-wing press, radio, and television." For nearly a generation now, Helms went on to say:

> There have been warnings from responsible quarters that America is being led into turmoil and chaos by the commu-

> nist propaganda apparatus. But leaders high in politics and government and higher education have shouted down the warnings. . . . Don't worry about communism, we have been told. The militants, the protestors we have been told—are not communists. Clear evidence of the communist leanings and affiliations of one militant after another has been suppressed by the news media.

Then Helms offered what he considered proof of the media being left-wing, even communist. "[Fonda] was asked how *she* would go about changing America to suit her fancy," Helms said, although he did not say where she had been asked this. He then said that Fonda had made the following statement which he had gotten "from television news film," although Helms did not identify the film, the place, or the time. According to Helms, Fonda had answered that question about changing America by saying, "I believe that we have to strive for a transition to a socialist society. First—" and then, in Helms's recounting, an interviewer broke in and asked Fonda "How far?" Helms said that Fonda had replied, "All the way to communism. I mean, I think we should all study what the word means and I believe if everyone knew what it meant we would all be on our knees praying that we would, as soon as possible, be able to live under, within a communist structure."[35]

Helms then turned directly to Raleigh's morning newspaper, the *News and Observer* and charged that it "constantly ridicules anyone opposed to, or apprehensive about, communism." The paper had a reporter present at Fonda's talk at Duke University, Helms said, but "the newspaper carefully avoided any reference whatsoever to Miss Fonda's all-out public endorsement of communism. In fact, the subject wasn't even mentioned in the newspaper story." Helms concluded his editorial by saying, "this is just one way that communist involvement in the strife and turmoil of

America has been hidden from the American people by the 'liberal' news media. Would you say that it's deliberate?"[36]

Several weeks later, FBI director J. Edgar Hoover received a transcript of Jesse Helms's commentary against Fonda on Channel 5. The name of the sender was blacked out but the transcript is on Helms's letterhead and was accompanied by a friendly note congratulating Hoover on his birthday and apologizing for not sending these items to him sooner. After Hoover received Helms's commentary with the alleged quotation from Fonda, Hoover sent instructions to FBI agents that, wherever Fonda spoke, they should "make every effort to obtain a verbation [sic] transcript of Fonda's talk . . . from the standpoint of possible violation of Sedition Law." If they could find a credible comment from Fonda endorsing communism and if they could show that she had any dealings with self-declared communists, the director believed that the FBI might have some success in silencing her or putting her behind bars on grounds of treason or conspiracy. FBI agents now trailed Fonda with tape recorders but they never recorded anything like the quotation Helms claimed to have heard on "television news film." Had the statement Helms cited existed, it is difficult to imagine that the FBI could not have, with Helms's help, located it.[37]

The next year, in 1972, Jesse Helms was elected to the U.S. Senate from North Carolina. He went on to win elections for the next twenty-five years and became one of the most powerful figures on Capitol Hill, a repeat offender in denouncing civil rights legislation and integration. He called imprisoned African National Congress leader Nelson Mandela in South Africa a communist who should stay behind bars. He launched a filibuster against a national holiday for Martin Luther King Jr. In the words of columnist David Broder, Helms won elections by picking "at the scab of the great wound of American history, the legacy of slavery and segregation," and inflaming "racial resentment against African Americans."[38]

Around the same time that Helms and Leibman were in touch with the FBI about their attacks on Fonda, journalist Lee Winfrey, who wrote for the *Detroit Free Press,* wrote an article about Fonda when she appeared at Michigan State University in November 1970. Winfrey also appears not to have interviewed Fonda directly, assembling instead his article from wide-ranging and unnamed sources. He belittled Fonda as a wannabe revolutionary and claimed that she told the thousands of students at the university meeting that "I would think that if you would understand what communism was, you would pray on your knees that we would someday become communist." No FBI transcript of Fonda's talks contain these remarks or any like them, even though J. Edgar Hoover sent out orders to agents to step up their examination of transcripts of Fonda's talks as well as "verbatim notes and statements from witnesses."[39]

The letters in the FBI files about the "Special Correspondents List" and the interest at the agency in Helms's and other media figures' attacks on Fonda raise questions about the role that the FBI played in fostering a network of right-wing print, radio, and television commentators that first emerged during the civil rights movement and the war in Vietnam. The FBI appears to have reached out covertly to people in the media who supported its right-wing politics and encouraged them to falsely attack liberals and progressives.[40]

In addition to the known FBI harassment, Fonda was plagued by unsolved thefts and burglaries while she was working to end the war. For example, she had moved to Detroit before the Winter Soldier Investigation to help organize the event. Shortly before the hearings opened, someone broke into the trunk of Fonda's car, where she had materials relating to the Investigation. The thieves took everything relating to the Winter Soldier Investigation, including a mailing list of supporters, a list of contributors with the amounts they had given, and the literature prepared for the hearings. Her Cleveland arrest also came just before her first appearance on her national fund-raising tour for the Winter Soldier Investigation.[41]

In 1972, the FBI gave Fonda's files, along with those of Dr. Benjamin Spock and civil rights leader Floyd McKissick, to its own reviewers, a Ms. Herwig, a Major Fryer, and a Mr. Kinley. These three were asked to review the files and assess whether the investigations should be continued. The FBI reviewers reported their conclusions in October 1972 and agreed that the investigation should end. Kinley flatly said it should be "terminated." And Fryer concluded that

> Given broad language of sedition statute (Fonda case) and unclear scope of Bureau jurisdiction in domestic intelligence, initiation of these investigations appears in each case to have been no more or less profitable than other investigations which have been/are being conducted for domestic intelligence purposes. However, in view of apparently sterile results, I recommend discontinuance of all three investigations.

Herwig struck a blow at the investigation itself:

> There are more dangerous characters around needing our attention. Unless D.J. [Department of Justice] orders us to continue, these investigations should be closed. The basis for investigation appears to be—pick someone you dislike and start investigating.[42]

Despite these critical assessments, the FBI continued its broad surveillance of Fonda. Indeed, she soon ended up on the Nixon White House "enemies" list.[43] Even so, for all its power, the FBI never succeeded in building a case against Fonda. If it pinned its hopes on trapping Fonda by uncovering secret activities, the FBI was blind to one obvious fact: Fonda had no secret political activities. She did her utmost to take her ideas into the public space, to articulate opposition to the war as persuasively as possible, to engage war supporters directly, and to respond to critics. Indeed, her antiwar action was a model of democratic dissent. Her attention was first drawn to the war by the voices of GIs and veterans, by the protests of ordinary people. Her courage to continue speaking out against the war was sustained by the support that she got from GIs, veterans, and the crowds that came out to talk about the war. She was arrested under false pretenses with additional false attacks on her reputation. But she didn't complain about the FBI surveillance, or about her false arrests, or about the lies her government spread about her. When possible, she used the courts to defend her rights and then kept working to end the war.

4

GOING TO VIETNAM

FONDA FIRST PLANNED TO VISIT North Vietnam in 1971, after her work against the war introduced her to many Americans who had already gone there. Most of the Americans who traveled to North Vietnam came out of churches and universities, from experience in the civil rights movement, and from established peace groups in the United States. They were pastors, teachers, students, and civil rights and antiwar activists, all looking for firsthand information about the war and about the Vietnamese. Many were women.[1]

Mary Clarke and Lorraine Gordon were the first Americans to go to Hanoi after Lyndon Johnson announced Operation Rolling Thunder in February 1965. Clark and Gordon belonged to Women Strike for Peace, a group founded in late 1961 when thousands of women across the United States walked off their jobs and out of their homes for a one-day strike protesting Washington's policy of testing atomic bombs by exploding them in the atmosphere. Clarke and Gordon spent three days in Hanoi in May 1965. Bombs were not yet falling on the city, but it was preparing for an air attack. The American visitors were startled by the burgeoning construction of air-raid shelters all over Hanoi. Some of the shelters were large enough to accommodate dozens of people but many were small units set along Hanoi streets at ten-foot intervals: concrete, cylindrical one-person bomb shelters with lids two inches thick left ajar for quick occupancy.[2]

After Clarke and Gordon's trip in 1965, more and more Americans traveled to North Vietnam. By 1972, nearly three hundred Americans had gone there looking for alternative information about the war at a time when the American media largely presented the official view from Washington. The travelers brought with them humanitarian supplies in open defiance of U.S. prohibitions against taking medicines, X-ray machines, or bandages to Hanoi, and they carried mail for the American POWs in Hanoi at a time when Washington made mail deliveries difficult.

In addition to the physical dangers and the sheer difficulty of traveling there, Americans who went to North Vietnam knew they faced government harassment upon return to the United States. North Vietnam was on the ever-changing list of countries that Americans were "banned" from visiting, a ban imposed by presidential fiat because Congress refused to pass restrictive travel laws. Federal agents confiscated the passports of travelers to Vietnam when they returned to the United States. It was knowledge of this likely outcome that kept Martin Luther King Jr. from traveling to Hanoi in 1967 with German theologian Martin Niemoeller and Presbyterian minister and antiwar activist A.J. Muste.[3]

Legal scholars almost unanimously agreed that the White House travel bans violated the Constitution. When Americans whose passports were seized sued to recover them, lower courts sided with them. Finally, in late 1967, the United States Court of Appeals in Washington, D.C., ruled against the government and for the citizens' right to travel. The ruling drew a distinction between the citizen and the passport, which was the property of the government. The Court of Appeals ruled that only passports could be prohibited from "traveling." If American citizens went to "banned" countries and their passports showed no evidence of their visits—no visas—then the government could not seize their passports. The court went further: if there was an offending visa in the passport, and if the government *did* seize the passport, it had to issue a new one as soon as that citizen requested it—even if the applicant openly declared an intention to take the new passport directly back to a banned country. Under these guidelines, seizing passports was pointless. By the time that Fonda went to Vietnam, the United States had largely ceased trying to prosecute such travel.[4]

The account of Fonda's trip to Vietnam, and the furor that it raised, illuminates other issues, including the way the Pentagon, at first, alternately endangered and neglected the American POWs in Hanoi. The Pentagon infiltrated mail that family members sent to POWs in Hanoi, putting contraband in that mail that included miniature parts for radios and receivers, coded writing kits, along with questions like; "What frequencies and times can you receive?" In no time, officials in Hanoi discovered these materials and they promptly told the world what they had found and laid out the items in the Museum of War in Hanoi. They believed that the Pentagon was sending these items to prisoners in Hanoi to try to pinpoint the location of the POW camps and then bomb the rest of Hanoi with impunity. Hanoi officials were also wary of the prisoners to whom these packages were addressed, suspecting them of working with the Pentagon to send out location information about the camps.

After the Pentagon put contraband in POW packages, officials in Hanoi decided that mail coming from the United States to the prisoners of war had to be X-rayed first. North Vietnam, a poor country by any standard, lacked even X-ray machines for mail so it told Washington to send POW mail first to Moscow, where it would be X-rayed and then passed on to Hanoi. The White House refused to ask the U.S. Postal Service to set up routing through Moscow; it refused to acknowledge that contraband had been smuggled into soap, toothpaste, and candy bars sent to the POWs; it refused to promise to stop the smuggling, and it called the Vietnamese liars. Hanoi refused, in turn, to accept further mail through the existing system.[5]

By 1969, American servicemen imprisoned in Hanoi were virtually cut off from communication with their families. Sometimes the Pentagon didn't even deliver the prisoners' mail to their families. For example, in 1971, the National Liberation Front in South Vietnam announced the early release of twenty-three-year-old POW, John Sexton Jr. Upon hearing the news, the Pentagon hastily released a letter to Sexton's family that he had written from his prison camp in South Vietnam two years earlier. John Sexton's father was angry. He hadn't heard anything from his son during his entire captivity. "We thought he was probably dead for those two years and here they [the Pentagon] had the letter all along," he said. Pressed for an explanation from Sexton's family, Pentagon officials said that they had been examining John Sexton's letter to see if it really was from him and if it had a "propaganda content."[6]

When American citizens returned from the War Museum in Hanoi and said that they had seen contraband items there from the Pentagon, officials in Washington flatly denied sending secret materials to the POWs and claimed the reports proved the treachery of the Vietnamese. So when Reverend William Sloan Coffin Jr. was in Hanoi, he took photographs of these items in the museum and wrote an article about it. A Pentagon spokesman said that Coffin's photos and news story were "too ridiculous to dignify with a reply." But the items were real enough. Some family members of the POWs in Hanoi later detailed how Pentagon personnel had inserted these items in packages and letters sent to POWs in Hanoi.[7]

After the White House refused to facilitate mail to and from Hanoi, families in the United States became desperate to hear from their missing men. A letter was usually the first sign that they had survived a shoot down. Family members wanted that letter. So when they heard through the news media that antiwar Americans were going to Hanoi, they called the activists and implored them to take letters for their fathers, their sons, or their husbands, and give it to Vietnamese officials in Hanoi. The families asked them to bring back letters as well.

At first, different groups of travelers to Hanoi responded to these family pleas on a case-by-case basis as best as they could, but by 1969, Women Strike for Peace was sending regular delegations to North Vietnam, and the media sometimes reported their upcoming trips. The group was soon inundated with calls from POW families, and before long they were, by default, the most regular mail couriers to the airmen imprisoned in Hanoi. By the time the prisoners were released in early 1973, Women Strike for Peace had carried over seven thousand letters to the POWs in Hanoi from their families, and just as many back to the United States. They also brought the first letters back from prisoners who had been captured in South Vietnam.

Women Strike for Peace kept a record of every prisoner's name that passed through their hands. They checked this list against the official Vietnamese list of POWs, adding names as they appeared, and asking the Vietnamese about them. Later, they even began forwarding to Vietnamese officials names that Americans had given them of family members who had been shot down and were now missing.

Women Strike for Peace was not secretive about its work. They wanted to work with the officials in Washington, but the officials were often hostile. In February 1970, for example, the Defense Department sent a letter to all families of POWs, warning them not to send mail through Women Strike for Peace. The letter said that "those who use such groups as an intermediary run the very real risk of personal harassment and have no assurance at all that welfare information will be received." The Pentagon's letter offered no hint as to what form this "personal harassment" might take, but FBI agents began visiting families of POWs and warning them personally against sending mail with Women Strike for Peace. When pressed for a reason not to send letters to her son, one FBI agent told a defiant mother that Women Strike for Peace "was felt to belong to the communist group."[8]

Fonda knew about the political impasse of the mail and how Women Strike for Peace was helping resolve it for the families. On her first trip to Vietnam, in March 1971, she planned to carry mail for POWs in Hanoi that family members had sent directly to Women Strike for Peace. When that trip was canceled after a renewed U.S. bombing campaign over North Vietnam, she hoped for another opportunity. It came in July 1972; by then, traveling to Hanoi had become more common. At this late stage in the war, with American troops almost completely withdrawn, more American journalists were going to Hanoi and writing reports that presented a more balanced view of the war. Some even expressed sympathy for the struggle of the Vietnamese people.[9] American scientists were also going to Hanoi to establish professional ties with Vietnamese scientists. Labor leaders went to Hanoi as well. Even U.S. business leaders went to Hanoi seeking opportunities.[10]

The Vietnamese Committee of Solidarity with the American People, which hosted most international visitors to Hanoi, invited Fonda to North Vietnam in 1972. The Vietnam Cultural Association and the Vietnam Film Artists Association invited her as well. These groups were made up of young photographers, poets, actors, singers, dancers, and other artists devoted to preserving Vietnam's folk culture. They traveled deep into the country, where they performed amid blasts of air-raid warnings. They invited international visitors to go with them.

In addition to carrying mail for American POWs, Fonda wanted to go to Vietnam to observe the war firsthand. This took on added urgency in the early summer of 1972 when reports came from Hanoi that American planes were dropping explosives on the dikes that held back the waters on the vast, fertile plains of the Red River Delta, where over fifteen million Vietnamese peasants lived and cultivated rice. When Radio Hanoi first broadcast news of this bombing, White House officials dismissed it as "enemy propaganda." Then Sweden's ambassador to North Vietnam, Jean-Christophe Oberg, told international reporters that he had seen the bomb-damaged dikes himself. He described the air attacks as "methodic." Jean Thoreval, a journalist covering the war for *Le Monde,* reported that American planes had dive-bombed a dike system while he was standing on it. He said it appeared to him that the attacks were "aimed at the whole system of dikes." Sven Oste, foreign editor of Sweden's largest newspaper, reported an even more ominous finding: some of the bombs dropped on the dikes were delayed-action explosives. These bombs, he said, burrowed into the earthworks around the rivers, lay there silently, then blew up without warning if workers used heavy machines to fill in the bomb craters. With the rainy season approaching, Oste said, the Vietnamese were forced to fill the deep craters slowly—by hand.[11]

The dike-bombing tactic deeply disturbed Fonda. She believed it was a savage tactic and wanted it to stop. She believed bombing dikes could kill untold thousands of Vietnamese whose survivors would, in turn, try to shoot down even more American planes and imprison the pilots. Bombing dikes indicated escalation, not the de-escalation the president kept promising. The Vietnamese would not give up their rice harvest lightly. In May, Nixon had ordered American planes to drop explosive mines in the harbors of Haiphong, Hanoi's link to the world. With the harbor of Haiphong now riddled with silent explosives, people there could not count on international food shipments if famine struck. If the dikes were bombed and the delta flooded, the Vietnamese would starve. Under these conditions, the young women and men at the antiaircraft emplacements around Hanoi were vigilant. The Vietnamese saw them as heroes—insurers of food security. The antiaircraft emplacements were their defense against famine. The American pilots bombing the dikes would pay the price.

Fonda went to Hanoi with personal and political interests—and over two hundred letters for the POWs there. Her personal interest was to carry mail to the American POWs, meet with Vietnamese musicians, writers, actors, and artists and learn about wartime life in Vietnam. Her political interest was to photograph the bomb damage done to the dikes in the Red River Delta and publicize the evidence. If the bombing of dikes was known, she believed, there would be an international outcry, but an international outcry was not enough. It would take a domestic outcry in the United States to stop the bombing. If stark evidence of the bombing reached enough Americans, she believed that they, combined with the international community, could put pressure on the White House to abandon the bombing before the rainy season began in August and September.

Fonda arrived in Hanoi on July 12 and stayed two weeks. By then, there were relatively few American troops left in Vietnam—the ground war was almost entirely Vietnamized. When Fonda arrived in Hanoi, in fact, the very last American combat troops were leaving South Vietnam. They left behind over forty thousand troops to support the Vietnamization effort, air crews for the bombing raids over North Vietnam, and over a hundred thousand American men and women elsewhere in Southeast Asia.

When Fonda reached Hanoi, she was following the trail between Hanoi and the United States left by the nearly three hundred Americans who preceded her. Like her, they had come to North Vietnam to learn firsthand about the war. Like her, they visited bombed schools, hospitals, villages, and antiaircraft emplacements. They, too, met with POWs in Hanoi and carried mail between them and their families. Like Fonda, their talks were broadcast on Radio Hanoi. The difference between Fonda and these other activists, some of them also well-known to the public, was that the White House and the Pentagon largely ignored them at that time, just as supporters of the war did afterward.[12]

The Vietnamese cultural groups who had invited Fonda introduced her to two aspects of Vietnamese life. One was the rich cultural life that continued under the bombardment: musical performances, dance, poetry readings, and plays that helped confront the war through art. The young people in the cultural groups performed American plays, they explained to Fonda, to help the Vietnamese people understand the United States better. While Fonda was in Vietnam, the Vietnamese Cultural Association was on tour performing Arthur Miller's play *All My Sons,* the story of an American manufacturer during World War II whose plant made airplane parts. He discovers that his airplane parts are faulty, but he keeps silent for fear of losing his government contract. As a result, planes crash and people are killed, including one of his own sons. A surviving son learns what his father has done and condemns him for his silence. There is no excuse for not living up to our responsibility, the son says, not money, not comfort, not family loyalty.

One afternoon while air-raid sirens sounded in the distance, Fonda sat on the lawn of an eleventh-century Vietnamese building and watched Vietnamese actors perform Miller's play. Afterward, she asked the performers why they had chosen this particular play. The performers said it was "so that people can see it and can understand better what Americans are like. The son is a good person. We make a distinction between the American government and the American people."[13]

The Vietnamese, Fonda discovered, tried to understand American society so they would not hate the American people or blame them for the war. When the bombs fell, the Vietnamese blamed Nixon. "Nixon's flying," they would tell American visitors as they pointed out the bomb craters and blasted buildings. "No give damn," they sometimes added defiantly. One Vietnamese official told his American guests that, in their war experience, "only our English has been 'Vietnamized.' "[14]

If the Vietnamese could see the American people as potential friends, Fonda believed, Americans might also see the Vietnamese as such. She thought about this as she saw the other aspect of Vietnamese life—its bombed side. The young Vietnamese took her to villages, to hospitals, schools, and residential areas in urban areas repeatedly bombed by planes that swept over the civilian population, leveling their homes and killing their children. Two days after arriving in Hanoi, Fonda went outside the city to a rural, rice-growing area where she donned boots and waded through rice paddies to see bomb craters on dikes built at the confluence of two rivers. Around the dikes were miles of threatened rice fields.

Fonda stood on the dikes and filmed the massive bomb craters. She filmed villagers carrying dirt to fill in the gigantic holes. Some had wheelbarrows and some carried their loads in baskets fastened to bamboo poles slung over their shoulders. They already needed more than three thousand cubic yards of dirt to fill the existing craters—and there were more bombings ahead. They worked furiously with their wheelbarrows and baskets because the rains were coming and the river would rise. Many days' work filling one bomb crater could be undone in seconds when the American planes struck again.[15]

At Hong Phong village, where Fonda went that same day, American planes had dropped over fifty bombs the week before. When asked about it in Washington, the Assistant Secretary of Defense insisted that the planes only hit military targets. Fonda did not see—nor did other reporters—military targets in the area. What they did see were destroyed peasant homes, smashed fruit trees, and dead farm animals. The attack came in the morning when most of the able-bodied villagers were out in the fields. It was the elderly and the very young who had stayed near their homes who were killed and maimed in that air raid. Some were killed outright, others too badly injured ever to work in the fields again. The village could never be the same. One bomb brings a thousand social problems in its wake, a Vietnamese guide once told Americans as they walked through a bombed village.

In Hanoi, Fonda went to Bach Mai, a large university hospital and research center that was still in service, but on a vastly reduced scale. Many of its buildings were damaged by bombs, and its staff used the hospital only for procedures and surgeries impossible to perform elsewhere. They had built a network of bomb shelters around and beneath the hospital and devised precise procedures to evacuate occupants to bomb shelters within minutes. The staff worked every day knowing the hospital was a marked target.

When Fonda visited in July, Bach Mai Hospital had only six months left. During President Nixon's Christmas Eve bombing of 1972, American bombers would strike the hospital one last time, leaving, in the words of a *New York Times* report, "rescue workers carrying patients piggy-back, cranes and bulldozers and people using only their hands, desperately clearing debris to reach victims still buried in the rubble, and the frantic hospital director running from one building to another."[16] One of the first bombs that Christmas Eve blew a building apart, exploding its concrete over a bomb shelter where Dr. Tran Do Trinh, the deputy director of the hospital, was teaching a class about mitral stenosis. Because the class was already in the bomb shelter, there was no place to go, so Dr. Trinh continued his lecture and the medical students continued taking notes until the concrete blasted the shelter area. "The living were mixed with the dead," Dr. Trinh said. "We had to break through the rubble that covered the entrances with our bare hands to remove the wounded. It took almost two weeks to extricate all of the dead, and the smell of the dead filled the hospital." Among the bodies that he had to carry out were three of his students.

When Fonda was at Bach Mai in July 1972, the hospital was

still functioning, the staff still optimistic, the director proud of their skill in providing health care and teaching medical students.[17] Fonda had not gone to Vietnam intending to speak on Radio Hanoi. She had wanted to speak to American pilots on the air bases in Thailand and South Vietnam when *Free the Army* was touring in the Pacific, but the U.S. government had prevented her from entering those countries. In Hanoi, she realized that she now had the opportunity to reach the American pilots who were even now bombing Vietnam and who might sometimes listen to Radio Hanoi's English-language programs. After her intense experience of viewing, day after day, heavy bomb damage in North Vietnam, Fonda wanted to ask the pilots to consider what they would see on the ground if they ever visited the places they had blasted.

She asked her Vietnamese hosts if she could tape-record a message to broadcast on Radio Hanoi, some description of the view below the bombs. They gave her a Sony tape recorder, and every morning Fonda sat down and spoke from her heart about what she had seen the day before. The scenes she described to the pilots were fresh in her mind. Sometimes she read from printed materials, including the *Pentagon Papers*. Usually she spoke without notes—as if informally addressing a small group.

The first of these recorded talks to American pilots were rebroadcast over Radio Hanoi on July 14. Fonda described what she had seen the day before in Hong Phong village where, a Pentagon spokesman had insisted, only military targets were hit. "In the area where I went yesterday," she said, "it was easy to see that there are no military targets, there is no important highway, there is no communication network, there is no heavy industry. These are peasants. They grow rice and they rear pigs. They are similar to the farmers in the Midwest many years ago in the United States. Perhaps your grandmothers and grandfathers would not be so different from these peasants." As she walked through the rice paddies to the dikes where the American bombs had fallen, Fonda said, she wondered how she would be received. But she saw and felt no hostility as she spoke to the women there, she said in her broadcast. "They seemed to be asking themselves, 'What kind of people can Americans be, those who would drop all kinds of bombs so carelessly on their innocent heads, destroying their villages and endangering the lives of these millions of people?' " Fonda then put in an earnest plea for the pilots to think about this. "All of you in the cockpits of your planes, on the aircraft carriers, those who are loading the bombs, those who are repairing the planes, those who are working on the 7th fleet, please think what you are doing. Are these people your enemy? What will you say to your children years from now who may ask you why you fought the war? What words will you be able to say to them?"[18]

Fonda never told the pilots—or any of the GIs she met, for that matter—what to do. She only asked them to think. Her broadcast after she visited the bombed hospital of Bach Mai described what she saw, how she felt, and she asked the pilots to think about that, too:

> I visited a hospital today, the Bach Mai hospital. I saw a huge bomb crater in the center of the hospital. It was obviously dropped there on purpose. With the kind of bombs, the kind of techniques that have been developed now, you know, particularly you pilots know, that accidents like that don't happen. This was no accident. It destroyed wards filled with patients. It destroyed hospital equipment. It killed some doctors. It is a terrible thing to see what has been done. Why? Why did you do this? Why do you follow orders telling you to destroy a hospital or bomb the schools?
>
> Do you know what happens to the women when the napalm that you're dropping lands on them? You have no idea.

Deformed hands, necks twisted out of shape, women with children who were working, women who are used to working with their hands, who were lovely and alive and graceful—the way Vietnamese women are with their long black hair—twisted out of shape, not dead, not spared the pain and the misery of living as a mutilated person, forever in physical pain.

Why is this being done? The victims in the hospitals with thousands of holes in their bodies from the steel pellets that are being dropped, and even worse now that the Nixon administration has gone one step further from the Johnson administration—the steel pellets have been perfected, they're now plastic, rough-edged plastic. Why? Because plastic doesn't show up on X-rays, which means that these people spend the rest of their lives with their bodies filled with plastic pellets and every time they move, it causes excruciating agony.

The women that I have talked to were not even under your bombs but came to help victims of the chemical bombs. The chemical toxic gases were so strong that even after the bombs, long after the bombs had exploded when these women came to save the other people, they got sick. And weeks and months later they still—they pass out, they have headaches, they are losing their memory. Women who, who were pregnant are giving birth to deformed babies.

How can it be that the people of the United States have caused this kind of terrible, terrible suffering on a nation so far away? On a nation that has caused us no harm? I mean, what do you think? That the Vietnamese people are going to row across the Pacific in canoes? So I ask you and I will continue to ask you as long as I am here and I ask you as an American and I ask you because I cry every night when I think of what these people have to go through, and I cry

> every night when I think of the danger that is being done to them because of the bombing of their kids. And I say, Why? And I say that the time has come for us to stop it.

On July 17 and 18, Fonda traveled to Nam Dinh district, an industrial area known throughout Vietnam for its textile production. Nam Dinh was a favorite of American bombers who had, only weeks earlier, reduced the textile plant to rubble. It was the second time the textile plant had been destroyed. When the French had left after their 1954 defeat, they had carried off, in revenge, most of the machines and equipment from the plant. That equipment had been laboriously replaced over the years, but the American bombers had blasted the entire rebuilt structure in minutes. Fonda walked among blocks of houses leveled by bombing and strafing runs where rubble replaced homes that once housed thousands of Vietnamese factory workers and their families. The bombs had fallen heaviest there, and then a second wave of planes had swept over the area and dropped antipersonnel weapons on the survivors who rushed out after the initial bombing. The high school was destroyed, as was an old pagoda and a kindergarten. The neighborhood was torn apart. Survivors were dazed. Children were orphaned; someone needed to care for them. The elderly were left without children. Someone needed to care for them, too. In Nam Dinh, once again, Fonda saw that the bombs had left behind a thousand social problems.

When Fonda returned from Nam Dinh, she tape-recorded an account of her visit, describing it precisely from the point of view of the people on the ground. When she was on Hang Tien Street, she said, she had found two women

> who were picking through the rubble left by the bombs and they came over and spoke to me. One of the women said that she'd been at the market when the bomb fell on

the top of her house. Her house has been turned into a huge bomb crater. Her husband and three children were all killed. Her oldest son was twenty-five years old, her next oldest son had been twenty-two, and her youngest son was eighteen. Three families in this area were entirely destroyed by the bombs. . . .

I saw a secondary school where six hundred students from fifth to seventh grade had been in class. That school had been hit by two bombs. I saw the center of a Chinese residential district, bombed, three planes, houses razed to the ground. The number one hospital of the city which had two hundred beds and it treated people from all over the city—large parts of it had been destroyed, particularly the pediatrics department and the supply department where the medicines had been kept. The large factory, the textile factories of Nam Dinh are in charred ruins. No one is allowed to go in there because there are delayed reaction bombs. . . .

I went to the dike, the dike system of the city of Nam Dinh. Just this morning at four o'clock it was bombed again, and I was told that an hour after we left the city, planes came back and re-bombed Nam Dinh. The dike in many places has been cut in half and there are huge fissures running across the top of it.

Again, I am talking about these things and I am describing to you what I am seeing on the ground because I think that you must not understand that the destruction is being caused to civilian populations and residential areas, to cultural centers. I saw the pagodas bombed in Nam Dinh. The area in which there are theaters where people come to rest, the recreation centers were all destroyed in Nam Dinh.

What are your commanders telling you? How are they justifying this to you? Have you any idea what your bombs are doing when you pull the levers and push the buttons? Some day we're going to have to answer to our children for this war. Some day we are going to have to explain to the rest of the world how it is that we caused this type of suffering and death and destruction to a people who have done us no harm. Perhaps we should start to do it now before it is too late.

Perhaps, however, the most important thing that has to be said about Vietnam is that despite all that Nixon is doing here and that Johnson has done before, despite all the bombs, the people are more determined than ever to fight.

This is very important to understand. Every man, woman, and child in this country has a determination like a bright flame, buoying them, strengthening their determination to go forward, to fight for freedom and independence.

And what interests me so much is that as an American, is that this is so much like the essence of the American people. The one unifying quality I believe about the American people, the common denominator that we all share, is the love for freedom and democracy. The problem is that definition of freedom and democracy has been distorted for us and we have to redefine what that means. But the Vietnamese who have been fighting for four thousand years know very well.

And as in Nam Dinh, for example, all the rubble and all of the destruction has not stopped them. It is fascinating to see. There are people still living there, there is still electricity in the city. The factory has been dispersed, but it is still working. The textiles are still being produced. Families are still producing food for a living. They are still going to the markets, and they are still ready to pick up a gun if necessary and defend their homes and their land.

As she traveled across North Vietnam, Fonda literally lived under the bombs. When her group spotted planes in the countryside, they took cover in the ditches. The air-raid sirens often sent her and those with her to bomb shelters where she waited, apprehensively, for her own country's planes to start on bombing above her. When her group was returning by road from the searing visit to Nam Dinh, air-raid sirens rang out. A family near the road offered the group the use of their own air-raid system—one small underground shelter built for each member of the family. Fonda shared a shelter with the family's young daughter as American planes roared overhead and dropped bombs within hearing range. The small bomb shelters were cramped but still better than the open ditches on the side of the road.

Fonda often met other international visitors in Hanoi's bomb shelters. Once she found herself with members of the International Control Commission, a United Nations group that had already lost one plane in the air corridor between Phnom Penh and Hanoi. There were always international reporters in the shelters. Fonda also met members of the American Friends Service Committee who had come to Hanoi to donate surgical equipment and medicines.[19]

Being on the bombed side of the war zone left Fonda feeling outraged that the war had been normalized into just another political game; that aerial bombardment of civilians—their homes, factories, power plants, and places of worship—was just another acceptable form of politics. While Americans disagreed about many things, their political leaders permitted them—their media, their business leaders, most of their entertainment figures—to object to war, but not to disrupt it. Fonda believed the war needed to be disrupted. She rejected a foreign policy that destroyed so many lives, that injected the hopelessness into entire societies, that crushed people's right to make their own history. She recorded another message on her Sony tape recorder:

> This is Jane Fonda. I have come to North Vietnam to bear witness to the damage being done the Vietnamese land and

to Vietnamese lives. . . . Nixon is continuing to risk your lives and the lives of the American prisoners of war under the bomb in a last desperate gamble to keep his office come November. How does it feel to be used as pawns? You may be shot down, you may perhaps even be killed, but for what, and for whom? Eighty percent of the American people, according to a recent poll, have stopped believing in the war and think we should get out, think we should bring all of you home. The people back home are crying for you. We are afraid of what must be happening to you as human beings. For it isn't possible to destroy, to receive salary for pushing buttons and pulling levers that are dropping illegal bombs on innocent people without having done damage to your own souls.

Tonight when you are alone, ask yourselves: What are you doing? Accept no ready answers fed to you by rote from basic training on up, but as men, as human beings. Can you justify what you are doing? Do you know why you are flying these combat missions, collecting extra pay on Sunday? The people beneath your planes have done us no harm. They want to live in peace. They want to rebuild their country. They cannot understand what kind of people could fly over their heads and drop bombs on them.

Did you know that the antipersonnel bombs that are thrown from some of your planes were outlawed by the Hague Convention of 1907 of which the United States was a signatory? I think that if you knew what these bombs were doing, you would get very angry at the men who invented them. They cannot destroy bridges or factories. They cannot pierce steel or cement. They only target is unprotected human flesh. The pellet bombs now contain rough-edged plastic pellets. Your bosses, whose minds think in terms of statistics, not human lives, are proud of this new perfection.

> The plastic pellets don't show up on x-rays and cannot be removed. The hospitals here are filled with babies and women and old people who will live for the rest of their lives in agony with these pellets embedded in them.
>
> Can we fight this kind of war and continue to call ourselves Americans? Are these people so different from our own children, our mothers, or grandmothers? I don't think so, except that perhaps they have a surer sense of why they are living and for what they are willing to die.

At the bombing sites, survivors asked questions that American visitors found hard to answer. "What would you do if our pilots bombed Pittsburgh?" a Vietnamese woman once asked. When a group of women, including poet Denise Levertov, were walking along the bombed dikes of the Red River Delta one day, an old Vietnamese woman carrying water asked the guide who these woman were. When the guide, Madame Be of the Vietnamese Union of Women, replied that they were Americans, her questioner recoiled. "Americans! Yankees!" the horrified woman exclaimed, shifting the weight of the carrying pole balanced on her shoulders. "Why do you want to bring such evil people here?"[20]

On one of the last days that Fonda was in Vietnam, her hosts took her to a rural area just outside Hanoi. One of their stops was at an antiaircraft emplacement to meet young women and men who lived there, trying to guard the rice fields and villages from aerial bombardment. Fonda spent about an hour at the site where journalists and photographers had come too, along with the usual Vietnamese artists, musicians, dancers, and writers. Some of the musicians sang a song at the site, and the bystanders, including Fonda, applauded when they finished. In a spirit of reciprocity, Fonda offered to sing a song to them in Vietnamese. It was a song written by a Vietnamese student imprisoned by the American-backed Saigon government in South Vietnam, and it was popular throughout the divided country. Fonda had learned the song from her hosts, who sang it often, and now she sang the song back to them. When she finished, the group burst into applause and appreciative laughter, moved that an American would take the trouble to learn the song in their own language. While they were laughing and clapping, they spontaneously invited Fonda to sit in the seat of the antiaircraft emplacement. When she sat in the seat, they continued to applaud and Fonda responded by thanking them for their generosity, talking briefly about the intense experience of life in the war zone.

Images of Fonda at the site and sitting in the emplacement seat were later—much later—deployed by her accusers, who claimed she had committed a crime by sitting, literally, in the seat of those who tried to protect their homes from American bombers. Many Americans who, like Fonda, had traveled to Vietnam and witnessed the terror that American bombs inflicted on the land and people, shared her belief that antiaircraft equipment was a defense that could save innocent villagers from being bombed and killed. That these emplacements were used to protect against American bombing of villages, dikes, and urban areas should have raised anew the issue of the American bombing policy. Instead, the image of Fonda at the antiaircraft emplacement was framed as though the scandal lay not in the bombing, but in those Americans who opposed it. By sitting in the place of the young people at the antiaircraft site, Fonda was expressing a solidarity with the realities of their lives. It was a sentiment partly expressed in an article American journalist Anthony Lewis wrote after he had traveled to Vietnam and saw the same things Fonda had seen. Lewis wrote, "With sympathy for the men who fly American planes, and for their wives and families, one has to recognize the greater courage of the North Vietnamese people who have been their targets."[21]

Before Fonda left Hanoi, her hosts asked if she would meet

with American POWs. Since 1965, American visitors to Hanoi had been meeting with American pilots imprisoned there. As antiwar activists turned into regular carriers of POW mail, these visits with the airmen became routine. By now, many of the POWs in Hanoi opposed the war and met readily with the activists. By 1970, antiwar sentiment within their camps was rising to levels approaching that of the general American population. This was partly true because the massive bombing raids of Vietnam in 1970 brought down new pilots who were less supportive of the war than many of the pilots who were shot down in the mid-1960s when support for the war was high in the United States. It was also partly true because the Vietnamese sometimes took the airmen out to the sites of villages, schools, and hospitals that their bombers had destroyed. Sometimes they took them to see the survivors, the bandaged, orphaned children, the old people left homeless and childless by the raids. Some of the airmen said that these visits convinced them that their bombing coordinates were not, as the Pentagon claimed, directed only at military targets.

The airmen in prison in Hanoi had plenty of time to read, and their prison library contained some of the same books about the war that Americans were reading at home. One small prison library carried titles by authors including Charles Dickens, Arthur Schlesinger Jr., Mikhail Sholokhov, and John Steinbeck, as well as the complete works of Shakespeare. It also had books on the war: Howard Zinn's *Vietnam: the Logic of Withdrawal,* George McTurnan Kahin's *The United States in Vietnam,* Don Luce's *Vietnam: the Unheard Voices,* Felix Greene's *Vietnam,* Townsend Hoopes's *The Limits of Intervention,* James Gavin's *Crisis Now,* the American Friends Service Committee's book on Vietnam, and others. Eventually, even the *Pentagon Papers* made its way to the prison library in Hanoi where the airmen read it at around the same time their fellow Americans were reading it.

Some pilots said that these books made them think about Vietnam as a country in and of itself for the first time. "Flying is exciting," one American POW said after his release, "especially when you're being shot at. There's a great sense of power in flying a jet; there's something almost sexual about it. You don't think about the people you're fighting, you think about the target. Otherwise you don't think about much else except your family, flight pay, and promotion. Only when you're shot down do you ask, 'What the hell was I doing up there?' "[22] In the prison camps with little to do but think, support for the war dimmed. By 1971, as many as half of the officers in Hanoi were openly disillusioned about the war.[23]

Many airmen in Hanoi, whatever their opinion of the war, met frequently with journalists and visitors from Western countries. It was a good way to get word out that they were captured, not dead. If they were photographed, their families could get a glimpse of them. Meeting with fellow Americans from home also helped normalize their lives in a small way, connect them to the world they hoped to return to soon. Some of the airmen who opposed the war and wanted Americans to work to end it said exactly that in the interviews with American TV film crews.

For example, in late 1970, Canadian journalist Michael Maclear interviewed two American POWs, Navy Commanders Walter Wilber and Robert Schweitzer. Both men were thoughtful, earnest, and open, Maclear said. They talked about getting mail through Women Strike for Peace and about messages they had taped for their families that went out over Radio Hanoi to be picked up by the CIA and forwarded to their families at home. They showed Maclear the volleyball and basketball courts set up in the courtyard inside their prison block. They showed him pictures of their families that they kept in their rooms. They had been taken to all of the museums in Hanoi, they said, the art museum as well as the museum of war. They had been taken to the Catholic

Cathedral on Christmas Eve for a service that was packed with Vietnamese. "We discuss the war very much," Wilber said, "because the war is very close to us here. We're all involved with it." He went on to say, quite deliberately, that the best way out would be for the United States to withdraw its troops and make peace with Vietnam. Schweitzer told Maclear that his prison experience had given him "the deepest discussions I've ever had in my life with my fellow prisoners here. We've had to go to the very core of our feelings on a number of things: loyalty, what is it? Where does it lie? Morality? Legality? In our affluent, rushed life in our country, I suppose, we don't normally give too deep a thought about it. But here we definitely do—I feel all of us do—and we've talked at great length about how we feel . . . I feel that the future of our country as well as Vietnam and Indochina cannot be served by the prolongation of this war." He had written to his wife, Schweitzer said, and urged her to join peace groups and read the books about Vietnam that they were reading in prison.[24]

In May, two months before Fonda reached Hanoi, some of the imprisoned airmen had sent out a handwritten letter with another group of Americans who had come to Hanoi. The airmen's letter was written for "the United States Congress and to all Americans:"

> Ladies and Gentlemen:
>
> Despite a bombing halt announced in 1968, the President ordered the resumption, and authorized the continuation of the bombing of the Democratic Republic of Vietnam, with a variety of excuses to justify the raids. On Sunday morning, 16 April 1972, the peace of Hanoi and Haiphong was shattered by American aircraft and bombs. Many innocent people died a totally needless and senseless death.

We, detained Americans in Hanoi, could not help but be struck by the futility of such action. We have come to know the Vietnamese people, and we know that no bombing, or threat of death, is going to still the spirit that lives in their hearts. We believe that widespread bombing of the Democratic Republic of Vietnam only serves to turn world opinion more strongly against the United States, and risks the death and capture of many more Americans, as well as endangering the lives of those already held captive.

No bombing of Hanoi and Haiphong will cause the Provisional Revolutionary Government of the Republic of South Vietnam and the Democratic Republic of Vietnam to come begging for peace, for while they truly desire peace it will not be peace short of freedom and independence.

No bombing of the Democratic Republic of Vietnam serves to make the withdrawal of American forces any safer, it only makes it more likely that they cannot be withdrawn at all, and serves only as an admission of the failure of the Vietnamization policy. We appeal to the American people to exercise your rights and responsibilities, and demand an end to the war now! We appeal to Congress to take firm, positive action, to go with the words already spoken against the war. The resumption of the Paris Peace Conference and serious negotiations based on the 7–point proposal of the Provisional Revolutionary Government are obvious first steps. Require these steps and much more, Americans! The hope of the world is in your hands. Bring us home now![25]

By the time Jane Fonda reached to Hanoi with mail for the imprisoned airmen there, it had long been routine for international visitors to meet with POWs, and it was ordinary for Americans to hear that the pilots in Hanoi were urging an end to the war. When Fonda's hosts asked if she would visit a group of POWs, she readily agreed. The seven men who met with her were not coerced into the meeting; indeed, many more pilots wanted to meet with her than were able. "The entire camp that I was in when Jane Fonda visited wanted to see her," former POW Edison Miller said, although he didn't even know who Jane Fonda was. Miller only wanted to see her because he knew she was Henry Fonda's daughter. In addition to Lieutenant Colonel Edison Miller, the airmen who met with Fonda were Navy Commander Walter Wilber, Air Force Major James Padgett, Navy Lieutenant Commander David Wesley Hoffman, Air Force Captain Kenneth James Fraser, Air Force Captain William G. Byrns, and Air Force pilot Edward Elias.[26]

The seven POWs and Fonda met around a large table surrounded by chairs, enough room for them, for Fonda, some members of a Japanese film crew in Hanoi at the time, a French photographer, and some members of the Vietnamese Cultural Association. It was a typical meeting between international visitors and American airmen: low-key, filled with small talk, inquiries from the airmen about particular bits of news and sports from home, conversations about their families, requests to call them and pass on a message. Because all of the pilots who met with Fonda were openly critical of the war, they also talked about the war in a meeting that lasted about an hour.

After she met with the airmen in Hanoi, Fonda recorded this message on her Sony tape recorder, and it was broadcast over Radio Hanoi the next day.

> Yesterday evening, July 19, I had the opportunity of meeting seven U.S. pilots. Some of them were shot down as long ago as 1968 and some of them had been shot down very recently. They are all in good health. We had a very long talk, a very open and casual talk. We exchanged ideas freely. They asked me to bring back to the American people their

sense of disgust of the war and their shame for what they have been asked to do.

They told me that the pilots believe they are bombing military targets. They told me that the pilots are told that they are bombing to free their buddies down below, but of course, we know that every bomb that falls on North Vietnam endangers the lives of the American prisoners.

They asked me to bring messages back home to their loved ones and friends, telling them to please be as actively involved in the peace movement as possible, to renew their efforts to end the war.

One of the men who has been in the service for many, many years has written a book about Vietnamese history, and I thought this was very moving, that during the time he's been here, and the time that he has had to reflect on what he has been through and what he has done to this country, his thoughts have turned to this country, the history of struggle and the people that live here.

They all assured me that they have been well cared for. They listen to the radio, they receive letters. They are in good health. They asked about news from home.

I think we all shared during the time that I spent with them a sense of deep sadness that a situation like this has to exist, and I certainly felt from them a very sincere desire to explain to the American people that this war is a terrible crime and that it must be stopped, and that Richard Nixon is doing nothing except escalating it while preaching peace, endangering their lives while saying he cares about the prisoners.

And I think one of the things that touched me the most was that one of the pilots said to me that he was reading a book called *The Draft* written by the American Friends Service Committee and that in reading this book he had

> understood a lot about what had happened to him as a human being in his sixteen years of military service. He said that during those sixteen years, he had stopped relating to civilian life, he had forgotten that there was anything else besides the military and he said in realizing what had happened to him, he was very afraid that this was happening to many other people.
>
> I was very encouraged by my meeting with the pilots because I feel that the studying and the reading that they have been doing during their time here has taught them a great deal in putting the pieces of their lives back together again in a better way, hopefully, and I am sure that when they go home, they will go home better citizens than when they left.

Fonda left Hanoi on July 22 and flew to Paris for a press conference before returning to New York. She carried with her reels of film and a soundtrack documenting her trip. The film showed her visits to the bombed dike system, the villages, the hospitals, and the children of Vietnam. It showed her meeting with the POWs.

At the same time that Fonda flew back to the United States, news accounts were surfacing that the United States military had tried to start firestorms to burn the mahogany forests of Vietnam. "Operation Sherwood Forest," it was called. First, the military dropped millions of gallons of herbicides from the air on the double-canopied rain forest, then dropped fire explosives to burn off the now-dead foliage and ignite gigantic firestorms. The project was a mixed success, the secret report noted, because the "moist tropical rain forest would not burn." Despite this drawback, the report went on, "the effect of the defoliant itself significantly improved visibility for [aerial] observation."[27]

The report of this attempt to destroy Vietnam's forests by fire was followed by another report that U.S. commanders in Vietnam operated under directives granting virtually unlimited powers to order strikes on anything at all, without warning. The directives were worded so that on paper it appeared that commanders were urged, even ordered, to avoid "unnecessary danger to civilians and destruction of civilian property." That said, the directives also authorized any attack if the commander decided that "friendly survival is at stake," or if it was "necessary for the accomplishment of the commander's mission." The more recent directives forbade use of the term "free fire zone," which had come under wide criticism. Commanders were instead ordered to use the term "specified strike zone."[28]

With these news reports as a backdrop, Fonda's work in filming bombing attacks on dikes came at a crucial moment. The administration had routinely denied that it oversaw bombing of dikes, but Fonda was returning with film that proved the contrary. Her recent success as an actor promised to attract media and popular attention to this documentary evidence. News of her trip and her focus on the bombing of the dikes had appeared in U.S. media throughout her stay in Vietnam.

Fonda's trip was not the only factor that fixed the world's attention on the bombing, but it was the one that tipped a low-level international concern into a high-profile issue that the White House could no longer ignore. While Fonda was in Hanoi, reporters raised questions at White House press briefings about her reports of bomb damage on dikes. Within days, Dr. Eugene Carson Blake, president of the World Council of Churches, called on the United States to stop the bombing. Then–UN Secretary General Kurt Waldheim appealed to the White House to "stop this kind of bombing which could lead to enormous human suffering, enormous disaster." The White House responded that all the charges were propaganda from Hanoi. On July 25, White House press secretary Ron Ziegler told reporters that "North Vietnam is having some success with their campaign to get the world to believe that American planes were bombing dikes."[29] The White House resented the public censure. Despite all the court rulings that forbade it, White House aide Charles Colson ordered the State Department to seize Fonda's passport when she returned to the United States.

When Fonda arrived in Paris from Hanoi, she held a press conference and showed film of her trip, including that of the bombed dikes around Nam Dinh. At one of the sites, she pointed out over fifty bomb craters shown on the film. The same day as Fonda's press conference in Paris, the State Department called its own press conference. Bringing numerous easels into its briefing room, the department promised to show reporters reconnaissance photos proving there was no bombing of the dikes of Vietnam. But late in the afternoon, the press conference was abruptly cancelled with no reason given. "The Administration realized," one reporter wrote, "that Hanoi also could produce photographs."[30]

The next day, when reporters grilled State Department spokesman Charles W. Bray about the dike damage, Bray was tight-lipped. He would only say that "any damage to the dikes was a result of legitimate attacks on military installations such as anti-aircraft sites." He said the air strikes that did occur had "the most incidental and minor impact on the system of levees." He said that the United States had "evidence" to back up his statements. He declined to share that evidence with newsmen. In recent days, a reporter concluded afterward, "the Administration has made no secret of its annoyance and frustration over the growing world concern that the American bombing of Vietnam might lead to catastrophic results during the current rainy season if the dike system breaks down."[31]

The State Department then released its own "intelligence report"on the dike system in Vietnam. The report named only one person: Jane Fonda. The State Department tried to discredit Fonda's report by saying that she had been escorted "by Hanoi" to view the dike damage. After dismissing her report, the State Department showed parts of reconnaissance photos that revealed bomb damage at only twelve locations. The intelligence report did not mention the total number of bomb craters at all the sites, but said that "a crew of less than fifty men with wheelbarrows and hand tools" could repair any individual bomb crater easily in a day. Journalists complained that the State Department report offered no evidence "other than the barest details of the dike system and some cursory conclusions drawn from reconnaissance photos." State Department officials replied that they had decided not to show more photographs because North Vietnam might then issue its own photographs, which might be "fabricated."[32]

The furor wouldn't die down. And so, on July 27, the president suddenly called a news conference. Nixon invited reporters into the Oval Office, stood upright behind his desk, and blamed every single death in Vietnam on "policies of North Vietnamese communists." He talked about the "restraint" the United States was exercising in its war against Vietnam and said that Americans "should perhaps realize that when we talk about morality that it is never an easy question." Fonda had reminded reporters who asked her about her trip that the Allies had executed a German official for bombing dikes in Holland during World War II. Now, the president told the newsmen a story about how, in 1951, as a young vice president, he had asked President Eisenhower about the morality of the deliberate bombing of German cities during World War II: Dresden, Essen, Hamburg, and Berlin. Eisenhower had told him then, Nixon said, that "the height of immorality would be to allow Hitler to rule Europe." It would be the height of immorality now, Nixon told the reporters, for the United States to leave Vietnam.

Nixon then went after the UN Secretary-General and what he called other "well-intentioned and naive people." "I note with interest," he said, "that the Secretary-General, just like his predecessor, seized upon this enemy-inspired propaganda." He called Waldheim's concerns "hypocritical" and said that "if it were the policy of the U.S. to bomb the dikes, we would take them out, the significant part, in a week." Nixon said that the North Vietnamese were "skillful at propaganda" because they invited people into their country "to the areas where they have found bomb damage." He charged the Vietnamese with hypocrisy because "they have not gone to any great pains to fill those holes, which they would naturally want to do before the possibility of rain and flood again comes to the North."[33]

The White House presented the dike-bombing issue as one of Vietnamese duplicity, American dupes, and UN meddling. It sent George H. W. Bush, its ambassador to the United Nations, to meet with Secretary-General Waldheim and tell him that "these allegations are part of a carefully planned campaign by the North Vietnamese and their supporters to give worldwide circulation to this falsehood." He had "put forth strongly the view that the bombing charge was part of a massive propaganda campaign," Bush told reporters after the meeting. He said that he had "reaffirmed to the Secretary General that in our opinion, Hanoi was doing everything they could to escalate these falsehoods."[34] The Secretary-General said little in public. He had already sent a memo to the Security Council stating that "the United Nations can no longer remain a mute spectator of the horror of the war and of the peril which it increasingly poses to international peace." Several days later, the Secretary-General indicated that he had "unofficial" proof of the bombing of the dikes and he called Bush in for a second meeting. That meeting was short and Bush emerged looking "subdued and troubled," telling reporters that "I think that the best thing I can do on the subject is to shut up."[35]

In addition to, and because of, this furor over the dike-bombing's, Nixon found his Vietnam policy under legislative attack in both houses of Congress as the once-modest band of antiwar congressmen threatened to become a majority. Congress was finally fed up with the war that, according to the White House, was always almost over, but never actually was. Even the president's supporters were frustrated into action. Kansas Senator Robert Dole, who also chaired the Republican National Committee, said of the prolonged war: "there's a feeling in the Senate that we have to do something, even if it's wrong."[36]

The Senate passed an amendment calling for all American troops to be withdrawn from Vietnam over the next four months, provided that the POWs were also released. The once reliably hawkish House Foreign Affairs Committee voted for a similar antiwar amendment. The Senate then voted to cut off funds for "any use of rainmaking or the creation of forest fires as a weapon of war." Ten senators sponsored a resolution that said that "the United States shall not bomb or otherwise attack by air or sea the dams, dikes, or hydraulic systems in North Vietnam."[37] Nixon, unhappy with these legislative actions, implied that these elected officials were siding with the enemy. "We would hope," he said after the congressional votes, "that Congress in its actions will not in effect give a message to the enemy: 'Don't negotiate with the present Administration. Wait for us. We will give you what you want in South Vietnam.' "[38]

Fonda lost all her film from this trip—or else it was stolen. She had gone to Vietnam to make a documentary of life in Vietnam, and she returned with ample footage for that project. On her flight home from Hanoi, she checked her heavy boxes of film and photographic equipment with the airline. When she got to Paris, the boxes containing the sound were missing, and so Fonda showed silent footage at her press conference in Paris, including the footage of her meeting with the POWs. She took that silent footage with her on her flight to New York, but it, too, soon vanished.

Fonda returned to the JFK airport on July 27 with 241 letters from American POWs in Hanoi to their families. She also carried part of an antipersonnel weapon made by defense contractor Honeywell that she had picked up in a bombed village in Vietnam. Customs agents were on the lookout for her. They followed the instructions of White House aide Charles Colson to seize her passport, and pored over every page for proof that it had been "used" in Vietnam. They found nothing—no visa from North Vietnam, no mark from that country on her traveling documents. Citizens had the right to travel, the courts had ruled, and a passport couldn't be confiscated if it had no "offending" visa stamp. The customs agent had no choice but to hand Fonda's passport back to her.[39] Fonda's trip to Hanoi and the resulting dike-bombing controversy had angered people in the Nixon administration and its supporters. Before long, they would try to have her charged with treason.

5

FALLOUT:
THE ORIGINS OF THE FONDA MYTH

FONDA CAME BACK from Hanoi with a strong sense of urgency and a heartfelt message about the war. She didn't try to conceal the emotions generated by traveling among the bombed and the dead. She had cried every night she was there. "I didn't cry for the Vietnamese," she said. "I cried for the Americans. The bombs are falling on Vietnam but it's an American tragedy. The tragedy is ours. And it's going to take the American people many, many years to undo the damage and wipe off the blight that has been put on our flag and on our country by the likes of Mr. Nixon. And I believe that one day, and I hope that it will be soon, that American history will be changed, and all the people who are speaking out today and the many more who will speak out tomorrow against these kinds of crimes will be the real patriots—are the real patriots."[1]

Fonda's trip to Hanoi became the pivotal event of her antiwar activism. It was used by some to attack her maliciously in the stream of treason charges that would ultimately depart altogether from reality. The charges against Fonda originated in the Nixon administration and the FBI's dirty tricks against her, then lost traction and virtually disappeared when the war and its realities—and Fonda's trip to Hanoi and its realities—were fresh in people's minds. But in later years, those realities blurred and yielded to a right-wing drumbeat that sought to create a narrative of "honor" about the Vietnam War by reviling its opponents. This reinterpretation of the war, and of the antiwar movement, steadily gained ground over the next decades, nurtured by veterans' associations, politicians, and makers of popular culture. Fonda's trip to Hanoi became the central image of this campaign to vilify her as a political dupe and betrayer of American manhood. The myths about Jane Fonda, originating in the Nixon White House and incubated on the far right of the political spectrum, slowly permeated military culture, both in active-duty and veterans' organizations, then emerged in the late 1980s in a full-throated roar.

When Fonda returned from Hanoi in 1972 the first charges of treason were flung down by State Department officials. She responded to those charges by refocusing on the conduct of the war. When a reporter brought up the administration's allegations that she had committed treason by speaking on Radio Hanoi, Fonda replied that "given the things that America stands for, a war of aggression against the Vietnamese people is a betrayal of the American people. There is the treason."[2] She appealed to the history of the first Americans and the wars once waged against them to encourage a longer view of the current war in Vietnam:

> Let's go back to the American Indian War. If an American had used whatever means of mass communications available at that time to speak out to the white settlers crossing the United States and say, "Let us consider what we are doing. Small tribes are being killed off, land is being taken away, their culture is being destroyed. . . ." If an American could have done that and saved the lives of the Indians, they today would not be viewed as traitors. The dikes were being bombed, and I was saying the dikes were being bombed. In order to discredit that, in order to make people stop hearing what I was saying there, I am being accused of being a traitor.[3]

Fonda's trip to Vietnam attracted the attention that it did partly because it came at a precarious moment for the Nixon administration. The war in Vietnam was dying down—for Americans—and the president wanted to keep it dying down in the media as well.

There was only one American combat unit left in Vietnam in July 1972 when Fonda was there, and that unit was packing up to leave. American deaths were now "only" two or three a week. But the bombing was as intense as ever. Vietnamese deaths, most of them civilian, numbered in the hundreds each week.[4] Fonda wanted Americans to remember that. Nixon wanted them to forget. He had the fall elections on his mind. Unpleasantness about the war—a wider public awareness that it would end without victory—could threaten his electoral success.

Historian and Nixon biographer Jeffrey Kimball said that Nixon believed, accurately, that after a peace agreement and American withdrawal, the U.S.–backed Saigon government would collapse. If there was a peace agreement well before the elections in November, the Saigon government might collapse before the fall elections and harm his reelection effort. Five days after Fonda returned to the United States from Vietnam, Nixon privately told his national security advisor, Henry Kissinger, that "South Vietnam probably can never even survive anyway." But he added that "winning an election is terribly important. It's terribly important this year, but can we have a viable foreign policy if a year from now or two years from now, North Vietnam gobbles up South Vietnam? That's the real question." Kissinger told the president that *they* could avoid the label of failure if South Vietnam could hold together for a decent interval after the United States military was gone. He told the president that "we've got to find a formula that holds the thing together a year or two, after which, Mr. President, Vietnam will be a backwater. If we settle it, say, this October, by January '74 no one will give a damn."[5]

Things unraveled for the White House that summer. The week that Fonda returned from Vietnam also brought the first public evidence that the burglars who broke into the offices of the Democratic National Committee on June 17 at the Watergate complex had ties to the White House: their telephone records revealed numerous calls to people at the Committee to Re-Elect the President. A Republican party spokesman denied all connections between his party and the burglars. But then G. Gordon Liddy, who worked for the Committee to Re-Elect the President, refused to answer investigators' questions about the break-in at the Watergate and resigned from the committee. Nixon's former attorney general, John Mitchell, who headed the committee, abruptly resigned, too. And so, the Committee to Re-Elect the President, which some people took to calling "CREEP," was in some disarray as questions about the Watergate break-in accumulated.

Watergate was becoming a problem for the Nixon presidency, but the more immediate obstacle to reelection was managing the public perception of the war in Vietnam. Elected officials in Congress were threatening to cut off funds for the war, and public support for the war sagged below 50 percent. In this political context, the media and the public was interested in Fonda's evidence about bombing of dikes and civilians. A political attack on her served to shift the focus away from the bombing, even away from the war itself.

While Fonda was still in Hanoi, State Department spokesman Charles Bray first sounded the treason alarm by publicly "rebuking" her. He told reporters that "it is always distressing to find American citizens who benefit from the protection and assistance of this government lending their voice in any way to governments such as the Democratic Republic of Vietnam—distressing indeed." Bray mentioned that the Justice Department was checking reports "that Miss Fonda made antiwar broadcasts during her visit to Hanoi." Bray acknowledged that, because Americans had the freedom to travel, "large numbers of Americans have visited Hanoi without special authorization." Even so, he continued to insinuate that Fonda had broken a treason law but refused to specify which one.[6]

The CIA had prepared transcripts of Fonda's broadcasts on

Radio Hanoi. When reporters asked for them, the State Department was at first happy to oblige. But the officials quickly discovered that publicizing the actual content of Fonda's broadcasts held certain pitfalls. The transcripts were packed with Fonda's compelling eyewitness accounts of the massive bombing damage on dikes and villages, cities, and rice fields. When the State Department distributed these transcripts, reporters incorporated her bombing reports into their news stories. Never having intended to publicize Fonda's eyewitness reports, the administration found itself in a quandary. Furthermore, a study of the transcripts contradicted the claims administration officials made about them. For example, a State Department spokesman initially told the press that Fonda had urged American pilots to "desert" and "go over to the other side." But no transcript substantiated this charge, and Fonda insisted she had never encouraged desertion.

Reporters also noticed that the State Department had two kinds of transcripts. Some were fairly straightforward, compiled by CIA employees, of Fonda speaking in English on Radio Hanoi. But other transcripts had been reworked through two translations before reporters got them. This was true because some of her talks were translated from English into Vietnamese by Vietnamese translators and read by Vietnamese journalists on Radio Hanoi. CIA translators in Washington, D.C., then listened to this once-translated recording and translated it back into English—but not, of course, into the same English Fonda had used. These twice-translated CIA transcripts are especially unreliable; the language is uniformly stilted and unlike the other broadcasts CIA officers claimed to have transcribed directly from Fonda's English broadcasts.[7]

The chief hindrance to the Nixon administration's effort to paint Fonda as a traitor came, unexpectedly, from its own Justice Department. The new attorney general, Richard Kleindienst, had succeeded John Mitchell when he left to head up the Committee to Re-Elect the President. Only five days after Kleindienst was sworn in as attorney general on June 12, the Watergate burglary took place. Kleindienst had not been involved in, nor informed of, the planned break-in. To Nixon's surprise, Kleindienst now ordered the Justice Department to cooperate fully with the Watergate investigation, no matter where it led. Tensions grew between the White House and Kleindienst, who continued to assert his independence by refusing to give in to political pressure on Fonda's case.

The Justice Department said that its lawyers could find nothing illegal in Fonda's actions on her trip to Hanoi, nor in her taped reports broadcast over Radio Hanoi. It refused to empanel a grand jury to indict her. Justice Department lawyers raised further questions about the legality of pursuing treason charges in an undeclared war like the one in Vietnam. Kleindienst himself told reporters that he "doubted that anyone, including former Attorney General Ramsey Clark and Jane Fonda, the actress, would be prosecuted." The attorney general then volunteered that "no evidence of any wrongdoing has been presented to the Department yet."[8] Justice Department officials told reporters that Fonda had not violated any statutes, including those that would punish anyone who "advises, counsels, urges, or in any manner causes or attempts to cause insubordination, disloyalty, mutiny, or refusal of duty by any member of the military or naval forces of the United States."[9]

Still, the White House continued pressing the Justice Department to bring treason charges against Jane Fonda. In this context, former Supreme Court justice Arthur Goldberg called a reporter to express his doubts about the White House charges against Fonda. "I'm a great believer in the First Amendment, of free speech," Goldberg said, "and it doesn't stop at the boundary's edge. Miss Fonda hasn't said anything [in Hanoi] that she hasn't said in this country." If the government insisted on prosecuting

Fonda for what she said in Hanoi, it must prosecute her for saying the same things in the United States. If what she said in Hanoi was treason, Goldberg emphasized, the government should have brought charges against her long before she ever went there.[10]

As it became apparent that the Justice Department saw no grounds to craft a legal case against Fonda, a few congressional members on the House Internal Security Committee—successor to the House Un-American Activities Committee—denounced Fonda and urged the Justice Department to investigate her. Fletcher Thompson, a Republican representative from Georgia, led the charge. Running for election to the Senate against Democrat Sam Nunn in a race that looked tight, Thompson raised the "Fonda in Hanoi" flag throughout the fall campaign in Georgia. He called her "Hanoi Hannah" and repeatedly accused her of treason. He called a press conference and told reporters that she had urged soldiers to desert and join the other side. He said that she had given "aid and comfort to the enemy."[11] Fletcher was wrong—Fonda never urged soldiers to desert—but he continued to make allegations about her tour of Vietnam, even as the transcripts of her talks and the Justice Department's findings disproved them. Thompson wanted his colleagues on the House Internal Security Committee to join him and subpoena Fonda to testify before them. Committee members were reluctant to go that far. Instead, they asked the Justice Department, which had already declined to prosecute Fonda, to dispatch "a complete report on Fonda's activities" by September 14.[12]

Fonda, unruffled, had already urged the State Department to release all of its transcripts of her talks in Hanoi, and she stood by them. After the House Internal Security Committee requested the Justice Department report, she said, "I welcome the Committee members studying the texts of my broadcast from North Vietnam. After a full examination, they have seen that there is no basis for the charges against me. I invite the Justice Department and any other agency to do the same. I have done nothing against the law." Fonda then turned the focus back to the president. "Furthermore," she added, "Nuremberg rules define Nixon's actions in Vietnam as war crimes and give every American citizen a legal basis and a moral right to resist what is being done in our names."[13] Fonda said that Fletcher Thompson was "trying to get himself elected to the Senate" by subpoenaing her to appear before "a committee whose very existence is unconstitutional."[14]

The Justice Department never did come up with a report on Fonda's trip. On September 13, it sent a letter back to the House Internal Security Committee stating that Fonda's trip was "still under active consideration" and that issuing a report would be inappropriate. The committee expressed disappointment that the Justice Department couldn't seem to complete its report in good order, and requested that Kleindienst come and testify. "Although it might be fairly said that public support for American involvement in the Vietnam conflict is steadily declining," the letter said, surely "the public" condemned Fonda's visit. The committee tried once more to nudge the Justice Department into building a case against Fonda by pointing out other potentially applicable laws, including the 1799 Logan Act.[15]

Kleindienst sent his assistant attorney general, A. William Olson, to Capitol Hill to answer the committee's questions. Once he settled into his witness chair, Olson turned himself into the committee's "treason tutor" by launching into a long discourse on what constituted treason. He first pointed out that under the English kings, "it was given a very broad scope," but that those who founded the United States "had made great efforts to define carefully the offense of treason, specifically limiting its scope." Olson spoke at length about the founders' concerns about the inherent dangers of treason charges. One concern, Olson told the committee bluntly, was that treason charges might be used to suppress political opposition. Another was that citizens might be convicted because of "perjury, passion, or inadequate evidence" in other words, out of revenge. For this reason, he said, the crime of treason had standards of proof that were "unique" among criminal statutes, one of which required two eyewitnesses to each charge. Another stated the words themselves must demonstrably "present a substantial danger." Whether "a member of the military actually received or was influenced by the publication or utterance" was immaterial, Olson said. Committee Chair Richard Ichord agreed with Olson. He said that he personally saw no words in Fonda's Radio Hanoi talks that incited military personnel "to do anything other than to think."[16]

Olson next turned to the Logan Act, which the committee had urged him to charge Fonda with violating. The Logan Act is named after George Logan, a Philadelphia farmer and congressmen who traveled to Paris in 1798 to confer with government officials there during the height of Washington's political hysteria over the XYZ Affair. Logan's goal was to elicit some concrete peace offer or clarification from the French government to stem Federalist efforts to declare war against France. The Federalists, who wanted war, attacked Logan's patriotism, called him a traitor, and instituted the Logan Act. It survives to this day, making punishable by fine and imprisonment for American citizens to travel to other countries and discuss with foreign officials matters relating to "disputes or controversies with the United States."[17]

Olson discussed the circumstances of the Logan Act's passage, the fact that it had never been successfully invoked against anyone in the nearly two hundred years since. He also asked that the committee "appreciate" the difficulty of securing evidence of treason in cases that involved conversations between a citizen of the United States and officials of a "hostile government." He ended by emphasizing that "uncorroborated admissions of a citizen concerning such conversations would be insufficient to support a prosecution under the Logan Act."[18]

Olson's testimony left little doubt that the Justice Department had no intention of bringing treason charges against Jane Fonda but rather saw the allegations against her as rooted in politics. When the committee pressed Olson to "be more specific" about when the department would conclude its Fonda investigation, he responded with a quotation from Justice John Marshall: "As there is no crime which can more excite and agitate the passions of men than treason, no charge demands more from the tribunal before which it is made, a deliberate and temperate inquiry." The committee asked Olson about other Americans who had gone to Vietnam and broadcast talks over Radio Hanoi. Olson said that of all the Americans who had gone to North Vietnam over the past few months alone, the Justice Department had only looked into Fonda's case. Indeed, he said, there were at least eighty-two Radio Hanoi broadcasts from Americans who traveled to Vietnam well before Fonda. When Massachusetts congressman Robert Drinan skeptically asked why Fonda had been singled out, Olson declined to comment.[19]

After Olson left, the committee called another witness, CIA contract employee Edward Hunter, who called himself "a leading authority on the techniques of Communism." Hunter claimed to have coined the word "brainwashing" to describe an alleged phenomenon on which he considered himself an expert. Hunter was more eager than Olson to address the House Committee on Internal Security about Fonda. He had read all her broadcast transcripts and his report was ominous. The damage Fonda had inflicted on the entire U.S. military was severe, he said. Hunter described American servicemen as somewhat naive, virtual blank slates in wartime, unable to resist information that countered the claims of their own government. "When the American citizen, especially one with the glamour and the prestige value of a Jane Fonda, can travel back and forth between the United States and the enemy capital without interference or arrest by the American authorities, the effect on military morale is devastating," Hunter argued. When soldiers in Vietnam learned that their fellow citizens were speaking out against the war in the capital city of the enemy, Hunter said, their enemy achieved a new level of "war propaganda." Fonda, like other travelers to North Vietnam, was able to operate "both on her own soil and in communist areas." Even in World War II, Hunter said emphatically, "neither Germany or Japan had this advantage." Because no name had been coined to categorize this new kind of "war propaganda," Hunter suggested calling it "enemy blue," a term "that just now arises in my mind," he said.

Hunter suspected elected officials of treason no less than he suspected Fonda. He, too, believed America was being defeated from within. He told the committee that Fonda's Radio Hanoi broadcasts particularly threatened the soldiers in Vietnam because they reinforced equally "treasonous" comments by elected officials at home. He said that American GIs registered Fonda's statements and then "saw or heard it repeated by prominent American figures, even in our legislatures." He called this another "dual approach" of communist propaganda and said that "a man's stamina must be strong, indeed, to be able to resist such a traumatic assault upon it without some conscious or subconscious impact being inflicted." Hunter's "analysis" of Fonda's broadcasts exposed them as "highly professional in structure and aims." He claimed that "any soldier who listened or read her dramatic presentations could not help but be at least subtly affected in present or future attitudes. Withstanding Fonda's broadcasts required GIs to be "knowledgeable in communist tactics," he said, but "practically all were too young to have had the time or opportunity for the exhaustive study required." GIs were confused when Americans with "prestige value" protested the war because soldiers did not anticipate "being deceived and lied to by fellow Americans." In wartime, Hunter said, "this is tantamount to being wounded."

Fonda's "prestige value," he said, "helped inject her subversive suggestions into the heads of the target audience."

Hunter doubted that Fonda was intelligent enough to have composed these speeches on her own. Her broadcasts, he said, were "so concise and professional a job that I most strongly doubt that she wrote it herself. She had to have been working on it with the enemy. Her movements and utterances disclose skilled indoctrination—a brainwashed mind—but even so, her work in Hanoi could not have been a unassisted effort." Committee Chair Richard Ichord agreed with Hunter. He said the proof of assistance was that Fonda "used a lot of military terms that wouldn't be within her knowledge."

After Hunter's grim report, the committee heard from retired Brigadier General S. L. A. Marshall. Marshall agreed that Fonda's antiwar activism "taxed" the loyalty of the troops, although he believed that some might have "discounted" her as a "half-cracked female." The situation in Indochina was "extremely sensitive," he warned, and probably without historical precedent. The condition of the man in uniform was too precarious to withstand ideas like Fonda's. When the "Chief of Staff, USA," had gone to Vietnam in 1970 to assess the situation, Marshall said, he felt "so much alarm" at the state of the troops that he had returned to tell the president that "anything might happen" including "large-scale mutiny." Where the balance is that delicate, Marshall concluded, "any act of aid and comfort to the enemy of the United States could become the fatal straw."[20]

Following this dire testimony, the committee concluded its hearings on a note of frustration, complaining that "the recent broadcasts of Jane Fonda over Radio Hanoi are only the latest of a continuing series of activities of U.S. citizens in North Vietnam which the Department of Justice seems unable to control." Despite the existence of the Logan Act, the committee said that "the record is barren of any completed prosecution . . . in the absence of optimism on the part of the Justice Department, we must seek other statutory remedies."

The statutory remedy that the committee sought was a brand-new bill to criminalize travel to certain countries, including North Vietnam, and the committee drafted the bill in record time. It levied fines of $10,000 and ten years' imprisonment for anyone who traveled without government permission to "countries engaged in armed conflict with the United States."[21] The bill was drafted entirely in reaction to Fonda's trip to Vietnam. The House Internal Security Committee placed the bill on the "suspension calendar," a procedure usually reserved for non-controversial items that required a two-thirds majority for passage. Chairman Ichord declined to call Fonda to testify before the committee about the bill. Some committee members told reporters that they did not want to allow her to testify publicly because they feared "it would provide a forum for her strong views against American involvement in Southeast Asia."[22]

When the travel bill came up on the floor of the house, Thompson and Ichord took turns hammering away at Fonda. Then Congressman Clarence Long, a Democrat from Maryland, rose quietly to his feet. He accused Thompson and Ichord of forcing the members to vote for the bill at the risk of being called "soft on communism." He said that he had "come to believe more and more that we are governed by fear, fear of a wretched little country, fear of going back home and being accused of disloyalty." He turned to face the Republican aisle. "My son went to war," he said. "A thousand members have served here in Congress since this war began. Only twenty-six sons of members went, and my son was the only one who was wounded. I am sick and tired of this fear." The floor debate sputtered out after his speech, and the anti-Fonda bill failed. Its defeat was "a pallid victory for civil liberties," columnist Mary McGrory wrote, "and the same for the prisoners [in Hanoi], who can go on getting letters every now and then, and visits from peace groups, if it's any comfort to them."[23]

After the anti-Fonda travel bill was defeated, a reporter asked Fonda if she would "welcome a commission of inquiry into your activities." Fonda said that she thought such a commission would be "a waste of time and of American tax dollars." There were more important things to do, she said. But she added that if she were called before such a commission, "I would certainly go. I would go and I would say what I have to say. I wish that they would publish, for example, my broadcasts, those broadcasts that they've been poring over to find if there's any crime that I've committed. I wish the American people could see what I have said. I wish that I could show my film to people in Congress."[24]

There would be no legal case against Fonda, but the harsh and unyielding attacks on her ensured that animosity toward Fonda was far from over. Congressman Thompson revealed his frustrations over his inability to have charges brought against her by saying "declared war or undeclared war, this is treason."[25] But it was during this time that three of the FBI's own reviewers drew an opposite conclusion and criticized the agency for continuing its investigation of her. They unanimously agreed that the FBI had no reason to spy on her and recommended strongly that it cease.[26]

With the administration unable to pursue treason charges against Fonda, others took up the task. The political campaign against Fonda in the nation's capital died down in the next months, but lingered in far-flung areas outside Washington, in local posts of the American Legion and the Veterans of Foreign Wars, where it was fanned not by Vietnam veterans but by older veterans of Korea or of World War II.

Fonda began to receive assassination threats directly. One letter came from an Art Jasky, who said he represented the "American Liberty League." He wrote to Fonda, "Because you are a traitor to the U.S., you are now destined for assassination." Jasky said that the American Liberty League members would henceforth keep Fonda under constant surveillance. "Someday, sometime, somehow," the letter promised, "when you are at the right place, at the right time, a shot will ring out ending your life. Every member knows that after he shoots you he will be caught and tried for murder, but he also knows that there is no more capital punishment, and his chance of getting out of the pen in seven years is very good and getting out sooner for good behavior. The assassin will be free while you are rotting in your grave." Another letter came on the letterhead of the West Covina Christian School in West Covina, California, and signed by one Clarence F. Stauffer, Principal. The letter said: "You are guilty of treason in your statement and actions in N. Vietnam and other places when you shoot off your infamous mouth. If your motives were honest, you would denounce the atrocities of your N. Vietnam chummies which have been documented. If you enjoy your commie murderers so much (as you seemed in your pictures sitting on an anti-aircraft gun) why not stay in N. Vietnam? We have had enough of you." The *Los Angeles Times* received letters calling for donations to "the Jane Fonda, Ramsey Clark assassination fund."[27]

While people were mailing Fonda anonymous death threats, a few state legislators were making threats against Fonda in public. In Maryland, state legislator William J. Burkhead told his colleagues on the floor of the legislature that Fonda's trip to North Vietnam was "weakening the bonds of civilization" and undermining "the cornerstone of this republic." He said that since "it was wise, manly and patriotic for us to establish a free government, it is equally wise to attend to the necessary means of its preservation."He then sponsored a bill that would put the General Assembly on record as not being "Fonda Jane," ban Fonda from the state of Maryland, ban all her films from the state, and grant the state the power to seize all money made from her films there. (It would have been the first "bill of attainder" ever to come before the Maryland legislature—bills of attainder having been outlawed by the federal constitution after the American Revolution.) He didn't really care what happened to Fonda, Burkhead said, as long as she is "made to keep her mouth quiet." Then he called her a "nice-looking girl" who was acceptable as an actress but said that "something's wrong with her as a citizen." In a kind of one-upmanship, Maryland legislator Michael Foley said that he could see no reason why Jane Fonda should not be "sentenced to death" for treason. Burkhead replied, "I wouldn't go so far as to say execute her, but I think we should cut her tongue off." Then Burkhead compared Fonda to an "Arab" terrorist and said, "I'm trying to get at these kind of people who believe in going around and killing people and overthrowing their government and so on and so forth." Not a single member of the Maryland house stepped forward to object to the delegates' extreme language or to oppose Burkhead's bill. But the members who listened in silence at least did not support the bill, which died in committee.[28]

In Colorado, state representative Michael Strang introduced a resolution that singled out Fonda and declared that she was "unwelcome" in Colorado. He said that Fonda, whom he had never met, was a "foul-mouthed offensive little Vassar dropout." In the Colorado state legislature, at long last, Fonda had a defender in Arie Taylor, the first African American woman ever to serve there. Taylor spoke up for Fonda by offering a "John Wayne amendment" to Strang's bill. The somewhat tongue-in-cheek amendment declared actor and Vietnam War supporter John Wayne "unwelcome" in the state of Colorado "unless, by an act of God, he were to become black, brown or poor." The Speaker ruled Arie Taylor's proposed amendment out of order, but the legislators did defeat Strang's bill as well. Some of them noted that its passage might have prompted a stream of outsiders to seek publicity by being banned in Colorado.[29]

State and local newspaper columnists and editors weighed in against Fonda, declining to engage her statements about the war and instead swinging easily behind the vague charge of treason. William Loeb, publisher of the Manchester, Maine, *Union-Leader*, ignored Fonda's arguments against the war and simply called her "an irresponsible publicity seeker." Then he went on to say that Fonda "should be tried for treason. She should be shot if a verdict of guilty comes in."[30] The *Arizona Republic* editorialized that the case against Fonda was "a clear case of overt treason." It concluded that, for her treason, she should "receive the full penalty." The full penalty, of course, was the death penalty.[31]

Almost all of the columnists and reporters who wrote contemptuous reports were male. They usually focused on what she looked like, and seldom on her ideas or the issues she raised. They described her as "shrill." She "harangued," she talked too fast, she filled her conversation with too many figures and facts about the war, she didn't smile enough, she didn't have a sense of humor. Brady Black, editor of the *Cincinnati Enquirer*, lamented that it appeared Fonda was "shielded in her despicable behavior by the legal technicality that the Vietnam conflict is an undeclared war" and he editorialized that "we have found ourselves sorely tempted in the past to react indignantly to Miss Fonda's incessant and abusive caterwaulings." In Peoria, Illinois, *Journal Star* editor C.L. Dancey said that Fonda had "the classic characteristic of the non-stop harangue, with absolute answers to every question." After her "brief, supervised visit to Hanoi she proclaims certain knowledge about a variety of things from one end of that country to the other, from 1954 to the present day, and from military to political, to which she could not possibly have had any exposure whatever except BEING TOLD." An editorial in the *Miami Herald* said that Fonda was embarked on a "wild new costume role with monkey hairdos and suede pantsuits." Columnist Sandy Grady said that "Jane Fonda should go back to play-acting, at which she is superb, and let somebody else handle the heavy oratory." The good news, Grady added, "is that Fonda looks 27 instead of 35, chestnut hair flowing, figure lithe as a fawn. The bad news is that she still talks like a high school senior demanding smoking rights in the girls' room. No matter how just the cause, that is a dumb waste." After writing that, Sandy Grady felt constrained to add that "libbers can stop rattling their castanets and hissing about male chauvinist piggery." *Saturday Review* columnist Goodman Ace watched Fonda on a talk show and called her "extraordinarily pretty and divinely feminine. But as I listened to her go into her favorite subject, Vietnam, I discovered that Jane Fonda is not a girl for dating." Ace criticized Fonda at length for referring to "Nixon." He said she should use the term "President Nixon." When she talked about Vietnam, Ace said, Fonda metamorphosed from an "extraordinary pretty butterfly" into a "caterpillar."[32]

Not all columnists who wrote commentary or articles about Fonda's work dismissed her casually. Columnist Milton Viorst went to hear Fonda for himself, and he was surprised at the gap between what he had been led to expect from fellow columnists and what he observed:

> I watched Jane Fonda the other day at Georgetown University. Some two thousand students had packed Gaston Hall, literally to the rafters. Daniel Ellsberg had appeared on the program with her. But it was Jane, without makeup and in jeans they had come for and who held them captivated. I was a little surprised by her manner—no dramatics, no hip slang, no affectation. Jane Fonda's message was that the United States, despite the withdrawal of American troops, was perpetuating a brutal war in Vietnam by its huge financial subsidies to the unpopular regime of President Thieu. "Most Americans think the Vietnam war is over," she said.

> "Our problem begins with letting Americans know that thousands of Vietnamese are still being killed every month with American arms and American money. How do you end a war that people don't even know about?"

"She conveyed optimism and faith in the democratic process," Viorst noted, "She got a standing ovation."[33] Ordinary women who responded to Fonda often admired her courage and related what Fonda was doing to their own widening realization of the world. In response to an attack on Fonda, a letter-writer to the Washington *Evening Star* said simply: "Jane Fonda is doing what everyone should be doing; waking up and finding we are not the 'all right' country we say we are. She is one of millions who would like to see the war ended. Because she is trying to help, she is immediately put down."[34]

In the midst of the political charges against Fonda in the fall of 1972, Jimmy Hoffa, former president of the Teamsters Union and ex-convict, was carrying forward his plan of self-rehabilitation by going to Hanoi himself. Hoffa had been serving a thirteen-year prison sentence for jury tampering and fraud, but Richard Nixon, looking for a Teamsters election endorsement, had commuted his sentence. Hoffa was on the street again, but the judicial terms of his commutation barred him permanently from any direct or indirect role in Teamster activities. Between the war in Vietnam and Richard Nixon's political ambitions, the ex-convict concocted a scheme to return to his old place as head of the Teamsters Union. While Fonda was in Hanoi in July, Hoffa arranged a meeting with Henry Kissinger and laid before him a plan to climb aboard a labor delegation, still to be formed, that would travel to Hanoi. If Kissinger, who was then the president's national security advisor, would put in a word with the Vietnamese officials in Paris, Hoffa hoped that Hanoi would release some American POWs early to his "labor" delegation. As a reward for bringing home POWs just before the fall elections, Hoffa wanted Nixon to permit him to head up the Teamster's Union, which had just endorsed Nixon's re-election bid.

Kissinger agreed to the plan. He informed Le Duc Tho, the Vietnamese negotiator in Paris, that an American labor delegation wanted to visit Hanoi and needed an invitation from the government there. Before long, Hoffa had his Hanoi invitation in hand. As a convicted felon, he needed to stay well within the technicalities of the law so he asked the State Department for a passport validated for travel to North Vietnam. Raymond Farrell, head of the Immigration and Naturalization Service, advised the State Department that a "hot case" was up for travel validation to North Vietnam and they should treat it "discreetly."

Discretion prevailed for a time. On the afternoon of September 7, Hoffa went to the passport office in the State Department and picked up his passport, already validated for travel to Hanoi. He was set to depart for North Vietnam that evening. But word of the affair reached Secretary of State William Rogers late that day. Rogers became, according to his subordinates, "irate." He withdrew Hoffa's validation, canceled the trip, and made sure that all these events reached the morning papers. Recriminations began immediately. Henry Kissinger denied everything. Passport officials blamed a "lower level official" whom they declined to identify for the travel validation. Other sources told reporters that Kissinger had, without notifying William Rogers, approved Hoffa's trip to Hanoi in hopes of widening labor support for Nixon in the fall elections.[35]

Jimmy Hoffa never got to Hanoi, and as his trip unraveled and politicians still talked of treason, Fonda set to work to help put together a new, nationally coordinated antiwar educational organization, called the Indochina Peace Campaign, or the IPC. American ground troops were now gone from Vietnam and the war was, as far as most Americans were concerned, primarily an air war. An air war meant comparatively fewer casualties for Americans, which the media had, in any event, virtually ceased mentioning. So the Indochina Peace Campaign arrived on the scene when public awareness of the war was waning and when many in the antiwar movement had folded up their banners and moved on to other causes: the women's movement, the environmental movement, the politics of the personal. But there were still thousands of local activists across the country who continued to resist this war specifically, and they were looking for a well-organized national association that could help them continue the struggle.

The Indochina Peace Campaign became just that. It gained steam in early September, 1972, as the presidential campaign was in full swing. The IPC began as a tour of Jane Fonda, Tom Hayden, folksinger Holly Near, and George Smith, a former POW in Vietnam released early by the National Liberation Front. The group embarked on an intensive tour of ninety-five cities between September 2 and November 6. As the tour went on, they drew in other antiwar speakers: Fred Branfman, Gloria Emerson, David Dellinger, Pat Ellsberg, Cora Weiss, Frances FitzGerald, Elizabeth McAllister, Dan Berrigan, Kevin Buckley, Phil Ochs, and Virginia Warner, the mother of POW James Warner.

In the space of two months, IPC speakers appeared at an average of four events a day. They spoke at over eighty schools and universities, appeared on over seventy TV and radio shows, held thirty press conferences, and were featured speakers at thirty large community events; they spoke at twenty-five churches and temples, nine outdoor rallies, and seven women's meetings; and they set up large booths at the state fairs in Michigan and Ohio. Their combined audience numbered over 160,000 people in these first two months alone.[36]

At IPC meetings, one of the speakers narrated a forty-five-minute slide show from Vietnam. After the slide show, they answered questions from the audience, talked about Vietnamese history and culture, the current state of the war there, and the importance of voting in the upcoming election, which pitted Richard Nixon against George McGovern, who had decried the bombing of the dikes in Vietnam during his acceptance speech at the Democratic Convention in late July. Holly Near sang folk and antiwar songs. The audiences were rarely hostile. By 1972, opposition to the war permeated Congress; even the president talked of the war only in terms of ending it. "Most *feel* the war is wrong," one IPC report said of their audiences, "and they are confused and frustrated about how to end it."[37]

Fonda's film from Vietnam had disappeared by this time, so the Indochina Peace Campaign could not screen it. But they did have a film from Vietnam called *Village by Village*, which had been made by a four-person delegation to Vietnam in May 1972, two months before Fonda's visit. The IPC made copies of *Village by Village*, showed it at many public meetings, and sold it to local groups for their own events. The Hanoi delegation that made *Village by Village* included Father Paul Meyer, a theologian at New York Theological Seminary; Reverend Robert Lecky, editor of *American Report*; Margery Tabankin, president of the National Student Association; and Dr. Bill Zimmerman, a former University of Chicago professor who now worked with Medical Aid for Indochina. Their on-site film showed schools, hospitals, urban residential areas, and agricultural areas that had been "carpet-bombed" by B-52s—bombing that was far from the "precise, laser-guided" bombing that the Pentagon claimed. Meyer's group itself came under seventeen bombing raids; even their brief conversation with Vice-Premier Nguyen Duy Trinh in Hanoi was interrupted by an air raid and had to be finished in an underground bomb shelter.[38]

Village by Village also showed a forty-five-minute meeting with eight American POWs in Hanoi who sent back a letter with the delegation asking the American people to call on Congress to end the war. The prisoners said that their food, housing, and medical care in Hanoi was adequate. They strongly disagreed with Richard Nixon's recent decision to mine the harbors of Northern Vietnam and escalate the bombing. Meyer said that his visit to Hanoi convinced him that "regardless of one's political position on the war, it would be impossible for an American to come away from North Vietnam without being amazed at what is being done to innocent people there. The laborers, nurses, shop keepers, mothers and children of North Vietnam are baffled by the viciousness with which they are being attacked. From what we saw, the main effect that the bombing has had on these people is to increase their unity and their determination to resist at any cost."[39]

The crowds that came to see the IPC tour over the next months took home with them literature about the war, much of it now produced by IPC, which distributed over two million leaflets called "Six Million Victims" on the toll of war in Indochina, two hundred thousand copies of a fifty-page *Pentagon Papers Digest*, and over a million copies of their *War Bulletin* newspaper. And IPC's first tour pulled in thousands at a time: three thousand to Cathedral Park in Buffalo, New York; five thousand at the University of California at Davis, four thousand at California State University in Sacramento, two thousand at Tufts University, where Fonda was the Tufts Lecture Series speaker.[40]

After Hanoi, Fonda's language became more urgent, more stark. She called the war in Vietnam a "lost cause." She called Nixon racist for crafting a military strategy, Vietnamization, that "removed the war from our minds while it is being inflicted on the bodies of others." The president was hoping, she said, that "we are so racist and so callous that we won't care as long as fewer whites are killed." The American POWs in Hanoi were not being brainwashed, she said; it was the American people in their own country who were being brainwashed by the president and his advisers. And she told her audiences that "the tragedy is that they who are under our bombs know so much about us, and we who are bombing them know so little about them." The war was lost, she said over and over, "and the question is when we are going to realize that." She repeated that "those who are trying to end the war are the patriots. We should not allow the right wingers to steal our flag away from us."[41]

The FBI opened a file on the IPC, labeling it "a recently-organized communist-infiltrated front group." It sent agents to local schools and warned them not to allow the IPC to show slides and film or to talk with students. In Columbus, Ohio, FBI agents went to the superintendent of the Catholic schools, Father David Sorohan, and warned him that some of the leaders in IPC were under active FBI investigation and that it would be to the advantage of the Catholic schools if they did not allow Fonda to speak there. Sorohan knew his local antiwar community better than that. He took the agents' warning visit as unnecessary harassment, and when Jane Fonda came to Columbus, she spoke to thousands of Catholic students in the diocese. Sorohan told her and other IPC members about the agents' visit, and a local paper published a story about the FBI efforts, complete with quotations from Father Sorohan. When the agents' actions were made public, W. Mark Felt, acting associate director of the FBI, contacted the field office and scolded them for not being "discreet."[42]

It was not just Sorohan who welcomed the IPC. Many churches opened their doors as well. For some, it was an easy decision because their members were already opposed to the war. For others, the decision was more difficult. Someone approached Reverend Calvin Van Kirk Hoyt at the Mount Calvary Episcopal Church in Camp Hill, Pennsylvania, after the worship service one Sunday morning in September 1972, and asked him if Jane Fonda could speak in his church a few weeks later. The question was the furthest thing from his mind at that moment, Hoyt said. His church was only fifteen miles from the United States Army War College in Carlisle, and some of his parishioners were still strong advocates of the war, including a retired general. On the other hand, Hoyt had led his congregation through a Lenten series that spring about Vietnam. If Jesus were eighteen and had a low draft lottery number, he had asked his congregation then, would he go to Vietnam? Hoyt had also welcomed into his church a performance of Father Daniel Berrigan's *Trial of the Catonsville Nine,* which told the story of antiwar activists who had poured homemade napalm over draft records in Catonsville, Maryland, and set them afire.

Hoyt's parishioners found the play thoughtful and moving, but a few of them objected to the church raising questions about the government's actions in war. And so, when he was asked if Jane Fonda could speak in his church, Hoyt thought about it for a bit, but it didn't take him long to say, "Yes, certainly." He then decided to tell his congregation the following Sunday about Fonda's upcoming visit and why, as he put it, the church was "the right place" for her presentation. "If the matters about which she will speak are important enough to kill people over," he said, "then these matters are important enough to be faced honestly in the Church of Jesus Christ, the Lord of Life." Hoyt told his parishioners that Jesus had said that "ye shall know the truth and the truth shall make you free" and, in that spirit, he was committed to "a quest for truth." Moreover, as a Christian, he said, he was not under the command of his nation or of his nation's military but under the authority of God who commanded him to be "a responsible critic of my government."

Hoyt had already invited the War College in Carlisle, not far away, to send someone who could present the case for the war. They had not responded, but the offer still stood—if anyone in the church wanted to speak or bring in a speaker "for the other side," Hoyt invited his congregation to do so. No one would be more pleased than he "to have President Nixon as next week's speaker." If his congregants would come out to hear Jane Fonda, see her slides from Vietnam, and listen to her tell of her experiences there, Hoyt said, they would "have nothing to fear but tyranny, and nothing to lose except ignorance."[43]

Officers at the War College never responded to Hoyt's request for a speaker to defend the case for war. So Hoyt asked a retired general in his congregation to contact the military brass he knew and ask for a speaker. That drew no response, either. Hoyt made other equally unsuccessful overtures to the United States Army. "They treated us with contempt," Hoyt said. The only response he received came from an officer who told Hoyt that his name was going on a list of suspects at the White House.[44]

And so Jane Fonda came to Mount Calvary Episcopal Church near the Army War College and drew a packed crowd that stood in the back and sat on the windowsills. There were no disruptions, no rudeness, Hoyt said, and the audience and speaker had a respectful exchange. Fonda spoke, as she often did, about the impact of the war in Vietnam on women. She talked about their lives, not only as war-torn, but infused with hope and optimism for a better life someday, free of war, making their own history. Reverend Norman Thorson of the Hamilton Area Ministry told people later that Fonda's talk "was low-key and gave fresh information. Any serious American patriot who wants a balanced, informational report on the war would not want to miss this program."

Before Fonda arrived, someone wrote "commie, commie, commie" on the church sign out front, but her talk drew more praise than criticism. Several days later, Hoyt received an unexpected visit from the town's eighty-year-old banker. Hoyt expected criticism from the banker, who had a reputation for being conservative and gruff. But the banker told Hoyt simply, "I admire your guts. I wish more people had it." Vietnam was an extremely controversial war, Hoyt said later, and it was often hard to know the right thing to do. But in looking back, he said, "having the courage to take on the whole issue of the war was the proudest moment in my life."[45]

Wherever they went, IPC speakers encouraged existing local antiwar groups and spurred the formation of new ones. IPC's 1972 fall tour facilitated meetings for twenty-five new local organizations and held fund-raisers for sixteen existing ones. It helped draw groups together under a national umbrella. It offered local groups contact with other local communities and a national organization. It worked with many churches and interfaith associations: the Methodist Peace Fellowship, Disciples Peace Fellowship, Church Women United, Clergy and Laymen Concerned About Vietnam, the American Friends Service Committee, and the Fellowship of Reconciliation, among others.

The campaign benefitted immeasurably from Fonda's willingness to work with it at all levels. She was willing to visit the smallest community and appear at a fund-raiser, speak at local events designed to kick off community antiwar programs, and help write local fund-raising letters and sign her name alongside those of the local organizers. At the main office in Santa Monica, California, she sat at the desk answering phone calls from local groups around the country. Local IPC files are filled with letters from people saying that "Jane suggested that I contact you. . . ." To help people in the antiwar community stay connected, she helped publish *Focal Point*, a monthly periodical geared to the antiwar activist community itself. *Focal Point* provided news not on the war, but on the activists who opposed it. Within months, *Focal Point* was distributed to activists across the nation and around the world, in Canada, Japan, Vietnam, Sweden, Hong Kong, England, Venezuela, Switzerland, Hungary, East and West Germany, and the Netherlands. IPC put together another periodical, *Indochina Report*, for public distribution. That periodical carried reports from Vietnam, photographs, and analysis of the war that the mainstream media had, by that stage, mostly relegated to the back pages.

Fonda protesters—not Vietnam veterans but usually older men who said they were members of the American Legion or VFW—now turned up occasionally when Fonda spoke. They carried signs reading "Hanoi Jane" or "Fonda is a traitor," perpetuating the unsupported charges that first emanated from the White House. Despite these few sign-carriers and the lingering furor over her trip to Vietnam, newspaper accounts and even the FBI informants regularly reported that her audiences were large and receptive, and gave her thunderous applause. If there were occasional hecklers, Fonda let them speak, acknowledged their differences, and then continued with her talk and program. She said she believed that what it meant to love one's country was to "stand up to lies so that another Vietnam won't happen again." One FBI agent, dispatched by the bureau to write reports on Fonda's IPC speeches, went out of his way to note that when her audiences included people who "took exception" to her statements, the atmosphere "remained friendly."[46]

6

COMING HOME: THE POLITICS OF PRISONER REPATRIATION

LEFT TO ITSELF, the controversy over Fonda's trip to Hanoi in all likelihood would have died out. But after the Paris Peace Treaty was signed in January 1973 and the American POWs came home from Hanoi, one of the seven POWs who met with Fonda in Hanoi charged that he had been tortured into meeting with her. That dubious charge, encouraged and promoted by Pentagon officials, became the single driving factor in the myth that Jane Fonda had harmed American POWs. Fueled by that charge, other false stories about Fonda picked up speed over the next decades as the nation remained torn over the war that passed into history, irretrievably lost.

The details of the POW homecoming in 1973 deserve examination because that homecoming became the backdrop for the incendiary accusation that a POW in Hanoi was tortured because of Fonda's trip to Hanoi. This single charge spawned false charges of other POWs in Hanoi being tortured, and even killed, because of Fonda. These charges all sprang directly from the misleading stories that a minority of hard-line POWs told when they returned in 1973. They were encouraged by Pentagon officials scheming to kill the promised United States' reconstruction aid to North Vietnam. They succeeded in this goal. But their collusion with the hard-line POWs swept up innocent people in a wide net and even led to the suicide of one former POW.

The tangled tale of Americans being systemically tortured in Hanoi began in 1969, well before the American POWs were released. In the first years of the war, the White House had played down the POW issue. But all that changed in May 1969, when the Fellowship of Reconciliation (FOR), an established interfaith peace organization, sent a study team to South Vietnam to examine the "variety of religious forces in South Vietnam and the range of political expression there." The study team soon discovered that it was impossible to visit the religious and political forces in South Vietnam without also visiting the burgeoning prisons in Saigon. At that time, the United States was implementing its "Phoenix Program," assassinating and arresting tens of thousands of "suspected communists" in a counterinsurgency designed to squelch the opposition.[1]

In the prisons of South Vietnam in 1969, the study team observed prisoners forced to wear badges: yellow ones for "criminal" activity, red ones for "communist" activity. Seventy percent of the 35,000 prisoners in the entire system were there for being "communists." Hundreds of prisoners were under the age of eighteen. Some were as young as four. A warden at one prison told the study team that, of his six thousand prisoners, one thousand were South Vietnamese soldiers accused of actually working for the National Liberation Front. Two thousand had never been charged, although they had been incarcerated for years. The remaining three thousand were civilians accused of working with the National Liberation Front.

When the FOR's study team returned to the United States in 1969, their sober and careful report about the prisons in Saigon attracted wide attention. They testified before Congress about the grim conditions there in prisons the United States controlled. Only months into his first term, President Nixon had to confront the study team's damning report detailing the cruel detention conditions of prisoners held by the U.S.–backed Saigon government.[2]

And then Don Luce exposed the "tiger cages" on Con Son

Island in South Vietnam. Luce, once director of International Voluntary Services in Vietnam, had resigned in 1967 to protest the war. He had already lived in Vietnam for eleven years, and he loved the country. "I could not become part of the destruction of a people I love," he said when he resigned. "It's become unbearable to witness the destruction of Vietnamese family life, the home, the agricultural system . . . we're defeating ourselves here." In 1969, Luce came back to Vietnam with the World Council of Churches. Tipped off about the location of the notorious "tiger cages" of Con Son Island, where the Saigon government kept prisoners shackled to the floor at all times, Luce led a small delegation of U.S. congressmen to these cages with inmates unable even to stand up. Years in these cages had left the prisoners with permanently withered limbs, so they could only crawl, crab-like, across the floor. *Life* magazine published graphic photos of the prisoners that fixed their images in the reader's mind. The U.S. military accused Don Luce of siding with "the enemy." He was expelled from Vietnam the next year.[3]

To undermine these expose's of the Saigon prison system the Nixon administration began to allege that American POWs in Hanoi were routinely and systematically tortured. The claims of POW torture in Hanoi worked for the White House on two levels. First, these attacks portrayed Americans who spoke out against the known torture in Saigon as enemy sympathizers. Second, these allegations helped explain why some American POWs were writing home from their prisons in Hanoi and urging their families to join the antiwar movement and work for a negotiated, not a military, settlement. The White House could now proclaim that the prisoners were tortured into making these claims. It was embarrassing to the Pentagon that it could not depend on its own troops to emerge from the prison camps committed to the war.[4]

In August 1969, just weeks after the FOR Study Team issued its report, Hanoi released two more POWs early, Douglas Hegdahl and Robert Frishman. With their release, the White House and the Pentagon enjoyed an opportunity to put faces to the vague torture charges issued after the study team's report from Saigon. After Frishman and Hegdahl were home for some weeks, and after they met numerous times with Pentagon officials, they both agreed to make charges of torture in Hanoi. The Pentagon arranged to have articles of their allegations published in magazines, including the December 1969 *Reader's Digest,* the most widely read periodical at the time. The Pentagon sent the two former POWs on tours around the country, where they charged that the Hanoi prison camps were "an ordeal of horror" characterized by beatings, starvation, and torture.

Journalists who covered Frishman and Hegdahl noted contradictions between the stories they told when they first returned home and those they told after their repeated visits with Pentagon officials. Hegdahl, for example, was interviewed extensively by his hometown newspaper when he first returned home. At that time, he said nothing about torture and told his hometown paper that he had lost some weight in prison because he had gone on a "hunger strike" in Hanoi after his cell mate was moved to another camp. He wanted another cell mate right away and, in protest, he didn't eat all of his food each day until he got another roommate. If he had eaten everything on his plate, he said, he would not have lost weight. But later, on the Pentagon torture tour, he began telling audiences that all the prisoners were on starvation diets and that was why he had lost weight. Despite his claims of being badly underfed during his time in prison, Hegdahl gained no visible weight in the months after his release, and his slight frame was the same as in earlier photos of him as a POW in Hanoi.

Journalist Seymour Hersh investigated Robert Frishman's torture claims and wrote a series of articles pointing out contradictions. Well into his Pentagon torture tour, for example, Frishman began alleging that Hegdahl's cellmate in Hanoi, Richard Stratton, had his fingernails torn out. But people who had seen Stratton said that his fingernails were intact. When Hersh confronted him with that information, Frishman denied ever mentioning Stratton's fingernails. When Hersh talked to Pentagon officials, he found out that some thought the torture tour was not a good idea. One official told Hersh that Frishman "was under strain when he was released. He had been interviewed [by foreign journalists in Hanoi] many times. He played ball the most and was therefore most torn." Hersh concluded that there was no evidence of systematic abuse of American POWs in Hanoi.[5]

When the American POWs returned to the United States in 1973, many had been imprisoned for two years or less. But the ones shot down in the mid-1960s came back to a country far different from the one they left. Homecoming was especially difficult for the minority of hard-line officers who were shot down early and had refused to accept, while in the prison camps in Hanoi, evidence that their own country had changed. Their responses to the changes in the country were influenced by their political outlook and experiences.

The outlook of the several dozen hard-line officers, most of them shot down over North Vietnam before 1968, was shaped by their decision to adhere, on and off, to the Pentagon's Code of Conduct and impose it on other POWs. The Code of Conduct was developed in the 1950s by Pentagon officials alarmed by the ease with which American POWs in Korea spoke out against the war, even admitting to waging biological warfare in Korea.[6] The Code called on POWs to carry the war into the prison camps with them, never surrender freely, never accept early release, resist continually, always endeavor to escape, and refuse all cooperation with camp officials, even in the smallest areas. Its provisions were so extreme that even the Pentagon eventually acknowledged it was unenforceable, and most POWs did not adhere to it.

But the hard-line POWs intermittently tried to abide by this Code and even to enforce it on others. Sometimes they challenged low-level camp guards by plotting to sabotage equipment, refusing to bow or to obey orders. One of these hard-liners later recounted the satisfaction of watching another POW unscrew the gas cap of a truck and pour dirt down the fuel tank. "We learned to reverse everything the guards said," one of them said later, adding that they kept their spirits up by "keeping the Vietnamese infuriated." Another hard-line officer said of the Vietnamese guards, "if they said 'quickly,' we interpreted it to mean 'slowly.' If one room was given cookies on a given day, the men tapped around other rooms to make sure they were not getting 'special favors.'" Captain Jeremiah Denton said, "We forced them to be brutal to us." These challenges represented a mark of their personal heroism and endurance—their equivalent of winning the war in Vietnam.[7]

Vietnamese camp authorities put these hard-line officers in solitary confinement or sometimes with a single cell mate. This was their most difficult time. Many of them later described the deep depression that accompanies solitary confinement, especially when they had no idea how long their incarceration would last. The relatively few hard-line POWs who later spoke of mistreatment in the prison camps said that their mistreatment ended by late 1969 when the camp system was consolidated and they were transferred to large rooms that held up to fifty POWs.[8]

Most of the American airmen in the prison camps were not zealous Code of Conduct adherents. Many of them said that their gravest physical danger in captivity came when they parachuted toward villagers they had just bombed. Vietnamese military officers often saved them from beatings and death at the hands of the villagers, they said. They expected worse. Combat pilots were routinely issued suicide pills in their "survival kit," and some of those who survived their ejection may well have used those, fearing torture or death in captivity. One American POW said later that he was grateful that his Vietnamese captor immediately confiscated his poison capsule when he was shot down.[9]

When the hard-line officers returned home in 1973, their reentry was not easy. They had heard of the antiwar movement, but attributed much of it to Vietnamese propaganda or the cravenness of the American media. It was a shock to come home to families where some had not only turned against the war, but had joined the antiwar movement and worked to defeat Richard Nixon in 1972. Hard-line POW Harry Jenkins said it was disconcerting "to find women wearing pants and men wearing women's hair styles." Seeing the long hair on ordinary people when he returned home, he exclaimed in dismay, "The hippies have won." Jenkins thought that even the military had become reprehensibly lax: no longer "a strictly disciplined, hard-hitting bunch of guys."[10] Hard-line POW Jeremiah Denton spoke almost longingly of the "duress" that he experienced in the camps as fortifying. Now, he thought the nation had gone soft in his absence and might be, he said after he was released, "in a stage where we are subject to a lack of physical duress."[11]

All the POWs came home in February and March 1973, to a tightly controlled, Pentagon-scripted drama called Operation Homecoming that, from the beginning, prioritized the stories that the few hard-line officers were prepared to tell. Accounts of sustained torture would overwhelm those of the vast majority of POWs who made no such claims, thanks to the publicity the Pentagon granted the hard-liners. With the Watergate tide rising, and the war in Vietnam sliding toward defeat, Richard Nixon needed a boost. The airmen came home at just the right time for him. Journalist Shana Alexander said that the return of the POWs resembled "a carefully prepared TV commercial on behalf of the White House."[12]

At the same time that the nearly six hundred American POWs

were released, thousands of political prisoners in Saigon, incarcerated by the American-backed government there, were also released. American journalists covered both stories. They reported that the newly freed prisoners in Saigon at first balked at boarding the American helicopters that were to ferry them out of Saigon, "principally out of fear that they were being tricked and would be pushed out of the choppers to their death." One of the American officers said, "I don't blame them, considering the nature of this war." Journalists who observed both prisoner releases agreed that the prisoners in the worst shape were unquestionably those imprisoned in Saigon by the U.S.–backed government in Saigon. One journalist described some of them as "shapes . . . grotesque sculptures of scarred flesh and gnarled limbs. They move like crabs, skittering across the floor on buttocks and palms."[13] *Newsweek* magazine said that "the Communist prisoners were, on the whole, in pitiful condition. Many were maimed, hobbling on homemade crutches with multiple wounds or missing limbs. Yet when repatriation came, the Communists were as jubilant as the Americans. A group of prisoners being returned to the north ripped off their maroon POW pajamas minutes after being released and, clad only in shorts, ran singing and cheering into the arms of their waiting comrades."[14]

As soon as the last American POW was home, the Pentagon orchestrated ten press conferences around the country involving twenty-nine POWs, almost all of them hard-line officers, and billed these press conferences as opportunities for the American public to hear about the total POW experience. The hard-line officers presented their experience in Hanoi as the norm for all POWs. They described long sessions of beatings, vicious attacks by guards, and systematic mistreatment that permeated their prison experience. A photo of Richard Stratton bowing to his captors had been widely published during his imprisonment in Hanoi. The hard-line officers considered bowing a sign of weakness and Stratton now said that he had only bowed because he had been tortured into doing so. He said that the Vietnamese should be tried for "war crimes" for mistreating him and forcing him to bow.[15]

For the first weeks after the POWs returned home, the Pentagon kept up a steady stream of reports from the hard-line POWs about mindless and unrelenting physical torture in the Hanoi prison system. The Pentagon arranged news conferences with these POWs, and faithful reports of their interviews ran in the weekly news magazines and national and local newspapers under headlines like "POWs: The Price of Survival," "How the POWs Fought Back," and "The Secret Agony of the POWs." Any of these headlines helped the White House more than ones along the lines of "The Growing Watergate Mess."

At their Pentagon-arranged press conferences, hard-line POWs scorned the Vietnamese as inferior and contemptible. They condemned the proposed reconstruction aid to Hanoi. Harry Jenkins said he felt "spiteful" toward the Vietnamese for "dragging the American giant down . . . the longer I was there, the less I liked them." He scoffed at the Vietnamese for saying they suffered from the air war. "They cry about their women and children getting killed. Hell, they should have thought of that before they started the war. Let's just say if anyone comes around collecting for North Vietnamese relief, they could get a black eye."[16] Former POW James Mulligan said, "I know what sleazy gooks those people are. When you live with them, you know what they are. I had more respect for the gooks the first day I was there, and every day since I lost respect. They're so bad, they're inferior. I would say that these guys are the most corrupt people I've ever seen around, corrupt from top to bottom. They know nothing about the truth, they have no allegiance to anything, they're really creepy people."[17]

The hard-line officers praised Richard Nixon for bringing them home "with honor" and derided Americans calling for a negotiated settlement as a "bunch of loud-mouth radicals." The officers felt plenty of anger about their imprisonment in Hanoi, but they directed none of it at the planners of the war. Instead, they blamed Democrats and peace activists. Alan Brunstrom said that opponents of the war "were all traitors—it's just cut and dried." Without advancing any evidence, Colonel Robinson Risner said that "beyond any doubt, those people kept us in prison an extra year or two." Harry Jenkins said that all of the activists who visited Hanoi "shamed our nation in the eyes of the enemy." One hard-line POW said that among "the most devastating blows" to his "morale" in Hanoi were quotations in American periodicals from "Senators Mansfield, Fulbright and McGovern." He could disregard the antiwar protesters, he said, but "when they started quoting *Newsweek, Time, Life, Look,* the *Washington Post* columnist Walter Lippman. . . ." He shook his head in disbelief.[18]

These officers held up their heroism in prison as evidence that the United States could still stand tall in the world. Asked at his press conference what purpose the torture stories served, one POW replied, "I want you all to remember that we walked out of Hanoi as winners."[19] Jeremiah Denton said that "our honor was preserved." And Lieutenant Colonel John Dramesi replied, "People over here have been screaming that the North Vietnamese are humane and their cause is just. Well, this shows how humane and just they are."[20]

One government official who worked with the POW families said that the extreme views of some hard-line pilots were worrisome. "It scares me in a way," he told a reporter. "If the prisoners are not careful they will destroy their credibility. They've been away so long, they don't realize the depth of division in this country. They're making too light of the antiwar movement, they don't give it the importance we all recognize it has."[21]

For some Americans at home, these torture stories began to

redeem the war. It now appeared, despite what activists had said about the horrors of war the Vietnamese endured—the grim stories of atrocities, the millions forced to leave their homes, the years of napalm and Agent Orange, the vast bombing raids, the millions killed by the war—after all this, now the real suffering, the truly gripping and heroic personal war stories, came from a few enormously brave American POWs whose tales of torture could wipe away the guilt of war and replace it with righteous anger at the Vietnamese, despicable torturers who deserved the bombardment that they got.

In this context, an unidentified "senior U.S. officer" among the returned POWs first alleged that Jane Fonda had harmed the POWs in Hanoi. That person, never named, told *Newsweek*'s Thomas DeFrank that torture was rampant in the camps and that the Vietnamese "beat others to force them to appear before visiting antiwar activists such as Jane Fonda and former U.S. Attorney General Ramsey Clark."[22] The alleged torture was said to have taken place during Fonda's and Clark's visits in July and August 1972. But in all the hard-line officer accounts in other contexts, they place all their torture stories during the time they were in solitary—and unobserved by other POWs. They agree that torture and mistreatment stopped in 1969, when they were placed in large cells with other POWs. The torture stories, advanced by the Pentagon to erode support for reconstruction aid to Vietnam, were thereafter easily altered to suit shifting political ends.

On March 30, 1973, in a television interview in Los Angeles, Fonda denied the charge made by the unidentified officer that some POWs were tortured into meeting with her. She said that the POWs who met with her did so voluntarily. It was more than the charge against her that concerned Fonda. She realized, sooner than many in the antiwar movement, what these torture charges signified: a bitter end to the war that would wipe out reconstruction aid to Vietnam along with the prospects of an unflinching national accounting of the war. Reconciliation efforts receded with each new torture account.

Fonda believed that some prisoners were mistreated, and badly, but she objected to the hard-line POWs who presumed to speak for the entire group of returned prisoners. "I'm quite sure that there were incidents of torture," she said in her March 30 interview. "Some of these professional pilots were probably beaten to death by the people whose homes and families they were bombing and napalming. But the pilots who are saying it was the policy of the Vietnamese and that it was systematic, I believe that that's a lie."[23]

Fonda's response to the anonymous charge against her infuriated some of the hard-line POWs. No sooner had her comments been carried in the national media then James Kasler told ABC News that he was tortured and forced to meet with an American delegation in Hanoi, although he declined to specify the torture, when it took place, or the American delegation in question.

To counteract Fonda's television interview, Pentagon officials arranged a press conference for David Wesley Hoffman, one of the seven airmen who had met with Fonda in Hanoi in July 1972. Hoffman had been a lieutenant commander on the USS *Coral Sea* when he was shot down over North Vietnam on December 30, 1971. His left arm was broken when he ejected from his plane. His arm was put in a cast and healed by the time of his release fourteen months later. During his months in prison in Hanoi, Hoffman met with a number of antiwar delegations and newsmen. He made numerous statements to visiting journalists and was shown on American TV news broadcasts more than any other POW, surrounded by his fellow airmen, speaking out against aerial bombardment and calling for a negotiated settlement that would allow the POWs to return home.[24]

Now, in 1973, after meeting with Pentagon officials, Hoffman told newsmen, truthfully, that he had met with Fonda and Ramsey Clark in Hanoi. But for the first time since his return, Hoffman now said that he had been coerced and tortured into the meeting. "I had a broken arm," he told the reporters, "it was in a cast." He claimed he did not want to meet with Fonda in July 1972, and so the Vietnamese had tortured him by hanging him from a hook in the ceiling by his broken arm. "I was hung by that broken arm several times and allowed to drop at the end of a rope from a table which was kicked out from under me," Hoffman told reporters. He said he had only met with Fonda in July 1972 because he was tortured, and he went on to repudiate everything that he had said in his Hanoi news conferences against the bombing. The three TV networks, ABC, CBS, and NBC, covered Hoffman's allegation, and his story was widely reported elsewhere.[25]

Hoffman's incendiary charge ignited others over the years, and helped obliterate the public memory of the many services Americans who traveled to Vietnam had performed for the POWs: ferrying letters between them and their families for over three years, carrying packages to them, and urging better treatment of them and early releases. Later, Hoffman appeared ambivalent about his own charges. Immediately after issuing the torture allegation about his meeting with Fonda, he stopped talking about it, altogether, refusing to discuss it ever again. Yet his claim lived on, despite all the evidence against it.[26]

To begin with, David Hoffman's crewmate Norris Charles had a different story. They were shot down and captured together in December 1971,and then shared a cell with others in Hanoi. Norris Charles was released early from Hanoi, in September 1972, due partly, officials in Hanoi said, to continued urging from antiwar activists for more early releases.[27] Soon after his release, Norris Charles talked about Fonda's and Clark's visits to Hanoi in July. Charles said that "the camp official asked us if we wanted to see Ramsey Clark. He came over to our building and called us together and asked us if we wanted to see Clark. Everybody said, 'Yes, great.'" As for Fonda's visit several weeks earlier in July, Charles said that in that case, "they came around and I wanted to see her, of course, but everybody couldn't go in my particular group. Guys came from different places to see her." Charles, Hoffman's roommate during the time that Hoffman alleged he had been severely tortured, said that he had never experienced torture in Hanoi and had never heard of or seen any while he was there. The other POWs who met with Fonda and Clark likewise denied having been tortured.[28]

Hoffman's claim that he was tortured into meeting with Fonda was also undermined by Nobel Prize winner Dr. George Wald's investigation. Wald, a professor and biologist at Harvard University, visited Hanoi in February 1972, about six weeks after Hoffman was shot down, and he met with Hoffman in Hanoi at that time.[29] Wald carried his tape recorder with him and recorded his conversation with Hoffman. When he returned to the United States, he transcribed the tape and sent a copy to Hoffman's wife. A year later, when Wald read about Hoffman's claim of being tortured into meeting with Fonda, he felt that something was wrong.

Wald had taken careful notes on his visit with Hoffman in February 1972, in addition to his taped records. His first observation about Hoffman, Wald wrote, was that his left arm was in sling that held it "propped up at right angles to his body." On the tape transcript, Wald asked Hoffman how his arm was. Hoffman replied that when he ejected from his plane, the large bone had been completely broken in two, but the medical staff in Hanoi had taken good care of it. "Originally," Hoffman told Wald then, "they had it in a cast with my arm down against my body and it was healing very rapidly. So they decided they'd better take the other cast off and put it up like this so that it would heal in both directions apparently. I don't understand the full medical details, and it's difficult when you can't talk to the doctor and understand what he's saying." Hoffman added that the doctors had indicated that when the cast came off, he should have full use of his arm again. "One of the doctors comes by every day at least and checks on us to make sure we're all right," he said. "For instance, I was having a problem with my [left] hand. When I go to sleep, the hand would droop and go to sleep and I'd wake up in the morning with it stiff. So they brought me this [showing a little wrapped paddle that slipped into the end of his splint] and it holds the hand up. Now, when I go to sleep, the hand at least stays straight and doesn't cut the blood off."

When Wald asked Hoffman how he was being treated, the airman said he was "amazed, frankly and honestly," at how well he had been treated. "I didn't know what to expect, honestly," he said, "from the time that I was shot down until this very moment my treatment has been superb." If Hoffman felt coerced into making these statements, he offered not the slightest hint at the time. A prisoner less than two months, he talked at length about wanting to go home. "Anyone who's here, any of the captives, captured pilots, aircrew, they're all anxious to go home," he said. "I think the biggest thing that our attention is centered on is the political campaign that is coming up [the 1972 election], what's going to happen. Is the country going to be able to elect a President who can end this thing. It seems to us that it's perfectly obvious that we have to withdraw, to end the war, and that's the only way we're going to go home. And we all want to go home, very, very much. That's the foremost thought in anybody's mind."

He didn't see how Nixon could be reelected, Hoffman told Wald, "unless I read American opinion very, very wrongly—and it hasn't been that long since I've been away." Hoffman said that he wished that

> some of the people that are here could go and tell the American people just exactly what's going on. . . . I think

> some of the pilots who have been here a while, some of the people that have been captured here a while, if they could go and tell the American people what they have seen in the way of treatment, what they see in the way of Vietnamese people, their attitudes, what they're fighting for. . . . After all, two hundred years ago our country fought for its freedom, now why can't our country allow these people to have what we fought for and are so proud of? I don't understand, I honestly don't. And frankly, I would have been hard pressed to explain to anybody why I was here before I was shot down. And now I would find it impossible to explain to anybody what I was doing here, aside from the fact that it was my job and somebody said, "Go do it." That doesn't make it very tasteful.[30]

When Wald returned to Boston in March 1972, he checked with two orthopedic surgeons, Dr. Clement Sledge, head of orthopedics surgery at Robert Bent Brigham Hospital, and Dr. Henry Mankin, head of services at Massachusetts General Hospital, and told them about the Vietnamese's treatment of Hoffman's broken arm, describing how the first cast had been replaced by a second one. Both surgeons told Wald that the treatment of Hoffman's broken arm made "good medical sense." They said that a cast that held Hoffman's arm as it appeared in Wald's photograph would provide better "articulation" after healing than the first cast.

So when, in 1973, Hoffman suddenly claimed he was tortured to meet with Jane Fonda in 1972, Wald went back to Sledge and Mankin to discuss Hoffman's allegation that he was hung by his broken arm from a ceiling hook several times. The surgeons told Wald that if Hoffman was hung by his broken arm even once, it could have torn off his arm, even if it had been in a cast. In the best of circumstances, his circulation would have suffered irreparable damage and take months to heal, even imperfectly.[31]

The many photographs of Hoffman in Hanoi nowhere suggest that his arm was re-broken, as he claimed. Hoffman met at least five times with Americans visiting Hanoi and at least three times with foreign news reporters at regular intervals during his fourteen months of captivity. Wald took a photo of Hoffman in February 1972, two months after Hoffman was shot down. That photo shows him with the cast Wald described in his report. In May, Hoffman met with an American delegation made up of Father Paul Mayer, Reverend Robert Lecky, Margery Tabankin, and Dr. Bill Zimmerman. Their film of their trip, called *Village by Village,* shows Hoffman without a cast, looking relaxed and healthy. In May, Hoffman also met with an international film crew. Photos of him wearing no cast and using his arm normally were broadcast on ABC, NBC, and CBS evening news on May 18. In July, Hoffman and six other POWs met with Fonda. At that meeting, Hoffman showed Fonda the arm that had been crushed when he ejected from his plane. He'd been afraid that he would lose his arm, he told her, but now it was out of the cast and he could use it well. He raised his arm up and down to demonstrate its flexibility to Fonda. He asked her to tell his wife that his arm was well. "She'll be very happy," he said. Once Fonda was back in the United States, she called Hoffman's wife to relay the good news.[32] In August, Hoffman met with Ramsey Clark and other international visitors. Hoffman's arm was out of the cast and he used it normally. In September, he met with an American group made up of Reverend William Sloan Coffin Jr., Father Harry Bury, Cora Weiss, and David Dellinger. Again, his arm looked healthy.[33]

George Wald considered this information relevant to Hoffman's torture claims. He sent a letter outlining his counterevidence about Hoffman's claims to Senator J. William Fulbright, chair of the Senate Foreign Relations Committee. Wald told the Senator that he believed the matter was important because the atrocity stories that several POWs were telling "have had, and are having, important effects upon our domestic situation and foreign policy." Fulbright sent Wald's letter on to William Clements, deputy secretary of defense, asking him to respond to the questions that Wald had raised about Hoffman's torture allegations. In response, Pentagon spokesman Jerry Friedheim acknowledged merely that "the circumstances surrounding interviews conducted while in captivity inside North Vietnam were considerably different from those in this country when the men were free."[34]

Fulbright persisted. He wrote to Clements, complaining that Friedheim's letter was "not responsive" to the issue. This time, Clements himself replied tersely, saying that the Department of Defense "does not intend to pursue the matter." As far as the Pentagon was concerned, Hoffman's charge that he had been tortured into meeting with Jane Fonda would stand, regardless of countervailing evidence.[35]

Wald tried to get his doubts about Hoffman's torture allegations into the media, which had circulated Hoffman's story, but found the fourth estate as unresponsive as the Pentagon. Wald finally wrote a short piece and sent it to the *New Yorker*, which had run a feature story on him several years earlier after he criticized the arms race in a speech at MIT. In his article, which the magazine declined to publish, Wald asked if the administration was acting in its own interest by fanning the torture charges or if the Department of Defense was "pursuing some end of its own counter to another part of the Administration." For the past weeks, Wald contended,

> the media were filled with atrocity stories of returned POWs. Let me say at once that I have no reason to doubt other such

> stories than the one I go into here. As I understand it, however, all other reports agree that instances of gross mistreatment virtually ceased by about October 1969. This one, that is said to have occurred in 1972, may stand alone. These stories have had and still have important effects upon our domestic situation and foreign policy. They have created in this country a hatred of North Vietnam and of the so-called Vietcong far exceeding any that existed during the war. Also, they became the basis for bitter attacks upon the peace movement, singling out for special invidium such vulnerable public figures as Jane Fonda and ex-Attorney General Ramsey Clark. Third, and I think it most important, these stories made it virtually impossible to carry out Article 21 of the ceasefire agreement, pledging that "the United States will contribute to healing the wounds of war and to post-war reconstruction of the Democratic Republic of Vietnam and throughout Indochina." After the atrocity stories it would take a hardy Congressman to vote funds for this purpose.

"Whatever the motivations and intentions may attach to the atrocity accounts," Wald concluded, "there can be no doubt of their effect. For many, they have largely obliterated any feelings of guilt for what we had done in our massive bombings, napalming and crop destruction, carried out on a defenseless civilian population by our fliers, including the POWs." The torture charges, Wald believed, encouraged Americans to think that "however bad the things we did, *they* were worse."[36]

Jane Fonda was also concerned about Hoffman's charges. She believed the POWs she met had not been tortured in prison. They had all told her that when she met with them, and after they were all released, they maintained that, with the sole exception of Hoffman. Willing to acknowledge Hoffman's mistreatment and torture if it were true, Fonda set out to find evidence to support his allegation. Many of the POWs had suffered broken limbs and other injuries when they ejected from their planes, and they had been x-rayed, first in Hanoi, and again at U.S. military hospitals when they were released in 1973. Comparing Hoffman's X-rays from Hanoi and from his post-release exam in the United States could offer evidence of Hoffman's allegations, since all the photos of him during his captivity argued against his torture claims. Fonda obtained copies of Hoffman's X-rays taken during his treatement in Hanoi. She sent a letter to Hoffman, saying that those X-rays from Hanoi were available and asking if he would release his medical records from Balboa Hospital in San Diego, where he was thoroughly examined upon his release. Fonda told Hoffman that if a doctor of Hoffman's choosing would examine both sets of X-rays and confirm Hoffman's account, she was willing to accept that judgment. Hoffman never replied to her letter.[37]

Was Hoffman's broken arm attached to a hook in the ceiling while he stood on a table, which was then kicked from under him several times, as he alleged? All evidence is against that story. What we do know is that after the POWs' release, some of the hard-line officers attacked Hoffman for meeting with Jane Fonda and Ramsey Clark in Hanoi. They were already announcing their plans to bring charges against some POWs who had defied their orders in Hanoi by calling for a negotiated end to the war. When he claimed that his meetings with Fonda and Clark were coerced by torture, Hoffman, who planned to stay in the military, may have believed he was deflecting a possible court-martial.[38]

After the flurry of torture charges from the hard-line officers, congressional support for aid to North Vietnam slumped. "The hell with 'em," Congressman John McCollister, a Republican from Nebraska, said. "I would not vote a bus token to North Vietnam. If the North Vietnamese want money, they can get their good friends Ramsey Clark and Jane Fonda to take a collection for them." Congressman Joel Broyhill, a Republican from Virginia, said the accounts of torture by the POWs "convince me that not a cent" of American money should be spent to help a country "apparently run by savages." Congressman Jerry Litton, a Missouri Democrat, seized the moment to inveigh against both Hanoi and draft resisters. He said the United States should "solve" the question of aid to Hanoi by deporting the draft resisters to Vietnam. "If those in America who evaded military service loved the North Vietnamese too much to fight them, perhaps they still love them enough to help them in their reconstruction program," he said.[39]

Having promised North Vietnam reconstruction aid, the White House now realized, too late, the lethal impact that the torture charges, which it had at first supported, would have on that aid package. One military official who knew early of some POWs' intentions to raise torture charges told a reporter that "if Richard Nixon thinks reconstruction is in trouble now, he'd better find himself a bomb shelter when these guys start blowing the whistle."[40] Caught off-guard by events that it had helped set in motion, the White House hastily arranged a press conference for Philip Manhard, the highest-ranking American diplomat held in Hanoi. Captured in January 1968, Manhard was of considerable interest to the Vietnamese because he had been an intelligence officer during the Korean War and had interrogated Chinese POWs then. Now, after five years of captivity in Vietnam, Manhard appeared before the news cameras in Washington and pleaded for aid to Vietnam. "I think that this country has an admirable tradition, a spirit of generosity and forgiveness, a Christian tradition, to heal the wounds of war," he said. "The Vietnamese people need this," he urged. "Human needs go beyond ideology and the hardships of the past. In spite of the hardships I and others underwent, I think the best interest of our country and people lies in trying to generate a stable, peaceful coexistence." The White House effort failed entirely. Three days after Manhard's public plea, the Senate voted overwhelmingly to deny President Nixon authority to grant reconstruction aid to North Vietnam.[41]

With aid to Hanoi firmly defeated, the hard-line POWs who had once tried to use the Code of Conduct to carry the war in Vietnam into the prison camps, now turned against some of their fellow POWs. Led by Lieutenant Colonel Theodore Guy, they accused other former POWs of treason, collaboration with the enemy, and refusal to obey senior officers—themselves—during their prison ordeal in Hanoi. They pursued these charges with a vindictiveness that surprised even seasoned Pentagon officials. The Pentagon wanted to kill reconstruction aid to Vietnam, but it didn't want the spectacle of courts-martial pitting a few hard-line officers against other POWs who had also just emerged from the Hanoi prison camps.

One Pentagon official who worked on the issue told journalist Seymour Hersh that there was "hard feeling" on the part of those filing the charges. The hard-line officers had, at times, been housed with enlisted men in Hanoi and had "attempted to pull rank on the enlisted men—they didn't take to it," the Pentagon officer said. He characterized the hard-line officers as "one-sided" and a "club," and said they were "looking for blood." Of the men the hard-liners were threatening to bring charges against, he told Hersh that "none of them are officers and some of them are black, so the club is going after them."[42] Some of the hard-line officers openly vented their rage to the press as well. Captain James Mulligan told a reporter there was clear distinction between him and the men who refused to retract their calls for a negotiated settlement while in Hanoi: "No one ever minds anyone breaking under torture. It's those guys who fink out who get you. Those guys will get what's coming to them. Any guy who goes to Hanoi and gets religion after he's shot down is a pure phony."[43]

Pentagon officers asked Theodore Guy not to file charges against any former prisoners. It would bring bad publicity, officers said, and they wanted harmony to "preserve the hero image of the returnees and diffuse the radicals and peace groups who are looking for a cause." But Theodore Guy still went ahead and filed charges against eight POWs in his camp for "aiding the enemy" and showing "disrespect toward a superior officer." Some of the men he charged said that if Guy charged them for making statements urging a negotiated end to the war, then he would have to charge all the POWs, including himself. The eight men never denied their statements in Hanoi. They believed they had the right to free speech, even in their prison camp.[44]

One of the eight former POWs Guy charged was Abel Kavanaugh, who had been imprisoned in Hanoi over five years. On June 27, 1973, facing a court-martial and the possibility of more years in prison after his long ordeal in Hanoi, Kavanaugh shot himself. The other former POWs Guy had accused carried his casket at the funeral. Kavanaugh's wife said bitterly that "the North Vietnamese kept him alive for five years, and then his own country killed him. I blame Colonel Guy and the Pentagon for this death." She was considering bringing wrongful death charges against Guy. Guy said that he had no regrets. He told the *New York Post* that he was "not afraid of anything. If they do sue, I think it would be very unfortunate for the people I charged. I think they are better off shutting up right now. They should quit while they are ahead." One of Guy's friends, hard-line officer Marine Captain James DiBernardo, said that none of them regretted filing charges against other POWs. "We have gained one thing," he said. "These men will be marked for the rest of their lives. We didn't want to see them go to jail but wanted to show them up for what they are. They weren't Americans, as far as I was concerned."[45] It was left to the Pentagon, finally, to stop Guy's charges. Six days after Kavanaugh's suicide, it formally dismissed all of Guy's allegations against the remaining GIs, citing lack of evidence.[46]

Even after Kavanaugh's suicide, another hard-line officer, James Stockdale, persisted in his own effort to bring charges against two senior officers, Navy Commander Walter Wilber and Lieutenant Colonel Edison Miller. They and others—including David Wesley Hoffman, who later made the charges against Jane Fonda and Ramsey Clark—had met with antiwar activists and sent back a letter calling on the American people and Congress to work for a negotiated, rather than a military, settlement to the war. Stockdale had filed his charges a few days before Kavanaugh committed suicide, but he still persisted in his efforts with breathtaking vindictiveness, spending most of his first six months of freedom trying to send two fellow POWs back to prison. Finally, in September 1973, Navy Secretary John Warner ordered Stockdale's charges dismissed.[47]

The torture allegations were deliberately introduced for political purposes: they were used to deny any reconstruction aid to Vietnam and to create an image of the Vietnamese as a barbaric enemy. The allegations helped poison attitudes in the United States against Vietnam, the effects of which still linger. They reframed the United States' war against Vietnam as a story whose primary reality was Americans suffering terribly at the hands of the Vietnamese. The torture charges involved much more than the treatment of individual POWs in Hanoi, and they deserve more scrutiny.

Journalist Steven Roberts interviewed many of the POWs soon after they returned home. He noted discrepancies between the hard-liners' stories and the other men's. He concluded it was "uncertain how the prisoners' fierce commitment to resist a despised enemy has colored their accounts of prison life." He said that

> the question of torture is difficult to place in perspective. Undoubtedly, many men suffered considerable pain, particularly the camp leaders. But some dissident prisoners feel that

> the intense hatred toward the "gooks" has caused some returned men to "exaggerate" their descriptions of torture . . . prisoners who absorbed the most punishment were folk heroes to their comrades, and the critics wonder whether some prisoners have inflated their stories, even unconsciously, to enhance their reputations as "tough nuts."[48]

Roberts noted that hard-line officers exhibited a "deep and almost desperate belief that the Vietnam War was worth it, and that the president would, in fact, gain 'peace with honor.' " He quoted Lieutenant Colonel James Hiteshew as saying, "maybe we developed it ourselves, that we spent so much time, that this time was not lost. I mean, we didn't want to feel that we spent six years there for nothing. That would be pretty difficult, and we'd be a pretty bitter bunch of individuals. So we came out and in our minds we had done what we intended to do, we had accomplished it and we wanted to tell everyone else that job has been accomplished."[49]

"The embittered veteran prisoners valued uniformity and discipline above all," Roberts concluded, "but the newer inmate—a whole generation younger, shaped in an entirely different era—stressed 'conscience' and 'morality.' " Some older long-term prisoners stressed conscience and morality, too. Roberts cited especially former POWs Walter Wilber and Edison Miller as senior officers who, out of conscience, questioned the war and signed statements in Hanoi calling for a negotiated settlement and an end to the bombing. In prison, the hard-line officers threatened Wilber and Miller with courts-martial when they returned home. But to some of the younger POWs in Hanoi, Roberts reported, these two men "were heroes." Air Force Captain Lynn Guenther told Roberts that Walter Wilber and Edison Miller "took a lot of heat and stood up for what they believed in." The paradox of the hard-line POWs, Roberts said, was that

> they survived because of their unity; they "lived on loyalty," as one put it. They "brainwashed" themselves to believe more fervently than ever in the wisdom of the war and the good intentions of the Government. As Colonel Hiteshew said, "We were always behind the Administration, no matter who it was." But the very war they were fighting caused at least some segments of the country to lose faith in that wisdom and those good intentions. During the time that prisoners spent in North Vietnam, the "credibility gap" became a national institution; skepticism became a pervasive attitude; people followed the dictates of their morality, not their Government, in a massive outpouring of public protest.

The hard-liners, Roberts concluded, wanted to heal the divided country with a resurgence of national pride and patriotism they felt had been lost. But to the other prisoners, the ones who had come to oppose the war, this approach seemed shortsighted: "They are afraid that in the rush to exalt the prisoners of war and recite the litany of 'peace with honor,' the hard-won lessons of Vietnam are in danger of being lost."[50]

Many of the torture stories generated when the POWs first came home evolved over time as some hard-line airmen published books about their prison experience. For example, when Air Force Major Fred Cherry ejected from his plane, his left arm and ankle were broken and his shoulder crushed. When he was released from Hanoi in 1973, Cherry told CBS newsman Morton Dean that he had not suffered personally in Hanoi, and he described his medical treatment for his injuries as good. But several years later, when John Hubbell interviewed him for the *Reader's Digest* book *P.O.W.*, which emphasized the torture stories, Cherry likened his medical treatment to a chamber of tortures. There was no anesthesia, he said, which was true throughout North Vietnam, but Cherry now claimed that when the Vietnamese doctors treated him in the hospital, they deliberately tried to make him suffer in the process—they wanted him to "scream." Cherry told Hubbell he didn't understand the Vietnamese language, but he just knew that when the doctors looked at his face as he lay on the operating table, they were saying, "He is not unconscious; he is not screaming!" And so, Cherry told Hubbell, he determined not to scream; each time they looked at him, "he made sure that he was smiling widely."[51]

Over a decade later, Cherry wove Jane Fonda into his torture story. He now said he was tortured regularly and that once, in the middle of "an extended torture siege" that he set at sometime in 1967, he heard Fonda's voice over the public address system in the camp and became so "enraged" that he "tried to tear [his] irons from the walls."[52] But this story could not be true. Jane Fonda was nowhere near Hanoi in 1967, and had not even become an antiwar activist yet. She was not in Hanoi until July 1972, long after even the hard-line officers like Cherry said their mistreatment had ceased. Fonda was becoming a convenient shorthand among some veterans and war supporters for all the humiliations and contradictions of defeat in Vietnam.

Other pilots who had not alleged any torture in 1973 began to claim, in the next decades, that they, too, had been tortured. For example, neither Captain Thomas Moe and his sometime cell mate Myron Donald said they had been tortured when they were released in 1973. Indeed, their early accounts of prison emphasize learning French and Russian from other POWs, determined not to "mope" but make the best of it. Donald even offers a semihumorous account of his initiation into the prison system, saying that for the first few days, he piled his dirty clothes on the spare bed in his cell, expecting a maid to come take his laundry away. But years later, after the hard-line POWs wrote books describing systematic torture, Moe and Donald, among other returned POWs, began to claim that they, too, were tortured into writing their statements urging an end to the bombing and a negotiated settlement.

In the mid-1990s, after tales of POW torture in Hanoi had permeated the culture, Thomas Moe wrote an account of his prison experience depicting it as a long nightmare of torture. He said "about 20 guards each took his turn beating me to a pulp. They pounded me for six or eight hours." After this beating, they bound him tightly in ropes with his arms behind him until his arms turned "black," and for the following "hours" slammed his face or the back of his head onto a concrete floor. Another guard kicked Moe's back "with all the strength he could exert." The next day, after he was untied, Moe said that "red fluid oozed out of every opening in my body . . . you could stick your finger into me up to your knuckle and pull it out leaving a hole that would slowly fill with fluid." When Moe was released in 1973, he had said nothing about these things and appeared physically healthy.[53]

Bracketing the American war in Vietnam is the haze of lies surrounding the Gulf of Tonkin at the beginning and the haze of torture charges at the end. In each case, the charge took on a life of its own. The Gulf of Tonkin falsehoods temporarily boosted support for a cause ultimately few supported, and the charges of POW torture at the end of the war spawned decades of official U.S. hostility toward Vietnam, capped a punitive, vengeful economic embargo. These charges also spiraled into false accusations that Jane Fonda and other Americans had caused the POWs suffering and torture, and left powerful images in the minds of ordinary Americans of Vietnamese as bloodthirsty, inhumane, and brutal torturers who got their due.

The controversy surrounding Jane Fonda's trip to Vietnam reflected and reinforced the decades-long process of reshaping the experiences of the prisoners in Hanoi, which represented some Americans' attempt to redeem a lost war. One of the first justifications for invading Vietnam had been to keep communist

China "contained." But then Nixon went to communist China, toasted its leaders, and proclaimed friendship between the two peoples. Why, then, one might reasonably ask, had the United States really gone to war in Vietnam? Richard Nixon and Henry Kissinger could not explain contradictions like these to an increasingly skeptical public. And when a military victory was denied in 1975, urgent new questions added to the old, unanswered ones. A war won requires little soul-searching. It calls for celebration and then glides into history. Defeat, however, requires an explanation, a somber accounting, before it can be laid to rest. The lost war in Vietnam never had that reckoning. It was smothered by Richard Nixon's parting gift to the political culture: the claim that defeat came from within—only Americans could defeat America. It was a skillful political move. When the search for internal scapegoats fired up, antiwar activists like Jane Fonda became the first suspects.

7

THE COMPLICATED LEGACIES OF FONDA'S ANTIWAR ACTIVISM

FONDA'S ANTIWAR ACTIVISM has bequeathed a complex legacy. One result has been the mythical account of her actions during the war and, by extension, of the antiwar movement generally. Following the lead of Richard Nixon, this account claims that it was Americans themselves who defeated America in Vietnam. Fonda was singled out to bear the weight of that charge: she was accused of destroying the morale of American troops in Vietnam, causing the torture of American POWs in Hanoi, and betraying her country. Politicians and pundits berated her for speaking out against the war, a subject they claimed she knew little about; some even called for her execution. Folklorist Carol Burke observed that the legend of betrayal constructed around Jane Fonda has been so tenacious because the mythological image of an attractive woman who "turns out to be a snake" is "the oldest story in the world."[1]

The deeper legacy of Fonda's antiwar activism is one of inspiration, a legacy of perseverance in the face of false charges and wrongful government pursuit. During the war, Fonda refused to allow the bitterly personal and emotional charges of treason deter her from continuing to openly and forthrightly oppose the war and the bombing of Vietnam. Indeed, even after being vilified for going to North Vietnam in 1972, she confidently returned in May 1974, with her husband, Tom Hayden, and filmmaker Haskell Wexler. They made a documentary film of life in Vietnam and called it *Introduction to the Enemy*. It was intended, Fonda said, to show the Vietnamese, not as victims but as people "filled with optimism, people who have survived, people who very consciously don't hate Americans." *New York Times* film critic Nora Sayre praised the film as "pensive and moving," as much personal as political with a mood of "restrained optimism" whose message was that "the Vietnamese do not hate Americans, they want to know more about us."[2]

The government's spying on Fonda came, at last, to an ignominious end. She had not known the extent of the spying until late 1973, when syndicated columnist Jack Anderson handed her an FBI dossier that someone inside the government had passed to him. The dossier outlined the illegal methods employed to get Fonda's bank records and alluded to other actions it was carrying out against her. The FBI never discovered how those secret documents reached Anderson, but the agency suspected a contract employee who was updating the Secret Service computer system and whose fingerprints were found on the dossier Anderson gave to Fonda. But pursuing the contract employee was out of the question. He was cleared to handle classified documents, and the FBI had no other evidence against him. The case was "embarrassing," one agent wrote, and the FBI dropped it. The administration was embroiled in the Watergate investigation by this time, and a vindictive pursuit of someone whose only crime was revealing the crimes of the White House and FBI appeared unwise.[3]

The FBI files exposed an intense, illegal, obsessive, and ultimately fruitless surveillance of Fonda that lasted years. FBI agents opened her domestic mail, tapped her phone, and hijacked her personal bank information by falsely telling bank officers that it was a matter of "national security." They planted false allegations that she used profanity in public speeches, prepared a false story that she advocated getting guns and killing the president, and phoned her home to determine her travel schedule and even the daily activities of her preschool-age daughter and of the preschool itself. They followed Fonda to an astonishing number of public meetings and made tapes and transcripts of her talks. FBI agents freely handed out copies of their illegal surveillance reports on Jane Fonda to government agencies, including the Secret Service, the State Department, the IRS, the CIA, and the White House, which put her on its enemies list.[4]

After Anderson gave her the FBI dossier, Jane Fonda filed a million-dollar lawsuit against Richard Nixon, Henry Kissinger, Charles Colson, and what she called "the entire Watergate crew" for conspiring to destroy her credibility and disrupt her life.[5] She called the FBI's plot "part of an organized systematic attempt to discredit me during the Nixon administration . . . to make those of us who opposed the Nixon administration appear irresponsible, dangerous and foul-mouthed. I never have and never will raise money or spend money for guns," she said. "I don't use foul language and I never said I wanted to kill Nixon. Those are totally fabricated for the purpose of slandering me and making me appear to be a violent and irresponsible person."[6]

In response, the FBI transferred all blame to Fonda. If no one had answered the FBI's calls, her privacy would not have been invaded, the agency said, adding that the calls spared her "the embarrassment of having it known" that the Bureau was investigating her. The agency said finding out where her daughter went to preschool was a matter "of legitimate interest in our security investigation"and that her bank should not be criticized for handing over her financial records to the FBI because it spared bank employees the "expense and time" of the paperwork that subpoenas for her records would have required.[7]

The CIA took another route, denying it had opened her mail or otherwise spied on her. But with the case proceeding to court, the agency revised its tactics and said that its denial was "in error." The change in tone came when Edward Christenbury, a Justice Department attorney was assigned to the case for the CIA. Christenbury had not been involved in the spying activities, and he appeared earnest about righting the wrong. He filed court papers that completely reversed the CIA's original claim of innocence and admitted the Agency had illegally intercepted her mail as part of its hitherto-secret "East Coast Mail Intercept Program." Leonard Weinglass, Fonda's attorney, said that it was "the first time in a legal proceeding that the CIA acknowledged taking action against an individual in the United States."[8]

Fonda's suit against the government's illegal activities against her also helped crack open another spying operation, the "Huston Plan," a vast, secret program orchestrated by White House aide Charles Huston and authorized by President Nixon. The Huston Plan began in 1970 and relied on burglaries, wiretaps, and mail surveillance to harass activist individuals and groups. As part of Fonda's suit against the president and the FBI, federal judge Malcolm Lucas ordered Charles Huston to reveal the names of other persons and groups targeted by his scheme.[9] Fonda's legal action also forced the IRS to stop harassing the United States Servicemen's Fund. The group funded coffeehouses for GIs near military bases and Fonda had raised much of the money for it. Someone broke into the Fund's office, ransacked its files, and turned them over to the House Committee on Internal Security, which published the names of the Fund's donors. IRS Commissioner Johnie Walters then used this dubious foundation to revoke the Fund's tax exemption status. As part of her lawsuit, Fonda demanded that the White House and the IRS reveal the extent of its spying activities against the Fund. Rather than comply, the White House ordered the IRS to reinstate the Fund's tax exemption status.[10]

On February 4, 1975, John Keegan, acting assistant attorney general in the Ford administration, ordered the FBI to "promptly discontinue your subversion investigation of Fonda," and the FBI eventually offered Fonda an out-of-court settlement. The FBI agreed to give Fonda all the files it had collected on her. It agreed to admit that it had undertaken a campaign of harassment and intimidation against Fonda because of her political views and activities. It acknowledged that the campaign against her and the tactics it used were wrong. It agreed to "cease and desist from these practices" and not employ them against Fonda or "others who are similarly active."

After the government finally agreed, in 1979, to release to her all the files it had gathered on her, and after it had admitted wrongdoing in her case, Fonda dropped her financial claim against the government. "It's not what we were going after," she said of the million dollars. "We were trying to illustrate a principle." Between 1973, when Fonda filed her suit, and 1979, when it was settled, Richard Nixon resigned, the Rockefeller Commission and the Church Committee held hearings on the CIA's intelligence-gathering methods, the Justice Department issued guidelines outlawing all the techniques used against Fonda, and Congress enacted laws requiring stringent procedures when bank records were seized. In the files that the FBI released to her in 1979, she finally received an impounded letter sent years earlier by *Chicago Tribune* columnist Jack Mabley praising her for having the courage to speak out against the war. Mabley said he had no idea why his letter to Fonda had ended up in the hands of the FBI, which distributed it to the Secret Service and other government agencies. "It's kind of incongruous," he said. "I fit in with the conservative image of the *Tribune*, but you've got to hand it to a lady like that. I admired her for having the guts to speak out."[11]

White House Counsel Charles (Chuck) Colson, one of the defendants named in Fonda's lawsuit against the government, made a personal appeal to her to drop the charges against him. Colson was known as Nixon's "hatchet man" because he was fiercely loyal to the president. "I would walk over my grandmother, if necessary" to ensure the reelection of Nixon, he said in 1972.[12] Colson's fingerprints were all over the dirty tricks spun from the

Oval Office. It was Colson, for example, who showed Nixon the FBI's illegally gathered files on activists for the president's private amusement. In 1973, as part of the Watergate investigation, Colson ended up pleading no contest to obstructing justice in the burglary of Daniel Ellsburg's psychiatrist's office. After his legal difficulties surfaced, Colson told the press that he had been born again: he was now a changed man and was leaving dirty tricks behind him. Then he invited Fonda to lunch, to see, as one reporter given advance knowledge of Colson's intent put it, "that he is a changed man, now that he has found Christ and joined a religious movement."[13] Colson wanted Fonda to drop his name from the lawsuit that she had filed against the government because of "his conversion to Christ." Fonda declined Colson's offer of a free lunch but offered to meet with him in his law office in Washington. After the meeting, Fonda told reporters the meeting was "very productive," although the two had not discussed Colson's conversion.[14]

When the war was over and lost, Jane Fonda and her antiwar work became a vehicle for some war supporters to reframe their own disquieting experiences during that time. Even Charles Colson was soon "remembering" his connection to Jane Fonda in a way that blatantly twisted the facts to present his illegal activities in the White House in an innocuous light. In 1988, when the Reagan administration was coming under scrutiny for spying on Americans in ways resembling those of the Nixon administration, Colson wrote a piece for *Christianity Today* about why the government spies on political activists, which began:

> I well remember that angry morning in 1971. I stood in my White House office, glaring at the photograph on the front page of the *Washington Post*: actress Jane Fonda, defiantly perched on a North Vietnamese antiaircraft gun used to shoot down American pilots. As an ex-marine,

> I was incensed; as an administration official, I was ready to prosecute. Seething, I called the state department to suggest that Ms. Fonda's passport be revoked. It seemed right to leave her in Hanoi, where she was obviously more at home. Fortunately, cooler heads prevailed, or else the Vietnamese might eventually have gotten all the exercise videos and diet books. At any rate, that episode makes it easier for me to understand how anger and paranoia can lead to intemperate government action. . . .[15]

Colson's rewriting of history got it all backward. It was not Fonda's trip to Hanoi (which was in 1972, not 1971) that prompted Colson's dirty tricks against her. The FBI, Colson, and the White House were spying on Fonda illegally and spreading false stories about her long before she went to Hanoi. Their efforts against her began over two years before her trip to Hanoi, prompted merely by Fonda's speaking out against the war. Indeed, when Fonda was arrested under blatantly false pretenses in Cleveland in 1970, it was Colson, as he acknowledged once under oath, who had handed the FBI's secret files on that false arrest to Richard Nixon in the Oval Office.

In Colson's account in *Christianity Today*, he ignored all of these facts in favor of a story that erroneously leads the reader to the conclusion that it was her 1972 trip to Hanoi that first sparked Colson's and the White House's animosity toward Jane Fonda. The reader is led to believe, from Colson's account, that "cooler heads" restrained him from acting on his outrage against Fonda. In fact, as Colson well knew, he and the White House continued to illegally spy on Fonda well after the State Department rebuffed his demand to seize Fonda's passport (which the courts had already said the government could not do in such a case), and they kept it up with unimpeded vigor as long as they could keep doing it in secret.

Colson's account is wrong on almost every point of fact—even about the photograph that he claims he saw on the front page of the *Washington Post*. There never was a picture on the front page of the *Washington Post* showing Fonda on the antiaircraft gun emplacement. Indeed, that picture was not much remarked on in 1972, nor in the years immediately following. Back then, it was her broadcasts over Radio Hanoi that most infuriated war supporters at home. What Colson said he "remembered" in 1988 reflects the myths that developed during the 1980s, myths fed in part by the White House Colson helped shape, more than it does Fonda's actual activities against the war.

Perhaps Fonda best summed up the context and the consequence of the government's campaign against her. When officials in the Nixon administration were attacking her personally and secretly plotting against her, she sometimes pointed out that she had never issued orders to drop Agent Orange on Vietnam. She was not the one who sent the troops there. She had not ordered pilots to bomb Vietnam, setting them up to be shot down and imprisoned. She had tried to awaken the nation to the futility and enormous cost of those tactics. Unlike the Nixon administration, she had not tried to keep her activities secret. And when, in 1974, a reporter asked her what she thought now that Watergate had brought down the people who had once harassed and defamed her, she said simply, "I'm still here. The last government's in jail."[16]

In the following years, those unable to come to terms with the U.S. defeat in Vietnam, spread myriad false claims about antiwar activists. They targeted no one more harshly than Jane Fonda. Their false stories gained little popular credence when the war and its horrors were fresh in people's minds in the 1970s, but as memories of the war waned and myths about the lost war took root in the 1980s, the stories proliferated. The idea that *Americans* had defeated America in Vietnam lurked beneath every charge against antiwar activists, especially against Jane Fonda.

The Byzantine process linking Fonda's name to defeat in Vietnam is tenuously connected to torture stories that some POWs told in 1973 and which were developed in detail over the next decades in books published by and about the POWs. The books produced by the returned POWs were written largely by hard-line officers, and they contain almost no references to Fonda. But the grounds for the Fonda myth are there, to emerge over time.

The first book purporting to provide an overall account of the POW experience in Vietnam was a *Reader's Digest* book called *P.O.W.: A Definitive History of the American Prisoner of War Experience in Vietnam, 1964–1973.* Written by John Hubbell and published in 1976, the book is far from the "definitive" account that it claims because it confines itself to the small minority of hard-line POWs whose stories the Pentagon had orchestrated in 1973.[17] Hubbell's book gives Fonda only a cursory reference, saying that "most of the [hard-line] prisoners" regarded the visit to Hanoi of Ramsey Clark "as more serious than Fonda's" because Clark was the former attorney general of the United States. Not only is Fonda's trip to Hanoi virtually unmentioned in this early account, but the hard-liners do not once refer to David Wesley Hoffman's claims that he was tortured because of her.[18]

By the late 1980s, many of the hard-line POWs had written individual narratives of their prison experience. These accounts vie to outdo each other in the severity of torture they describe. Many of the hard-line officers had lived in solitary confinement for long periods up to, and including, 1969, and they allude occasionally to the extreme depression and despair that life in solitary imposed on them. Some of them describe long periods of hallucinations during that time and an absolute sense of hopelessness. But, with the exception of David Wesley Hoffman's one-time allegations at a Pentagon-arranged press conference in 1973, the hard-line POWs themselves seldom included Fonda in their narratives of torture, and on the rare occasions they did, their allegations are oblique and disputed by other evidence.[19]

Jane Fonda was first firmly introduced into the POW torture narrative in Lionel Chetwynd's 1987 melodramatic feature film, *The Hanoi Hilton*. The film bills itself as a faithful depiction of the overall POW experience, but it is instead a faithful follower of Hubbell's book with experiences of the vast majority of the POWs ignored in favor of the stories that the hard-line officers told. The film, written and directed by Chetwynd—who says that he, too, spent a lot of time with the hard-line POWs—broke with Hubbell in an important respect by writing into the script the role of an actress obviously understood to be Jane Fonda. In Chetwynd's film, a few unwilling POWs are brought in one by one to meet "Fonda" in Hanoi, and she lectures them shrilly about their obligation to "apologize" to the Vietnamese people for bombing civilians. With the exception of David Wesley Hoffman's single charge in 1973, the POWs who actually met with Fonda said that they did so willingly and that many more POWs wanted to meet with her. In Chetwynd's film, the POWs who meet with the Fonda stand-in loathe her. One of them, an African American who is supposed to represent Fred Cherry (who never met Fonda), angrily stalks out on her. Other POWs tell her that the food in prison is dreadful and that they are being tortured. The actress scornfully contradicts the prisoners and then "betrays" them to torture by telling the camp commander that they complained of bad food.[20]

Chetwynd's depiction of Fonda's trip to Hanoi is wrong in every respect. For example, Fonda, who went to Hanoi alone and returned alone in 1972, shows up at the POW prison accompanied by two men, one of whom is obviously supposed to be her future husband, Tom Hayden. Chetwynd adds another fabricated scene in which the Vietnamese release three POWs to Fonda. The film had limited popular appeal, but it was widely shown to veterans groups and at the annual gatherings organized by hard-line Vietnam POWs. Those who viewed it may well have believed it was an accurate account. The mythical portrait that later became embedded in Internet Web sites of Jane Fonda in Hanoi as a naive, wilfully ignorant woman who is obviously a traitor, comes straight out of this film, itself a product of Chetwynd's imagination.[21]

Buttressed by Lionel Chetwynd's fiction, feelings of betrayal and anger over defeat in Vietnam smoldered into resentment of Fonda. That rage tipped over late in 1987, after *The Hanoi Hilton* was released, when the town of Waterbury, Connecticut, got word that Jane Fonda was coming there the following year to film *Stanley and Iris*. Gaetano "Guy" Russo, World War II veteran and leader in the Waterbury Veterans of Foreign Wars post, immediately wrote a letter to a local newspaper, the *Waterbury Republican*, urging his fellow citizens to "defend the standards" of Waterbury and not give "comfort and support to Jane Fonda." Russo's fellow World War II veterans from the VFW supported him by sending a flood of letters to the paper that called Fonda a "commie lover" and framed her filming stint in Waterbury as a direct slap at veterans.[22]

This sudden outcry against Fonda amazed other townspeople who had not seen the film and had no idea that emotions about Fonda ran so high. They wrote letters to the newspaper defending Fonda. "Give me a break," one of them said, "perhaps these people have forgotten that it was people like Jane Fonda who actively protested that unnecessary war that helped stop the killing of our men." Waterbury resident Edith Ruskin called Fonda "a very courageous person. She was using her reputation as an actor in something that is the highest form of democracy, putting her in a category where she could have sacrificed her career and been punished to express a view."[23]

Russo was determined to prevent Fonda from coming to

Waterbury, and he called on other VFW posts across the country to help him. That network proved a powerful force behind the Waterbury Veterans post, with letters to the local paper arriving from veterans across the nation calling Fonda a communist and a traitor and congratulating the veterans of Waterbury for their outcry. "It's about time the veterans did go after Jane Fonda," one of them wrote.[24] The letters grew harsher, adding charges that Fonda had "undermined" an American military victory in Vietnam and that hosting her would be "an insult" to veterans. She should be tried for treason and "her sentence should be death by firing squad or hanging," one argued. VFW member Dominic Romano claimed Admiral John McCain once told him that his son, POW John McCain, had been "senselessly beaten" in Hanoi because he refused to meet with Fonda. If Fonda came to Waterbury, Romano said, the veterans "will be there in force."[25] Members of VFW posts from as far away as Louisiana came to Waterbury to swell the ranks at public protests, holding signs that read, "I'm not Fond'a Hanoi Jane." Some of their children and grandchildren waved signs with messages like "Thanks to you Jane, some kids don't have dads." Russo's language turned venomous. He said that Fonda should be "executed."[26] This severity attracted local members of the Ku Klux Klan, who joined the planning meetings and rallies against Fonda. Klan leader James Farrands, echoing Russo, said that Fonda should be "tried for treason and summarily shot."[27]

The town's clergy grew alarmed by the angry rhetoric. Reverend David Halmer said the invective against Fonda was creating a climate of violence, and it was time to put things in perspective. At an overflow town meeting called to discuss the issue, Father Edmund Nadolny said that the anger against Fonda was really generated by feelings about the war in Vietnam. "There's a much bigger issue here and that's not being discussed," he said. "Instead, all of this anger about Vietnam is being directed at Jane Fonda." The day before, Nadolny said, he had attended a rally against Fonda in the public park and held a sign that said simply, "Forgive." While he was just standing there, he told the packed room, "I had people spit on me and call me a son of a bitch, just because I was holding a card that said 'forgive.' And that was directed at me—what's going to happen when Jane gets here?" he asked.[28]

Despite efforts to turn the town against Fonda, the citizens of Waterbury gave her a warm welcome when the film crew came to town. Some formed a "Welcome Jane Committee" and printed up T-shirts that said "I'm fonda Fonda." They organized special showings of Fonda's films and held rallies in her support. At a town hall meeting where twenty-three townspeople spoke in her favor and only three against, the Board of Aldermen voted to give her an official welcome. Two separate polls showed that the people of Waterbury welcomed Fonda by wide margins and that half of the veterans in Waterbury welcomed her, too.[29]

In response to the Waterbury flare-up, Fonda arranged an interview with Barbara Walters on ABC's *20/20* program that aired on June 17, 1988. She didn't think, Fonda said, that "we've ever resolved what the war meant. There are still festering wounds and a lot of pain. And for some, I've become a lightning rod." Fonda said that she believed that "those who went to Hanoi and got documentary information that wasn't getting out, helped end the war . . . the POWs got out sooner. The killing stopped sooner. So I feel we played a part in bringing them home." She was proud of most of what she did, Fonda told Walters, and she was sorry for some of it. Fonda admitted she had regrets. She regretted sitting on the antiaircraft gun emplacement and she regretted "criticizing the POWs or at least some of the POWs when they came back because whether or not all of the POWs were tortured is beside the point . . . they suffered, they suffered enough," she said. "They didn't need to hear from me." She concluded by saying she wanted to tell the men who were in Vietnam

> who I hurt, or whose pain I caused to deepen because of the things I said or did. I feel I owe them an apology. My intentions were never to hurt them or make their situation worse. It was the contrary. My intention was to help end the killing and the war. But there were times when I was thoughtless and careless about it, and I'm very sorry that I hurt them, and I want to apologize to them and their families.[30]

Fonda also asked for a meeting with Vietnam veterans in Waterbury so she could "hear what they have to say to me directly." Reverend John McColley, rector of St. Michael's Episcopal Church in Waterbury, offered his church as a meeting place. Because the issue involved the Vietnam War, only Vietnam veterans were invited to the meeting and Gaetano Russo and the veterans who had stirred up the protests were not present. The Vietnam veterans at the meeting described it as "respectful" and "civilized." Many of them wanted to talk not about Fonda or what she did, but about their own experiences and unresolved feelings about Vietnam. They told Fonda they resented being seen by the public as "drug-crazed baby killers" (a motif popular in movies about Vietnam by this time) and that Americans needed to know that "the North Vietnamese committed massacres far worse than the My Lai massacre by American troops." Fonda talked about her antiwar work and why she had been opposed to the war. She told them that she was sorry for any harm the photos of her in Hanoi and her radio broadcasts had caused anyone. The Vietnam veterans in Waterbury harbored little rancor. They left the meeting expressing satisfaction, saying that "everybody learned a lot from everybody else."[31]

After the Waterbury tumult, it was clear that Fonda's image loomed largest in the imagination of the older veterans and others for whom the outcome of the Vietnam War was deeply unsettling.

The rising hostility toward her was embedded in deeper anger over the loss of the war in Vietnam, and no apology from her could ever alter that outcome in Saigon. Indeed, every apology she made only seemed to stir up further animosity. In Waterbury, the older veterans scorned her apology, saying it wasn't enough. Some of them said if she were really sorry, she had to "prove" it by going to Vietnam and finding the men "still missing in action."[32]

In the 1990s, the emergence of the Internet helped feed a virtual explosion of Fonda-related mythology that was generated almost entirely within the military and among veterans, many of them Vietnam veterans who, by now, had learned to despise and scorn her too—or, at least, they had learned to despise the caricature of her that they believed to be true. In her study of post-Vietnam military culture, Carol Burke notes that Internet Web sites created by veterans are not infrequently locales for images of Jane Fonda in crosshairs, "as if she were the sole enemy from an unfinished war." Burke points out that stories about Fonda continue to multiply and circulate widely "among active-duty soldiers and veterans" and that "thirty years after her trip to North Vietnam, veterans fill cyberspace with their resentment and new recruits learn that being a real warrior and hating Jane Fonda are synonymous."[33]

The Fonda myth continually generated new themes. One element of the evolving Fonda story involved spitting, which borrowed from another myth about the war, the myth that antiwar activists spat on Vietnam veterans upon their return home. These spitting stories emerged first in fiction—in movies about the war during the 1970s and 1980s—and were entirely separate, at first, from the Fonda myth.[34] After films picturing spitting on veterans were widely viewed, some veterans began to claim that antiwar activists had spit on them when they returned from Vietnam. *Chicago Tribune* columnist Bob Greene requested stories from veterans about being spat upon, and in 1989, he published the results in *Homecoming: When the Soldiers Returned from Vietnam.* Greene had received sixty-three responses from veterans claiming to have been spat upon, and sixty-nine responses from other veterans saying they had never heard of such a thing.

Greene's book interested sociologist and Vietnam veteran Jerry Lembcke, who tried to corroborate the allegations of spitting. In his book *The Spitting Image*, Lembcke reports finding no documented case of veterans being spat on during the war by war protesters. The widespread spitting allegations emerged only after they had first been "seen" in the movies in the late 1970s and into the 1980s. Lembcke did, however, find documented references, photos, and some news items of spitting during the war, but it was always of antiwar veterans or activists being spat on by war supporters. Among these is a news story and photo showing someone standing outside the U.S. Embassy in Stockholm in December 1972 throwing a can of red paint on Jane Fonda as she marched by in a large crowd of antiwar activists. Fonda simply wiped the paint from her face and eyes, continued the march, and never complained about it.[35]

As more people gained access to the Internet and realized how easy it was to spread stories anonymously, the spitting myth and the Fonda myth were fused. In some cases, the anonymous writers had Fonda spitting on POWs, but in the most common spitting story, a POW spat on her. In that Internet story, a POW was pressured by Vietnamese guards to meet with Fonda in Hanoi, but he refused. The guards then dragged him to the room where Fonda waited. When the American POW saw Fonda, he spat on her. At that point, his guards dragged him away and beat him so ferociously he nearly died. Another Internet story had four POWs in Hanoi agreeing to meet with Fonda because they hoped she would help them. They secretly passed her slips of paper on which they had printed their Social Security numbers. In this story,

Fonda jeered at the POWs and then handed their pieces of paper to the Vietnamese guards. Again, the men were severely beaten until three of them died, leaving only the fourth one to tell the tale, so the stories went.[36]

On the Internet, such stories spread rapidly through e-mail, helped along by mainstream conservative commentators, including columnists Jeff Jacoby, William Buckley, and Jonah Goldberg, eager to pass them along to their readers in reputable newspapers.[37] But these stories also contained the seeds of their own undoing. Emboldened, perhaps, by the venom directed against Fonda in military networks and by the common assumption that all POWs were tortured, the anonymous creators of the stories began to name actual hard-line POWs in their Internet postings. Jerry Driscoll was named as the POW who allegedly spat on Fonda, and Larry Carrigan was identified as the fourth POW who did not die from his beating after Fonda "betrayed" him and his three fellow POWs.

The hard-line POWs had never before spoken out against the false stories about Fonda but now, with their own names dragged into the publicity storm, Jerry Driscoll and Larry Carrigan forcefully repudiated those accounts, saying they never happened and urging an end to the Fonda tales. Mike McGrath, president of a group of Vietnam POWs, finally sent out an e-mail saying that Jerry Driscoll and Larry Carrigan "asked that we get their names off that bunch of crap . . . there were never any POWs killed on account of Jane. (Did anyone ever provide a name of one of those tortured fellows?)" The worst that had happened, McGrath said, "was that we had to listen to the camp radio (Radio Hanoi and Hanoi Hannah) with the Fonda propaganda. It pissed us off, but I doubt you can call that 'torture.' "

Even though hard-line POWs were willing to demand that their own names not be part of the false stories about Jane Fonda, some of them continued to give credence to the story that David

Wesley Hoffman told, although without mentioning his name. And former POW Mike Benge, who had been captured in Laos in 1968 while working for either USAID or the CIA, began to belatedly claim, around 1999, that he had been tortured because he refused to meet with Fonda in Hanoi, although when pressed for details, he backed off from that claim.[38]

Many of these false and discredited stories about Fonda were peddled on Internet sites of dubious repute. Since these stories implicating Fonda in POW torture had origins in the Pentagon during the Nixon administration, it is one of history's ironies that the Web site of the Nixon Library in California continues to peddle these false allegations about Fonda. Long after Richard Nixon's death, his presidential library keeps these stories alive by posting writings of Bruce Herschensohn, who worked briefly in the Nixon White House after making Cold War propaganda films for United States Information Agency. Herschensohn's posted articles on the Nixon Library Web site repeat long-discredited allegations about Fonda, including one that David Wesley Hoffman made for the first, and last, time in 1973. Herschensohn supplies no corroborating evidence for his posting alleging that POWs were tortured because of Fonda, claiming only that these stories were told to him by POWs, whom he does not name, when they returned from Hanoi in 1973. Herschensohn also attributes to Fonda statements allegedly made over Radio Hanoi that do not appear in the CIA transcripts, and he uses the twice-translated quotations, first from Fonda's English statements into Vietnamese and then by CIA translators back into English, while asserting that these are "direct quotes."[39]

Perhaps the low point in the attacks on Fonda came with the publication of Henry M. Holzer and Erika Holzer's 2002 book, *"Aid and Comfort": Jane Fonda in North Vietnam*. The book's dubious premise is that Jane Fonda, thirty years later, should now be tried for treason. The Holzers, to their credit, do acknowledge that allegations that POWs were tortured because of Fonda have been discredited by the POWs themselves, but then, with the help and endorsement of Mike McGrath, the former POW who had helped to discredit the stories implicating Jerry Driscoll and Larry Carrigan, the Holzers introduce new, but similar, charges that POWs were tortured because of Fonda. The Holzers attribute these new allegations to sources they do not identify, saying only that these charges came via e-mails. The e-mail senders remain anonymous in the Holzers' citations, demonstrating once again that the single constant in the Fonda stories has been spurious sourcing.[40]

The single-minded, relentless pursuit of Fonda by right-wing demogogues may seem less singular when viewed over the course of American history. Indeed, a personalized anger against women who speak out against violence and war is a distinct thread throughout American history. The women who nearly defeated Andrew Jackson's Indian Removal Act of 1830 endured alternately condescending and harshly personal mockery from supporters of the "Trail of Tears," including president Andrew Jackson. And when Jane Addams went to Europe in 1915 to denounce the carnage there as "an old man's war," in which young men were given rum to brace them before bayonet charges, American political and military men charged her with everything from being a subversive and a communist to "urging the abolition of private property." For years after World War I, right-wing men from the American Legion and the Army's Chemical Warfare Bureau made a virtual career of slandering Jane Addams for her internationalist perspective.[41]

There is no question that the efforts to twist and reframe the history of Fonda's antiwar work have borne bitter fruit. Since the war in Vietnam, noisy right-wing charges have back-washed into public memory and pervaded media reporting of mass movements against America's later wars. Those who opposed the wars in Iraq in the early 1990s and in 2003, for example, had to combat assumptions that the antiwar movement during the war in Vietnam had not supported the troops and had been far out of the mainstream. The support that the antiwar movement had given the troops during the war in Vietnam, the fact that the first counseling centers for returning vets were funded by Fonda through the coffeehouses, that fact that Americans who traveled to Hanoi had carried most of the mail and packages that meant so much to the POWs there, the fact that many antiwar rallies were marked by prayers and candlelight vigils, the fact that the antiwar movement was firmly rooted in the churches—all of these things, and many others, were virtually forgotten. When George W. Bush ordered the American military to invade Iraq in 2003, much news commentary on the antiwar movement centered on avoiding the "mistakes" of the Vietnam antiwar movement and of Jane Fonda in particular. One reporter began a story on the antiwar movement in 2003 thus:

> As the United States readies for war, the antiwar movement faces a dilemma. Mindful of the hostility that greeted actress Jane Fonda when she returned from a trip to Hanoi in 1972, at the height of the Vietnam War, antiwar leaders held a conference call this week to plan their strategy. With many Americans feeling a tug to rally round the flag in a time of conflict, the antiwar movement is planning to emphasize its support for U.S. troops. Angry rhetoric-filled protest rallies are giving way to more prayerful actions—including silent marches, like the one planned for Saturday in New York, and candlelight vigils, like the one held Sunday in 140 countries. . . . Opponents of war are reluctant to acknowledge that the shadow of Fonda's trip hovers over their strategic decisions, but Norman Ornstein, a scholar at the American Enterprise Institute, said the incident has left an

imprint on political memory. "We're not going to have a steady stream of visitors to Baghdad sending out radio broadcasts telling soldiers to defect," he said. Jennifer Duffy, analyst at the Cook Political Report, a nonpartisan newsletter on American politics and elections, said Fonda's antiwar legacy is still debated in Washington. Recalling a recent conversation among political types discussing the forthcoming Academy Awards, she said, "We were wondering how many people will use their time at the podium to say their piece, and whether they will turn into Jane Fonda."[42]

In fact, Fonda's acceptance speech when she won her Oscar for *Klute* in 1971 was a model of brevity and understatement: "There's a lot I could say tonight," Fonda told the crowd at the Academy Awards when she stepped forward to receive her award, "but this isn't the time or the place. So I'll just say, 'Thank you.' "[43]

Despite the concerted efforts of die-hard critics, Jane Fonda today remains a much-admired icon. In 1973, after her trip to Hanoi, she turned up on the Gallup public opinion poll as one of the most admired women in America, and she kept that position for years. In 1999, ABC News and *Ladies Home Journal* named her one of the "100 Most Important Women of the 20th Century." And despite long, concerted efforts by some to characterize Fonda's activism as un-American, even treasonous, a 2005 Gallup poll found that nearly three-quarters of Americans believe that celebrities who act against war are not anti-American.[44] Some of that sentiment may well be credited to Jane Fonda's achievement in opposing the war with composure and courage despite the intense pressure against her and the risk to her career. "It's not radical to be against the war," she said more than once, "it's patriotic to be against it."[45] There was widespread admiration for Fonda and others like her who, during the war in Vietnam, spoke out against it and did not wilt under aggressive government pursuit. Columnist

Emmet Watson once reported an encounter that illustrates this reaction well. When Fonda was passing through an airport terminal in 1974, a man "who happened to be a chief in the U.S. Navy" stopped her and asked to say a few words. "I agree with a lot of what you've said," he told her, "but I hope that you're not completely anti-military. We're having a tough time of it these days." Fonda told him that she wasn't anti-military. "What I have to say comes from the soldiers themselves. I respect them," she told the officer. After a brief conversation, he reached out and shook her hand. "Keep up the good work," he told her as he left. Many Americans, like this naval officer, were not proud of the war in Vietnam and they respected and admired people with the courage and self-discipline to work for its end.[46]

Jane Fonda's antiwar legacy is complicated. On the one hand, there are the destructive elements in which the resentments of national defeat were exploited to rewrite the history of the broad antiwar movement and of Jane Fonda's antiwar activism in particular. This legacy lurks primarily on the fringes of the far right, but it has permeated the culture to the extent that each new antiwar movement is ritually reminded by reporters and pundits "not to be like Jane Fonda," even though her real activism during the war is barely known to them.

The more enduring legacy of Jane Fonda, the one that rests on her actual activities and accomplishments, is an empowering one, a reminder that progress in American history most often comes from individuals who are willing to challenge harmful government policies, even the policies of war, and who speak up with conviction against injustice and violence in times of crisis. If even architects of the war have concluded, in retrospect, that the Vietnam War was "terribly wrong," it would seem long overdue to cease efforts to blame Americans for the nation's defeat in Vietnam.[47] If the war itself is not something for which Americans can be proud, we can be proud of those Americans, like Jane

Fonda, who worked to end the war and who struggled, sometimes at considerable cost to their own comfort and reputation, to spare the lives of soldiers and civilians—those of the "enemy" and those of our own. As our nation finds itself settling ever more fixedly into the role of empire with all its certain violence, we would do well to consider Jane Fonda's challenge to the ideology of empire that once called for victory, at all cost, in Vietnam.

NOTES

1. BECOMING AN ACTIVIST

1. University of Pennsylvania's National Annenberg Election Survey conducted March 1–15, 2004. See Al Kamen, "In the Loop," *Washington Post*, March 19, 2004, A21.

2. On the myth that American POWs were left behind in Southeast Asia, see H. Bruce Franklin, *M.I.A.: Mythmaking in America* (Brooklyn, NY: Lawrence Hill Books, 1992). On allegations that returning veterans were spat on by antiwar protesters, see Jerry Lembcke, *The Spitting Image: Myth, Memory, and the Legacy of Vietnam* (New York: New York University Press, 1998). Lembcke, himself a Vietnam veteran, argues that the spitting stories did not surface until the late 1970s, and that the only documented cases of spitting during the war were of antiwar activists being spat on by war supporters.

3. The *Rambo* movies, along with POW "rescue" movies like *Uncommon Valor* and *Missing in Action*, turned what had been a fringe political issue into a widely accepted assumption—that POWs were still in Vietnam—and nurtured a feeling that the United States' defeat in Vietnam stemmed from unmanly weakness. After President Ronald Reagan saw the opening of *Rambo* in 1985, for example, he said, "Boy, I saw *Rambo* last night. Now I know what to do the next time this happens." Even members of Congress invoked the film during floor debates. See H. Bruce Franklin, *Vietnam and Other American Fantasies* (Amherst: University of Massachusetts Press, 2000), 193–95.

4. For a look at some of the more outrageous manifestations of malice against Fonda, see Carol Burke, *Camp All-American, Hanoi Jane, and the High-and-Tight* (Boston: Beacon Press, 2004), 177–87.

5. On news coverage of the chemical and gas warfare against civilians, see *In the Name of America: The Conduct of the War in Vietnam by the Armed Forces of the United States as Shown by Published Reports* (New York: E.P. Dutton & Co, 1968). The Pentagon trained other militaries in chemical and biological warfare as well, including those of South Vietnam, Saudi Arabia, Thailand, West Germany, Greece, England, and Australia. See Robert M. Smith, "Gas War Training Given Foreigners," *New York Times*, January 25, 1970. See also Frank Harvey, *Air War—Vietnam* (New York: Bantam, 1967).

6. George Gallup, "Pat Nixon Tops 'Admired' List," *Washington Post*, January 1, 1973, A12. See also Chuck Conconi, "Personalities," *Washington Post*, December 11, 1985, C3.

7. "Why Famous Actress Became a Peace Activist," *Philadelphia Sunday Bulletin*, October 1, 1972, 4.

8. Ibid.

9. Leroy F. Aarons, "Jane Fonda: Looking Back with Understanding," *Washington Post*, July 19, 1973, K2.

10. Martin Kasindorf, "Fonda: A Person of Many Parts," *New York Times Magazine*, February 3, 1974, 19.

11. Evan Thomas, "War Stories," *Newsweek*, February 23, 2004.

12. In early 1969, there were 500,000 American soldiers in Vietnam. By mid-1972, their numbers had dropped sharply. The U.S. Army pulled its last combat troops out on August 12, 1972 (only two weeks after Fonda was in Hanoi), leaving behind 43,000 Air Force and support personnel. For Vietnamization and other American polices in Vietnam, see Marilyn B. Young, *The Vietnam Wars: 1945–1990* (New York: HarperPerennial, 1991).

13. Elizabeth Becker, "Kissinger Tapes Describe Crises, War and Stark Photos of Abuse," *New York Times*, May 27, 2004, 1.

14. Gardner left the coffeehouse movement after the national conference of GI organizers offered workshops on sexism, an issue he considered unimportant.

15. See David Cortright, *Soldiers in Revolt: The American Military Today* (New York: Anchor Press, 1975).

16. "The Shelter Half," Letters, *New York Review of Books*, January 29, 1970.

17. "The Covered Wagon," Letters, *New York Review of Books*, December 30, 1971.

18. *Colorado Springs Sun*, April 22, 1970.

19. See Donald Duncan, "The Whole Thing Was a Lie," *Ramparts*, February 1966. See also Mary Hershberger, *Traveling to Vietnam: American Peace Activists and the War* (Syracuse, NY: Syracuse University Press, 1998), 63–67.

20. Richard Eder, "U.S. Says Raid Site May Be Cambodian," *New York Times*, August 17, 1966.

21. President Nixon told Secretary of State Rogers to hand over the list of the 250 protesting employees, but Rogers refused.

22. Nancy Zaroulis and George Sullivan, *Who Spoke Up?* (New York: Holt, Rinehart, and Winston, 1984), 318.

23. Juan de Onis, "Nixon Puts 'Bums' Label on Some College Radicals," *New York Times*, May 2, 1970, 1.

24. William Safire, *Before the Fall* (New York: Doubleday, 1975), 189; Henry Kissinger, *White House Years* (New York: Little, Brown, 1979), 487.

25. John Kifner, "4 Kent State Students Killed by Troops," *New York Times*, May 5, 1970.

26. Richard Nixon, *RN: The Memoirs of Richard Nixon* (New York: Putnam, 1978), 457, 459.

27. "Jane Fonda Blasts U.S. Asian Policy," *Albuquerque Journal*, May 5, 1970.

28. Ibid.

29. Eric Lucas, "National Guard Injures 10," *New Mexico Lobo*, May 11, 1970, 5.

30. Max Frankel, "A Frustrated and Angrier Mood," *New York Times*, May 10, 1970.

31. John Herbers, "Big Capital Rally Asks U.S. Pullout in Southeast Asia," *New York Times*, May 10, 1970, 24. See also Zaroulis and Sullivan, *Who Spoke Up?*, 329.

32. Only four students were shot and killed at Kent State University. In the first few weeks after the shootings, there were news reports that a fifth person died of bayonet wounds, but this turned out not to be true.

33. Nat Henderson, "Actress Barred from Ft. Hood," *Killeen (TX) Daily-Herald*, May 12, 1970, 1.

34. For the violent attack on an antiwar rally in New York City on May 8, see Homar Bigart and Martin Arnold, "War Foes Here Attacked by Construction Workers: City Hall Is Stormed, Police Were Told of Plan," *New York Times*, May 9, 1970.

35. The film's iconic title led to a host of books with similar titles, including *They Shoot Writers, Don't They?*; *They Shoot the Messenger, Don't They?*; *They Shoot Intruders, Don't They?*; and *They Shoot Economists, Don't They?*. The film won the New York Film Critics Award but no Oscars. Some speculated that the film received no Oscars because of Fonda's antiwar activism.

36. Leticia Kent, "It's Not Just 'Fonda and Company,' " *New York Times*, March 21, 1971, II, 1. See also Lawrence Baskir and William Strauss, *Chance and Circumstance: The Draft, the War, and the Vietnam Generation* (New York: Alfred A. Knopf, 1978); and Richard Moser, *The New Winter Soldiers: GI and Veteran Dissent During the Vietnam Era* (New Brunswick, NJ: Rutgers University Press, 1996).

37. John Rechy, "Lieutenant on the Peace Line," *The Nation*, February 21, 1966.

38. The three were James Johnson, twenty years old; David Samas, twenty; and Dennis Mora, twenty-five.

39. "3 G.I.'s Lose Suit to Avoid Vietnam," *New York Times*, July 12, 1966, 6. A year earlier, Army officer Richard Steinke refused to follow military directives in Vietnam, saying that the war was "not worth a single American life." He was court-martialed and dishonorably discharged. In October 1966, Army Captain Doctor Howard Levy refused to train Special Forces soldiers bound for Vietnam. Dr. Levy said training men to kill would violate the Hippocratic oath. He was court-martialed and jailed.

40. Richard Halloran, "Army Orders the Seizure of Antiwar Mail Sent to G.I.'s in Vietnam," *New York Times*, March 31, 1971, 4.

41. GI Office, press release, August 8, 1970.

42. Identification with antiwar activists is pronounced in the writings and testimony of members of VVAW.

43. George Haddad-Garcia, *The Films of Jane Fonda* (Secaucus, NJ: Citadel Press, 1981), 158.

44. Andrew Hunt, *The Turning: A History of Vietnam Veterans Against the War* (New York: New York University Press, 1999), 60.

45. Ibid., 17–18.

46. Ibid., 5.

47. William Crandell, "They Moved the Town," in *Give Peace a Change: Exploring the Vietnam Antiwar Movement*, ed. Melvin Small and William D. Hoover (Syracuse, NY: Syracuse University Press, 1991).

2. GI JANE: WINTER SOLDIER AND *FREE THE ARMY*

1. The massacre was covered up in the chain of command for over a year and a half. Photographer Ron Ridenhour had taken photographs at My Lai, and he talked to Army officials about it. They ignored him, so he talked to members of Congress. Eventually, a few legislators began to take the massacre seriously. Faced with legislative pressure, the military finally announced the massacre in November 1969, eighteen months after the fact, and said that Lieutenant William Calley would stand trial for it.

2. "Carnage and the Incarnation," editorial, *Christian Century*, December 24, 1969, 1633.

3. After news of My Lai, some members of the Russell War Crimes Tribunal had called on Americans to hold their own inquiries into war crimes. The GIs were responding to that call.

4. Homar Bigart, "Antiwar Soldiers Face Army Trials," *New York Times*, January 25, 1970, 8.

5. See Tod Ensign, "Organizing Veterans Through War Crimes Documentation," *Viet Nam Generation Big Book* 5, no. 1–4 (1994). See also Philip S. Balboni, "What Every Vietnam Vet Knows: My Lai Was Not an Isolated Incident," *New Republic*, December 19, 1970.

6. See William Crandell, "What Did America Learn from the Winter Soldier Investigation?" *Vietnam Generation* 5, no. 1 (1996): 5.

7. For more information on the Winter Soldier Investigation, see Andrew Hunt, *The Turning: A History of Vietnam Veterans Against the War* (New York: New York University Press, 1999).

8. Crandell, "What Did America Learn from the Winter Soldier Investigation?"

9. See testimony in the *Viet Nam Generation Big Book* 5, no. 1–4.

10. Jerry M. Flint, "Veterans Assess Atrocity Blame," *New York Times*, February 15, 1971, 17. See also "The Terrible Reality: Letters From a GI in Vietnam," *The Progressive*, January 1970, 14–18.

11. Flint, "Veterans Assess Atrocity Blame."

12. See Nelson's account in Mary Hershberger, *Traveling to Vietnam: American Peace Activists and the War* (Syracuse, NY: Syracuse University Press, 1998), 150–54. See also John Moran, "Two Months with the NLF," *WIN*, February 15, 1971, 31–33; and "Excerpts from a Talk by Marjorie Nelson," May 21, 1968, AFSC–Vietnam, American Friends Service Committee Archives, Philadelphia, PA.

13. Peter Michelson, "Bringing the War Home: Veterans Testify Against the Atrocity in Indochina," *New Republic*, February 27, 1971, 21–22; Women's League for International Peace and Freedom newsletter, March 1971.

14. Michelson, "Bringing the War Home," 22.

15. More than one million Vietnamese lived under the toxins during the war. The U.S. government never compensated them for the chemical warfare it waged in Vietnam. In February 2004, Vietnamese civilians for the first time filed suit against Dow Chemical and Monsanto, the U.S. companies that produced Agent Orange. By that time, the American government was paying disability benefits to more than 10,000 American veterans who had worked with the chemicals in

Vietnam. See "Vietnam's Agent Orange Victims File Suit," Associated Press, February 4, 2004.

16. *Detroit Free Press*, February 2, 1970, 1.

17. Flint, "Veterans Assess Atrocity Blame."

18. Donald Duncan, closing statement, in Ensign, "Organizing Veterans Through War Crimes Documentation." Guenter Lewy, in his 1978 book *America in Vietnam*, presented the Winter Soldier Investigation in a misleading way that cast doubt on the veterans' testimony. Lewy's sole source was what he cites as a "Naval Investigative Service report" from the Marine Corps director. He provided no archival documentation for this report and no one else, including Lewy himself, has since been able to produce it. Paul O'Donnell, a Naval Criminal Investigative Service public affairs specialist, could find no evidence that the report ever existed. There is no evidence that any Winter Soldier witness was an impostor. Indeed, the status of all of them was verified by the *Detroit Free Press* at the time. For the alleged source that Lewy cites, see Guenter Lewy, *America in Vietnam* (New York: Oxford University Press, 1978), chap. 9, n. 28. O'Donnell made his statement to Andrew Seifter of Media Matters for America. See G.W., "Fox's Garrett Boosted Discredited Swift Boat Vets Allegation," http://mediamatters.org/items/200409030004.

19. Senators Mark Hatfield and George McGovern, Congressmen Ron Dellums and John Conyers Jr., and former senator Ernest Gruening were VVAW's strongest sympathizers in Washington.

20. Marvin E. Gettleman, ed., *Vietnam and America: A Documented History* (New York: Grove Press, 1985), 453. The following day, more than seven hundred veterans marched from their campsite on the Mall and threw their medals over a makeshift wall.

21. Senator Mark Hatfield of Oregon in the Senate of the United States, April 5, 1971, *Congressional Record.*

22. See *Los Angeles Times*, March 1, 1971. More than one thousand U.S.–backed Vietnamese soldiers and 176 Americans were killed in the invasion of Laos, which culminated in a hasty retreat. Michael Maclear, in *The Ten Thousand Day War* (New York: St. Martin's Press, 1981), 299, says that "only the deployment of every available US helicopter to evacuate the ARVN prevented a greater tragedy—and the overloaded helicopters were coming back with soldiers desperately clinging to the landing skids."

23. FBI files, transcript of speech by Jane Fonda at Madison College, Harrisonburg, VA, February 13, 1971.

24. Daniel C. Hallin, *The "Uncensored War": The Media and Vietnam* (Berkeley: University of California Press, 1989), 147.

25. FBI files, transcript of speech by Jane Fonda at the University of Alabama, Tuscaloosa, AL, February 11, 1971.

26. Robert Heinl, "The Collapse of the Armed Forces," *Armed Forces Journal*, June 7, 1971, 30–38.

27. "Hope Reminiscent," *Newsweek*, January 10, 1966, 41.

28. Alvin Shuster, "G.I.'s in Vietnam High on Hope's Marijuana Jokes," *New York Times*, December 23, 1970.

29. Lacey Fosburgh, "Antiwar Troupe Formed to Tour Bases," *New York Times*,

February 17, 1971, 20. *Free the Army* operated under the aegis of the United States Servicemen's Fund, established in 1967 to support antiwar military personnel.

30. "Left Face," *New Republic*, March 13, 1971, 9.

31. "Jane Fonda Antiwar Show Staged Near Fort Bragg," *New York Times*, March 14, 1971, 73.

32. Michael Kernan, "GI Movement: A Show to Call Its Own," *Washington Post*, March 15, 1971, B2. The *Los Angeles Times, Life* magazine, the TV networks, and the Canadian Broadcasting Company also covered *Free the Army*'s first performance.

33. Daniel Berrigan, *The Trial of the Catonsville Nine* (Boston: Beacon, 1970).

34. Kernan, "GI Movement."

35. Leticia Kent, "It's Not Just 'Fonda and Company,'" *New York Times*, March 21, 1971, II, 1.

36. Gary Arnold, "F.T.A.: The Fonda Way," *Washington Post*, June 28, 1972, E9.

37. Kernan, "GI Movement."

38. Ibid.

39. FBI files, LA 157-5089, 20.

40. FBI files, SAC report, LA 157-5089.

41. Fosburgh, "Antiwar Troupe Formed to Tour Bases."

42. Kernan, "GI Movement."

43. "4,000 See 'Free the Army,'" *Honolulu Advertiser*, November 26, 1971, A6.

44. Hershberger, *Traveling to Vietnam*, 191–92.

45. Arnold, "F.T.A."

46. Kent, "It's Not Just 'Fonda and Company.'"

3. SPYING ON FONDA

1. In 1969, Angela Davis was fired from her position at UCLA as an assistant professor of philosophy for being a member of the Communist Party. After George Jackson, one of the Soledad Brothers, was killed during an attempted escape from San Quentin prison, Davis was charged with kidnapping, murder, and conspiracy in connection with that event, and Richard Nixon condemned her before she ever came to trial. An all-white jury acquitted her of all charges.

2. FBI files, SAC, Los Angeles (157-4054) to Director, FBI, April 27, 1970; Director, FBI to SAC, Los Angeles, (157-4054), April 5, 1970. See also "Jane Fonda Cites FBI Ploy on Her," *Washington Post*, December 17, 1975, A3.

3. Joyce Haber, "Miss A Rates as Expectant Mother," *Los Angeles Times*, May 19, 1970, 12.

4. Seberg committed suicide in 1979. Her husband, Romain Gary, sued the FBI for her wrongful death.

5. Ward Churchill, *The COINTELPRO Papers: Documents from the FBI's Secret Wars Against Dissent in the United States* (Boston: South End Press, 1990); Nelson Blackstock, *COINTELPRO: The FBI's Secret War on Political Freedom* (New York: Random House, 1976); *Hearings Before the Senate Select Committee to Study Government Operations with Respect to Intelligence Activities*, 94th Cong. (Washington, DC: Government Printing Office, 1975).

6. For the Espionage Act, see Sheila Suess Kennedy, ed., *Free Expression in*

America: A Documentary History (Westport, CT: Greenwood Press, 1999), 55–56.

7. From his federal prison cell, Debs ran for president in 1920 on the Socialist ticket and garnered nearly one million votes. In 1921, after the high passions of war had waned, President Harding ordered Debs released.

8. The nine were George Darwin, Gary Lee Simzak, John William Barnes, Larry Thomas Zanger, Jack Hammond, Stanton Conrad, La Verne Mondt, Dan Greer (a chaplain's assistant), and Marilyn White, the liaison director between the Peak Service Club and the Inscape Coffee House. FBI files, SAC, Los Angeles (157-4054).

9. Before going to Fort Carson, Fonda participated in a thirty-six-hour "Fast for Peace" in Denver that was organized by the Mountain States Vietnam Moratorium Committee.

10. FBI files, LA 157-5089, LA T-9, May 8, 1970.

11. Valerie Bonge, "Fonda Visits Fort Carson, Speaks to Soldiers," *Colorado Springs Sun*, April 22, 1970.

12. FBI files, M.A. Jones to Bishop memo, RE: Jane Fonda, May 15, 1970, 3–4.

13. FBI file #157-5089, report of Richard Wallace Held, October 10, 1970, LA T-13 (August 17, 1970).

14. FBI files, J. Edgar Hoover to United States Secret Service, October 9, 1970.

15. FBI files, SAC, Los Angeles (157-4054), 20.

16. Fred Lawrence Guiles, *Jane Fonda: The Actress in Her Time* (New York: Doubleday, 1982), 165.

17. FBI files, SAC, Los Angeles to FBI Director, "Re: The Silent Ones," October 28, 1970.

18. Barbara Pumphrey and Al Thompson, "Jane Fonda Jailed after Scrap Here," *Cleveland Plain Dealer*, November 3, 1970, 1.

19. "Jane Fonda Accused of Smuggling," *New York Times*, November 4, 1970, 52.

20. *NBC Evening News*, November 3, 1970; ibid.

21. Pumphrey and Thompson, "Jane Fonda Jailed after Scrap Here."

22. "Court Needs SRO Sign for Jane Fonda Fans," *Cleveland Plain Dealer*, November 5, 1970; FBI files, "Confidential Source on Jane Fonda," December 3, 1970.

23. Barbara Pumphrey, "Jane Fonda Pleads Innocent in Scrap," *Cleveland Plain Dealer*, November 4, 1970, 1.

24. Ibid.

25. "Charges to Be Refiled Against Jane Fonda," *Cleveland Plain Dealer*, June 24, 1971.

26. "Jane Fonda Returns, Finds Slate Clean," *Cleveland Plain Dealer*, July 19, 1971.

27. FBI files, Richard Wallace Held, Field Office File 157-5089. See also "CIA Expected to Admit Opening Fonda Mail from Abroad," *Washington Post*, February 18, 1975.

28. FBI files, SA 100-12183.

29. Ibid.

30. Ibid.

31. FBI files, Director, FBI to SAC, Los Angeles, "Jane Fonda—Key Activist," March 11, 1971.

32. FBI files, Director, FBI to SAC, Richmond, January 21, 1971 and Director, FBI to SAC, New Haven, January 28, 1971.

33. FBI files, Marlin Johnson to Morris I. Leibman, January 26, 1971.

34. Eric Bates, "What You Need to Know About Jesse Helms," *Mother Jones*, May/June 1995.

35. FBI files, Jesse Helms commentary, "Viewpoint," December 17, 1970, in Director (100-459279), January 22, 1971.

36. Ibid.

37. FBI files, Director, FBI (100-459279), January 22, 1971.

38. See David S. Broder, "Jesse Helms, White Racist," *Washington Post*, August 29, 2001, 21.

39. See Lee Winfrey, "Jane Fonda—an LP Record with a Socialist Sermon," *Detroit Free Press*, November 22, 1970, 1.

40. See, for example, Kenneth O'Reilly, *Racial Matters: The FBI's Secret File on Black America: 1960–1972* (New York: Free Press, 1989); and James Kirkpatrick Davis, *Assault on the Left: The FBI and the Sixties Antiwar Movement* (Westport, CT: Praeger, 1997).

41. *Jane Fonda v. Richard Nixon*, U.S. District Court, Central District of California, Civil Action No. 73-2442-MML, July 28, 1978.

42. U.S. Department of Justice memorandum, October 6, 1972.

43. That list of names also included reporters Mary McGrory and Daniel Schorr; Paul Newman; John Kenneth Galbraith; Senators J.W. Fulbright, Edmund Muskie, and Edward Kennedy; and historian Arthur Schlesinger, among many others. Some said that they would have been "insulted" had they been left off. Edward Walsh and Philip A. McCombs, "Members of 'Enemies List' Cover Broad Spectrum," *Washington Post*, June 28, 1973, A11.

4. GOING TO VIETNAM

1. For a fuller account of the Americans who went to Vietnam, see Mary Hershberger, *Traveling to Vietnam: American Peace Activists and the War* (Syracuse, NY: Syracuse University Press, 1998).

2. For Women Strike for Peace's campaign against nuclear testing, see Amy Swerdlow, *Women Strike for Peace: Traditional Motherhood and Radical Politics in the 1960s* (Chicago: University of Chicago Press, 1993). When President Kennedy signed the Limited Test Ban Treaty in 1963, his science adviser Jerome Wiesner said that Women Strike for Peace was more influential in the president's decision than his arms "experts."

3. A.J. Muste to Martin Luther King Jr. memo, 1966, Papers of A.J. Muste, Box 43, Swarthmore College Peace Collection.

4. See, for example, Detley F. Vagts, "The Logan Act: Paper Tiger or Sleeping Giant?," *American Journal of International Law* 60 (Summer 1966): 268–302; Kevin Kearney, "Private Citizens in Foreign Affairs: A Constitutional Analysis," *Emory Law Journal* 36 (Fall 1987): 285–355. The White House responded to the Supreme Court ruling by implementing restrictions on spending American money in the banned countries.

5. "American Prisoners of War in Southeast Asia," *Hearings Before the Subcommittee on National Security Policy and Scientific Developments of the Committee on*

Foreign Affairs, 92nd Cong. (Washington, DC: Government Printing Office, 1971). See also Hershberger, *Traveling to Vietnam*, 177–82.

6. "U.S. Held Up Letter by P.O.W. Two Years," *New York Times*, October 12, 1971.

7. See, for example, Jim Stockdale and Sybil Stockdale, *In Love and War: The Story of a Family's Ordeal and Sacrifice During the Vietnam War Years* (New York: Harper and Row, 1984).

8. Women Strike for Peace called their POW mail-delivery system the Committee of Liaison. "American Prisoners of War in Southeast Asia," 181, 245. Women Strike for Peace eventually sued the CIA for illegal interference with their international mail. The CIA settled by paying them an undisclosed cash settlement. Ethel Taylor, "Inquiry into War Crimes: Vietnam Veterans Against the War," March 28, 1974, Series A.8, DG-115, Swarthmore College Peace Collection.

9. Journalist Anthony Lewis, for example, went to Hanoi in May 1972, just two months before Fonda did. His report in the *New York Times* on May 15 described seeing hospitals with red crosses painted on the roofs that were bombed. Lewis called the bombing "a cruel act of technological bad temper" and said that "in the face of bombing and years of war it is impossible for this visitor to detect any atmosphere of fear."

10. For some of these accounts, see Hershberger, *Traveling to Vietnam*.

11. "North Vietnam: Thin Line of Distinction," *Time*, August 7, 1972, 32.

12. See Hershberger, *Traveling to Vietnam*. See also James Clinton, *The Loyal Opposition: Americans in North Vietnam, 1965–1972* (Boulder: University Press of Colorado, 1996).

13. Jane Fonda, "A Vietnam Journal: Birth of a Nation," *Rolling Stone*, July 4, 1974, 53.

14. Hershberger, *Traveling to Vietnam*.

15. FBI files, transcript of a press conference given by Jane Fonda in New York City on July 28, 1972. See also Ramsey Clark, "What I Saw and Heard in North Vietnam," *Life*, August 25, 1972, 39–41.

16. Telford Taylor, "Hanoi Is Reported Scarred but Key Services Continue," *New York Times*, December 25, 1972, 1.

17. Hershberger, *Traveling to Vietnam*, 223. See also William Broyles Jr., "The Road to Hill 10," *Atlantic Monthly*, April 1985, 94.

18. Fonda's radio broadcasts were recorded by the CIA, which transcribed them and gave copies to the State Department. The transcripts are printed in "Hearings Regarding H.R. 16742: Restraints on Travel to Hostile Areas," *Hearings Before the Committee on Internal Security*, House of Representatives, 92nd Cong., 2nd Sess., September 19 and 25, 1972 (Washington, DC: Government Printing Office, 1972), 7644–72.

19. In Hanoi, Fonda also met with Vietnamese political officials, including Vice Premier Nguyen Duy Trinh in a meeting filled with small talk—the premier asked about her family and her visit to Vietnam thus far.

20. Denise Levertov, "Glimpses of Vietnamese Life," *American Report*, March 1973, 18–20.

21. Anthony Lewis, "At Home and Abroad," *New York Times*, January 6, 1973.

22. William Sloan Coffin, "Three Return," *American Report*, October 23, 1972, 4.

23. John G. Hubbell, *P.O.W.: A Definitive History of the American Prisoner-of-War Experience in Vietnam, 1964–1973* (New York: Reader's Digest Press, 1976), 549.

24. *CBS Evening News*, December 27, 1970, TV News Archives, Vanderbilt University.

25. "Text of Letter from Eight U.S. Pilots Detained in North Vietnam, May 1972," DG-84, PCPJ, Box 3, Swarthmore College Peace Collection. The letter was signed by Edison W. Miller, Lieutenant Colonel, U.S. Marine Corps; James D. Cutter, Captain, U.S. Air Force; Edwin A. Hawley Jr., Captain, U.S. Air Force; Norris Charles, Lieutenant (Junior Grade), U.S. Naval Reserve; Walter E. Wilber, Commander, U.S. Navy; David Hoffman, Lieutenant Commander, U.S. Navy; Kenneth Fraser, Captain, U.S. Air Force; and Lynn Guenther, Captain, U.S. Air Force. The Americans who brought back the letter were Father Paul Meyer, professor of theology at New Theological Seminary; Margery Tobankin, president of the National Student Association; Robert Lecky, editor of *American Report*; and Boston psychologist William Zimmerman. They went to Hanoi in May 1972 to discuss the possibility of beginning a program to send volunteers from the United States to North Vietnam to become witnesses to life in the bombed areas. See Hershberger, *Traveling to Vietnam*, 206–7.

26. FBI files, transcript of Fonda press conference, July 28, 1972.

27. The *New York Times* obtained an uncensored copy of the report, which it published on July 21, 1972, on the front page.

28. Ted Szulc, "Rules on Air Strikes in South Vietnam Allow Leeway," *New York Times*, July 17, 1972, 3.

29. Transcript of *NBC Evening News*, July 25, 1972, TV Archives, Vanderbilt University.

30. "U.S. Terms Damage to Dikes Minor and Accidental," *New York Times*, July 27, 1972, 3.

31. Ibid.

32. Darius S. Jhabvala, "US Admits Damaging 12 N. Viet Dike Sites," *Boston Globe*, July 29, 1972, 1.

33. Bernard Gwertzman, "Nixon, Criticizing War Foes, Calls Waldheim 'Naive,'" *New York Times*, July 28, 1972, 10.

34. Robert Alden, "Dikes Hit, Waldheim Says; Rogers Quickly Denies It," *New York Times*, July 25, 1972, 1; *NBC Evening News*, July 25, 1972, TV Archives, Vanderbilt University.

35. "Strain Grows: Waldheim, Bush Discuss Dikes," *Los Angeles Times*, July 29, 1972, 14; Robert Adden, "Waldheim and Bush Meet after Criticism by Nixon," *New York Times*, July 29, 1972, 2.

36. "The Doves Draw Blood," *Time*, August 7, 1972, 17.

37. "10 Senators Seek Halt to Dike Bombing," *New York Times*, August 5, 1972; "Senate Votes to Cut Off Funds for Rain-making," *New York Times*, July 29, 1972; "Dykes Only Slightly Damaged, Americans Say," *London Times*, July 29, 1972.

38. *Time*, August 7, 1972, 17.

39. See "Memorandum to the Committee on Internal Security Relating to Travel to North Viet-Nam," *Hearings Before the Committee on Internal Security*,

House of Representatives, 92nd Cong., 2nd Sess., September 19 and 25, 1972 (Washington, DC: Government Printing Office, 1972), 7563–64.

5. FALLOUT: THE ORIGINS OF THE FONDA MYTH

1. *ABC Evening News*, July 25, 1972, TV Archives, Vanderbilt University.

2. "Jane Fonda Says POWs Fear Nixon," *Washington Post*, July 26, 1972, 14.

3. Leroy F. Aarons, "Jane Fonda: Looking Back with Understanding," *Washington Post*, July 29, 1973, K3.

4. See "Only One U.S. Unit Left in Vietnam Combat Role," *New York Times*, July 26, 1972; and "Week's American War Toll Is Put at 10 Dead, 9 Hurt," *New York Times*, July 28, 1972.

5. See Jeffrey Kimball, *Nixon's Vietnam War* (Lawrence: University Press of Kansas, 2002). Nixon continued the war for domestic political reasons, Kimball says, despite his belief that the United States would not win. See also "Tape: Nixon Mulled Vietnam Exit in 1972," Associated Press, August 8, 2004.

6. "State Dept. Reprimands Jane Fonda," *Washington Post*, July 15, 1972, 3.

7. FBI transcripts of Fonda's talks in the United States are also plagued with errors. The tape quality was often poor and the transcribers sometimes had to guess at what she said. In one instance where there were two transcriptions of the same Fonda appearance, one transcript has her (when discussing racial issues in the South) referring to the city of "Augusta." The other transcript contains a reference to "Moscow."

8. "Kleindienst Doubts Action on Clark or Miss Fonda," *New York Times*, August 24, 1972, 52.

9. Sanford Ungar, "U.S. Won't Prosecute Jane Fonda," *Washington Post*, August 26, 1972, 2.

10. "People," United Press International, August 28, 1972.

11. *New York Times*, July 19, 1972, 43.

12. "House Panel Holds Off on Fonda Subpoena," *Washington Post*, August 11, 1972, 18. As a sign of how concerted the White House effort against Fonda was, First Lady Pat Nixon, who rarely held a news conference, had one on August 8, at which her main emphasis was criticism of Jane Fonda. Pat Nixon told the press that Fonda "should have been in Hanoi asking them to stop their aggression. Then there wouldn't be any conflict." "Mrs. Nixon Asserts Jane Fonda Should Have Bid Hanoi End War," *New York Times*, August 9, 1972, 12.

13. United Press International, press release, August 18, 1972.

14. Mary McGrory, "Fonda 'Booking' Foiled," *Washington Evening Star*, August 14, 1972.

15. "Hearings Regarding H.R. 16742: Restraints on Travel to Hostile Areas," *Hearings Before the Committee on Internal Security*, House of Representatives, 92nd Cong., 2nd Sess., September 19 and 25, 1972 (Washington, DC: Government Printing Office, 1972), 7539–42.

16. Ibid., 7552.

17. Scholars of constitutional law have long agreed that the Logan Act is too vague and allows too much prosecutorial discretion to be enforceable in the courts. See Detley F. Vagts, "The Logan Act: Paper Tiger or Sleeping Giant?,"

American Journal of International Law 60 (Summer 1966): 268–302; Kevin M. Kearney, "Private Citizens in Foreign Affairs: A Constitutional Analysis," *Emory Law Journal* 36 (Fall 1987): 285–355.

18. "Testimony of A. William Olson," *Hearings Before the Committee on Internal Security*, House of Representatives, 92nd Cong., 2nd Sess., September 19 and 25, 1972 (Washington, DC: Government Printing Office, 1972): 7542–46.

19. On the eighty-two broadcasts, see *Hearings Before the Committee on Internal Security*, House of Representatives, 92nd Cong., 2nd Sess., September 19 and 25, 1972 (Washington, DC: Government Printing Office, 1972), 7693.

20. Edward Hunter, "Analysis of Jane Fonda Activities in North Vietnam," *Hearings Before the Committee on Internal Security*, House of Representatives, 92nd Cong., 2nd Sess., September 19 and 25, 1972 (Washington, DC: Government Printing Office, 1972), 7581–602.

21. "H.R. 16742," *Hearings Before the Committee on Internal Security*, House of Representatives, 92nd Cong., 2nd Sess., September 19 and 25, 1972 (Washington, DC: Government Printing Office): 7606–7.

22. Ungar, "U.S. Won't Prosecute Jane Fonda."

23. Mary McGrory, "Wings of Doves Remain Unclipped," *Washington Evening Star*, October 3, 1972. Passage of the bill required a two-thirds majority and it fell short: 229 to 141.

24. "Why Famous Actress Became a Peace Activist," *Philadelphia Sunday Bulletin*, October 1, 1972.

25. Ungar, "U.S. Won't Prosecute Jane Fonda." Fletcher Thompson was defeated by Sam Nunn in the fall elections in Georgia, and he returned to his law practice.

26. U.S. Department of Justice memorandum, October 6, 1972.

27. FBI files, Acting Director, FBI to SAC, Los Angeles (9-4932), October 21, 1972; *Los Angeles Times*, August 11, 1972. Fonda's public relations agent Steven Jaffe turned over to the FBI stacks of hostile and threatening letters that she received over the next months. FBI files indicate that no action was taken.

28. Stuart S. Taylor Jr., "To Punish Actress, Out with Her Tongue," *Baltimore Sun*, March 7, 1973, 15; Edward Walsh, "Jane Fonda Likened to Arab Terrorist; Md. Legislators Snicker," *Washington Post*, March 7, 1972, C2.

29. "Notes on People," *New York Times*, April 6, 1973, 37.

30. Cited in Leroy F. Aarons, "Jane Fonda: Looking Back with Understanding," *Washington Post*, July 29, 1973, K1.

31. "A Clear Case of Overt Treason," editorial, *Arizona Republic*, July 25, 1972.

32. Brady Black, "The Justice of Public Opinion," *Cincinnati Enquirer*, July 31, 1972; C.L. Dancey, "Jane Fonda, Fanatic," *Peoria Journal Star*, October 20, 1972; "Un-Plain Jane's Solutions to Practically Everything," editorial, *Miami Herald*, November 18, 1970; Goodman Ace, "Top of My Head," *Saturday Review*, June 5, 1971.

33. Milton Viorst, *Washington Star-News*, November 11, 1974, A13.

34. "Letters to the Editor," *Washington Evening Star*, August 12, 1972.

35. See Fred Graham, "Officials Chagrined by 'Lawyer' for Hoffa in P.O.W. Discussion," *New York Times*, September 12, 1972, 1; and Benjamin Welles, "Hoffa Lawyer Sought Deal on Trip," *New York Times*, September 12, 1972, 1.

36. "November 21, 1972, Statement by Tom Hayden, L.A. Press Club," Inter-

national Peace Campaign Papers, Box 5, Folder 25, State Historical Society of Wisconsin, Madison, WI (hereinafter IPC Papers).

37. "The Tour and the Resources," IPC Papers, Box 5, Folder 25.

38. People's Coalition for Peace and Justice, press release, May 30, 1972, DG-84, Box 3, Folder Coordinating Committee, Swarthmore College Peace Collection.

39. Ibid.

40. *Courier Express*, October 12, 1972; *Sacramento Bee*, November 2, 1972, B1.

41. "Fonda Decries Vietnam Situation," *Tufts University Observer*, October 20, 1972.

42. FBI files, W. Mark Felt, to SAC, Cincinnati, November 30, 1972.

43. Reverend Calvin Van Kirk Hoyt, "The Church's Involvement with the Society in Which She Must Live," October 1, 1972, IPC Papers, Box 4, Folder 8.

44. Telephone interview with Reverend Calvin Van Kirk Hoyt, September 13, 2004.

45. Ibid. See also Indochina Peace Campaign report, September 27, 1972, IPC Papers, Box 4, Folder 7.

46. November 10 and 11, 1972, at the University of Georgia, Athens, GA. The term "Hanoi Jane" turned up as early as July 26, 1972. See Reg Manning's editorial cartoon in the *Arizona Republic*, July 26, 1972, 6. Also see, for example, "Antiwar Stance Not Unpatriotic, Jane Fonda Declares," *St. Louis Globe*, October 17, 1972, 5.

6. COMING HOME: THE POLITICS OF PRISONER REPATRIATION

1. The study team was made up of thirteen people, including Alfred Hassler, FOR's executive director; civil rights activist Reverend James Lawson; Annalee Stewart and Elsie Schomer with the Women's International League for Peace and Freedom; Edwin Dahlberg, president of the National Council of Churches; Elmira Kendricks, president of the National Student Christian Federation; Jacob Weinstein, president of the Central Conference of American Rabbis; and Harold Bosley, dean of Duke Divinity School. They were joined in Vietnam by Pastor Martin Niemoeller and Andre Trocme. On the Phoenix program, see Douglas Valentine, *The Phoenix Program* (New York: William Morrow & Company, 1990).

2. See "U.S. Study Team on Religious and Political Freedom in Vietnam," *Congressional Record*, June 17, 1969. The State Department's response to the study team's findings offered no specific refutation, but attributed the gross conditions in the Saigon prisons to problems of "modernization" and "severe wartime pressure," combined with the fact that the legal system in Vietnam was based "more on the French Napoleonic Code" than on American law. See "Comments on Report of U.S. Study Team on Political and Religious Freedom in Viet Nam," Clergymen's Emergency Committee, FOR, Swarthmore College Peace Collection.

3. See "The Tiger Cages of Con Son," *Life*, July 17, 1970; and Holmes Brown and Don Luce, *Hostages of War: Saigon's Political Prisoners* (Washington, DC: Indochina Mobile Education Project, 1973). See also Don Luce and John Summer, *Vietnam—the Unheard Voices* (Ithaca, NY: Cornell University Press, 1969).

4. In 1965, two of the first American prisoners released early from Vietnamese POW camps had emerged to say they believed the war was wrong. The Army

placed both men under house arrest in Okinawa and threatened them with courts-martial. See George Smith, *P.O.W.: Two Years with the Vietcong* (Berkeley: Ramparts Press, 1971). Smith and his fellow prisoner Claude McClure were eventually discharged from the army in 1965. Smith spent the next years in the antiwar movement in the United States. For accounts of other early POW releases that the Pentagon mismanaged, see Mary Hershberger, *Traveling to Vietnam: American Peace Activists and the War* (Syracuse, NY: Syracuse University Press, 1998), 47–48, 142–43, 155–56, 161–65, 215–19.

5. See Seymour Hersh, "The P.O.W. Issue: A National Issue Is Born," *Dayton (OH) Journal-Herald*, February 13–18, 1971. Hersh's series also appeared in the *Chicago Sun-Times* and the *Cleveland Plain Dealer*, among other newspapers.

6. See Stephen Endicott and Edward Hagerman, *The United States and Biological Warfare: Secrets from the Early Cold War and Korea* (Bloomington: Indiana University Press, 1998), 155–85.

7. See Steven Roberts, "P.O.W.'s Felt Their Mission Was to Resist," *New York Times*, April 30, 1973, 1; and Steven Roberts, "Former P.O.W.'s Charge Torture by North Vietnam," *New York Times*, March 31, 1973, 4.

8. The POW memoirs include Jay Jensen, *Six Years in Hell* (Bountiful, OH: Horizon Publishers, 1974); Gerald Coffee, *Beyond Survival: Building on the Hard Times—a POW's Inspiring Story* (New York: G.P Putnam, 1990); Everett Alvarez Jr. and Anthony Pitch, *Chained Eagle* (New York: Donald Fine and Company, 1989); John M. McGrath, *Prisoner of War: Six Years in Hanoi* (Annapolis, MD: Naval Institute Press, 1975); Eugene B. McDaniel, *Before Honor: One Man's Spiritual Journal into the Darkness of a Communist Prison* (Philadelphia: A.J. Holman, 1975); Howard and Phyllis Rutledge, *In the Presence of Mine Enemies* (Old Tappan, NJ: Fleming H. Revell, 1973); Robinson Risner, *The Passing of the Night* (New York: Random House, 1973); John Dramesi, *Code of Honor* (New York: W.W. Norton, 1975); Zalin Grant, *Survivors* (New York: W.W. Norton, 1975); Larry Guarino, *A P.O.W.'s Story: 2801 Days in Hanoi* (New York: Ballantine Books, 1990); Geoffrey Norman, *Bouncing Back: How a Heroic Bank of POWs Survived Vietnam* (Boston: Houghton Mifflin, 1990); James Rowe, *Five Years to Freedom* (New York: Ballantine Books, 1991); Ernest Brace, *A Code to Keep* (New York: St. Martin's Press, 1988); Sam Johnson and Jan Winebrenner, *Captive Warriors: A Vietnam POW's Story* (College Station: Texas A & M University Press, 1992); Jim and Sybil Stockdale, *In Love and War* (Annapolis, MD: Naval Institute Press, 1984); Dave Carey, *The Ways We Choose: Lessons for Life from a POW's Experience* (Wilsonville, OR: BookPartners, 2000); Spike Nasmyth, *2355 Days: A POW's Story* (New York: Orion Books, 1991); Jeremiah Denton, *When Hell Was in Session* (New York: Reader's Digest Press, 1976); and Ben and Ann Purcell, *Love and Duty* (New York: St. Martin's, 1992). For a non-hard-line account of the POW experience, see James Daly, *A Hero's Welcome: The Conscience of Sergeant James Daly Versus the United States Army* (New York: Bobbs-Merrill Company, 1975). See also John Hubbell, *P.O.W.: The Definitive History of the American Prisoner-War Experience in Vietnam, 1964–1973* (New York: Reader's Digest Press, 1976); Stuart Rochester and Frederick Kiley, *Honor Bound: The History of American Prisoners of War in Southeast Asia, 1961–1973* (Washington, DC: Office of the Secretary of Defense, 1998); and Vernon Davis, *The Long Road*

Home: U.S. Prisoner of War Policy and Planning in Southeast Asia (Washington, DC: Office of the Secretary of Defense, 2000).

9. See Hershberger, *Traveling to Vietnam*, 169.

10. Steven Roberts, "Two Pilots, Two Wars," *New York Times Magazine*, June 10, 1973, 16.

11. Steven Roberts, "Ex-P.O.W.'s Say Ordeal Was Not in Vain," *New York Times*, February 24, 1973.

12. James Sterba, "Managing the P.O.W.'s: Military Public Relations Men Filter Prisoner Story in a Careful Program," *New York Times*, February 20, 1973, 3; Shana Alexander, "Prisoners of Peace," *Newsweek*, March 5, 1973, 32.

13. "Vietnam: The Other Prisoners," *Time*, March 19, 1973.

14. "Home at Last," *Newsweek*, February 26, 1973, 20. One American POW got to see some of the conditions under which the U.S.–backed government in Saigon held its prisoners. John McCain went to Saigon in 1974 and Saigon officials promised him that he could go anywhere he wanted. McCain asked for a tour of Con Son Island prison. The Saigon officials looked "as if someone had come up behind them and walloped them with a two-by-four," McCain told journalist Arnold Isaacs. There is no record of what part of the prison system he saw, but he told Isaacs that it "wasn't quite as grim as the North Vietnamese camps he had been held in—but grim enough." Isaacs said McCain sounded "guarded" when he came back from his guided tour. There wasn't enough space there for them to exercise, he said. Arnold Isaacs, "My Measure of the Man," *Washington Post*, January 9, 2000, B2. In the 1990s, John McCain, now a Republican senator from Arizona, worked with Democratic Senator John Kerry, Vietnam veteran and former leader of Vietnam Veterans Against the War, to restore diplomatic and trade relations between the United States and Vietnam. In 1994, thanks in large part to their work, the United States ended its punitive trade embargo against Vietnam, and restored diplomatic relations in 1995. Former POW Douglas "Pete" Peterson was named the first U.S. ambassador to Vietnam the following year.

15. *New York Times*, March 30, 1973.

16. Steven Roberts, "Two Pilots, Two Wars," *New York Times Magazine*, June 10, 1973, 16.

17. See *New York Times*, March 29, 1973, March 25, 1973, and March 11, 1973.

18. Stuart Rochester and Frederick Kiley, *Honor Bound: The History of American Prisoners of War in Southeast Asia, 1961–1973* (Washington, DC: Office of the Secretary of Defense, 1998), 181.

19. Steven Roberts, "The P.O.W.'s: Focus of Division," *New York Times*, March 3, 1973, 16.

20. Roberts, "Former P.O.W.'s Charge Torture by North Vietnam."

21. Roberts, "The P.O.W.'s: Focus of Division."

22. "POWs: The 'Peace Committee,'" *Newsweek*, April 2, 1973, 27. The hard-line officers were particularly outraged at Ramsey Clark who, when he visited the POWs in Hanoi, told them correctly that the Pentagon would not bring charges against any of them for calling for an end to the war. The threat of courts-martial had been the only threat that the hard-liners could wield over junior officers and enlisted men and Clark's information took that away. See Steven Roberts, "Antiwar

P.O.W.'s: A Different Mold Scarred by Their Combat Experiences," *New York Times*, July 15, 1973, 1; and Daly and Bergman, *A Hero's Welcome*, 232–33.

23. "Jane Fonda Grants Some POW Torture," *New York Times*, April 7, 1973, 11.

24. David Wesley Hoffman appeared on *NBC Evening News*, January 6, 1972; *CBS Evening News*, February 15, 1972; *ABC Evening News*, May 18, 1972; *NBC Evening News*, May 18, 1972; and *CBS Evening News*, May 18, 1972. He was photographed in Hanoi by George Wald on February 19, 1972, and by Father Paul Meyer in May 1972. In October 1972, he met with a delegation from the United States that included Reverend William Sloan Coffin.

25. *CBS Evening News*, Friday, April 13, 1973; *ABC Evening News*, April 13, 1973; *NBC Evening News*, April 13, 1973; "Ex-POW: Fonda Blind on Torture," *Washington Post*, April 13, 1973.

26. In preparation for this book, I asked Hoffman to discuss his 1973 charges. He declined to respond. Family members told me he had consistently refused to discuss them.

27. See Hershberger, *Traveling to Vietnam*, 215–19.

28. Norris Charles interview with Steve Jaffee, October 12, 1972, *Indochina Peace Campaign Report*, 1973.

29. Wald, along with Haldan Hartline of the United States and Ragnar Granit of Sweden, received the 1967 Nobel Prize in Physiology and Medicine for work on the chemistry of vision. Wald was an outspoken opponent of the war in Vietnam and landed on Richard Nixon's enemies list.

30. "Interviews in Hanoi with Two Captured American Pilots," Papers of George Wald, HUGFP 143, Box 46, Folder "POWs," Harvard University Archives.

31. Ibid.

32. *Santa Barbara News & Reviews*, June 15, 1973, 1.

33. "Before We Make Them Heroes," *Indochina Peace Campaign Report*, July 1973.

34. Letter from George Wald to William J. Fulbright, April 30, 1973, Papers of George Wald.

35. Letter from William P. Clements to George Wald, August 7, 1973, Papers of George Wald.

36. George Wald, "Did One POW Lie?" Papers of George Wald.

37. See "Before We Make Them Heroes."

38. *Los Angeles Times*, April 13, 1973.

39. Bernard Gwertzman, "A Torture Victim Asks Aid to Hanoi," *New York Times*, April 3, 1973, 5.

40. "POWs: The 'Peace Committee.'"

41. Gwertzman, "A Torture Victim Asks Aid to Hanoi. Manhard told reporters that after his capture in Hue during the 1968 Tet Offensive he had been "strung up" at first because he had refused to answer questions relating to the ongoing battle of Hue. But he had never been tortured after that, he said, during all his years in Hanoi.

42. Seymour Hersh, "Eight May Face Courts-Martial for Antiwar Roles as P.O.W.'s," *New York Times*, March 16, 1973, 1.

43. Seymour Hersh, "Pilot Recalls 'Bad Attitude' Made Him Suffer in Hanoi," *New York Times*, April 1, 1973, 1.

44. "Colonel's Change Denied by P.O.W.'s," *New York Times*, May 31, 1973, 11. See also *New York Times*, July 4, 1973, 22. The specific charge of "showing disrespect" that Guy cited was based on an incident in Hanoi when the eight POWs he later charged were going to wash dishes in the prison courtyard and passed a group of officers shaving there. Major Edward Leonard shouted out to the eight that they must "stop all forms of cooperation and collaboration with the enemy." According to Major Leonard, one of the men shouted back cynically, "Who is the enemy?" When Guy, who considered himself the senior officer in that particular camp, threatened the men by saying that the Pentagon would bring charges against them when they returned home, they rebuffed him, telling him they knew he had made similar statements on Radio Hanoi, calling for a negotiated rather than a military settlement to the war. After Guy filed charges against these POWs, some of them handed out transcripts of statements in which Guy acknowledged the heavy costs of the war for the Vietnamese. See Hubbell, *P.O.W.*, 575. See also Rochester and Kiley, *Honor Bound*, 561–63; and "POWs: The Peace Committee," *Newsweek*, April 2, 1973, 27.

45. Roberts, "Antiwar P.O.W.'s"; James Sterba, "P.O.W.'s Wife Says U.S. Killed Him," *New York Times*, June 29, 1973, 9.

46. Daly and Bergman, *A Hero's Welcome*, 259–60.

47. "U.S. Drops Changes," *New York Times*, September 27, 1973.

48. Roberts, "P.O.W.'s Felt Their Mission Was to Resist."

49. Ibid.

50. Ibid.; Seymour Hersh, "P.O.W. Recalls 'Pressure of Conscience,'" *New York Times*, April 2, 1973, 3. See also Roberts, "Anti-War P.O.W.'s"; and Seymour Hersh, "P.O.W.'s Maintained Discipline but Had Their Quarrels," *New York Times*, February 23, 1973, 1.

51. Hubbell, *P.O.W.*, 194–96.

52. *Washington Times*, April 3, 1989, cited in Rochester and Kiley, *Honor Bound*, 181. This story is repeated briefly in James Hirsch's *Two Souls Indivisible: The Friendship That Saved Two POWs in Vietnam* (New York: Houghton Mifflin, 2004), 122.

53. Thomas Moe, "Pure Torture," *Notre Dame Magazine*, Winter 1995–96. On the development and content of the torture stories, see Elliott Gruner, *Prisoners of Culture: Representing the Vietnam POW* (New Brunswick, NJ: Rutgers University Press, 1993), 171, 179; and Craig Howes, *Voices of the Vietnam POWs: Witnesses to Their Fight* (New York: Oxford University Press, 1993). Howes uses all the POW memoirs to show how the hard-liners, afraid of being greeted as traitors when they returned home, developed a collective account of torture while still in prison.

7. THE COMPLICATED LEGACIES OF FONDA'S ANTIWAR ACTIVISM

1. Carol Burke, *Camp All-American, Hanoi Jane, and the High-and-Tight* (Boston: Beacon Press, 2004), 186.

2. See Nora Sayre, "Film: Vietnam Lesson," *New York Times*, November 15, 1974, 32.

3. FBI files, memo from A.B. Fulton to W.R. Wannall, February 28, 1974.

4. See Jack Anderson, "When the FBI Calls, Everybody Talks," *Washington Post*, May 12, 1973, D21; and Edward Walsh and Philip McCombs, "Members of 'Enemies List' Cover Broad Spectrum," *Washington Post*, June 28, 1973, A11.

5. *Jane Fonda v. Richard Nixon, etc., et al.*, October 18, 1973.

6. "Jane Fonda Cites FBI Ploy on Her," *Washington Post*, December 17, 1975, A3.

7. FBI files, Director, FBI, "RE: *Jane Fonda v. Richard M. Nixon, etc., et al.*," February 12, 1974.

8. Kenneth Reich, "CIA Did Open Mail, Fonda Lawyer Says," *Los Angeles Times*, February 15, 1975.

9. "Judge Tells Huston to List Targets," *Washington Post*, July 24, 1974, A10.

10. Jack Anderson, "Jane Fonda Wins Bout with IRS," *Washington Post*, March 13, 1974, D19.

11. Frederick Tulsky, "FBI Settles Jane Fonda's Suit," *Los Angeles Herald-Examiner*, May 8, 1979, A7.

12. FBI files, memo from Leonard Weinglass to Jane Fonda, April 19, 1979.

13. Maxine Cheshire, "No More 'Mr. Tough Guy'?," *Washington Post*, February 7, 1974, C2.

14. "It Was Productive," *Washington Post*, February 8, 1974, B3.

15. Charles Colson, "Who's Afraid of Hanoi Jane?" *Christianity Today*, April 8, 1988, 64.

16. Indochina Peace Campaign Papers, Box 7, Folder 2, State Historical Society of Wisconsin, Madison, WI.

17. Despite its shortcomings, Hubbell's book unwittingly provides a window into how the hard-line POW torture narrative was developed in the camps by a few senior officers in early 1971. These senior officers who had been insisting that they had followed the Code of Conduct heard from more recent shoot-downs that the Pentagon was actually encouraging them not to follow the Code in captivity. The hard-line officers, Hubbell wrote, found that "it was difficult to avoid a sense of betrayal, a feeling that the Department of Defense and the services had broken faith with men who long had been fighting hard on the POW 'extension of the battlefield.'" They then put together a "lengthy oral POW history, each man contributing all that had happened to himself and what he knew had happened to others." The narrative that they constructed referred to events that they claimed had occurred earlier when they were living largely in isolation with no one to witness first-hand the events of torture they describe. According to Hubbell, these POWs now went to other POWs with whom they had shared larger prison quarters for a year and, for the first time, told them this newly woven POW narrative of past torture. "The history took several hours to relate," Hubbell continues, and the unsuspecting POWs who had known these men for months but who were now hearing these stories of torture from them for the first time, "were badly shaken by the revelations, seemed almost unable to grasp the magnitude of the brutality that was described to them or to understand why they had been treated so differently." By now, Hubbell says, "the old hands knew the United States to be riven with dissension over the war. They guessed that a lot of the new shoot-downs did not share the hardline attitude toward the war of most of the old POWs, that some, perhaps even many of them, opposed the war." The hard-liners "hoped that any new arrivals who opposed the war would be military

men enough to keep their opinions to themselves, at least until the war ended and they were free." See John Hubbell, *P.O.W.: The Definitive History of the American Prisoner-War Experience in Vietnam, 1964–1973* (New York: Reader's Digest Press, 1976), 577–85.

18. Ibid., 585.

19. For example, Gerald Coffee says that he heard Fonda call the POWs "war criminals" over his prison radio. The CIA transcripts never show Fonda using language like that, although Vietnamese announcers who broadcast news and commentary in English did, and the POWs in Hanoi regularly heard those broadcasts. See Gerald Coffee, *Beyond Survival: Building on the Hard Times—a POW's Inspiring Story* (New York: G.P. Putnam, 1990), 244.

20. Lionel Chetwynd also wrote and directed the television drama *DC 9/11: Time of Crisis*, which misleadingly portrays President George W. Bush as tough-talking, decisive, and confident from the first instant of the national tragedy on September 11, 2001.

21. Shortly after Chetwynd's film was released, the Pentagon commissioned a book purporting to "offer a comprehensive, balanced and authoritative account of what happened to the nearly eight hundred Americans captured in Southeast Asia." The book was written and later revised by Stuart Rochester and Frederick Kiley and called *Honor Bound: The History of American Prisoners of War in Southeast Asia, 1961–1973* (Washington, DC: Office of the Secretary of Defense, 1998). The book also follows Hubbell's "mis-lead" by focusing on the hard-line POWs. Inexplicably, even the jacket of *Honor Bound* is misleading. It shows what appears to be an actual American POW in Hanoi, severely emaciated and ill. But it is actually a photo of a realistic-looking, but fake, POW. The photo comes from a POW exhibit at the U.S. Capitol in June 1970, organized by Texas billionaire H. Ross Perot and displaying two life-size models of emaciated men purporting to be POWs in Hanoi. The book jacket notes that the photo comes from that exhibit, but does not reveal that the real-looking figure in the photo is not an American POW in Hanoi, but rather a picture of a model made and photographed in the United States. See "Exhibit to Stir Opinion on P.O.W.'s Open in Capitol," *New York Times*, June 5, 1970, 8.

22. See Guy Russo, "Work to Keep Fonda Out of City," Letters to the Editor, *Waterbury Republican*, November 12, 1987.

23. Richard Hanley, "Activists Give Fonda Support," *Waterbury Republican*, November 19, 1987, B1; D.H. Zackermna, "Jane Fonda Is Welcome Here," *Waterbury Republican*, November 25, 1987.

24. Elmer Noyer, "It's About Time Veterans Protested Jane Fonda," Letters to the Editor, *Waterbury Republican*, December 18, 1987.

25. Dominic Romano, "Veterans, Not Fonda, Deserve Support," Letters to the Editor, *Waterbury Republican*, November 27, 1987.

26. Richard Hanley, "Veterans Lambasting Jane Fonda," *Waterbury Republican*, December 5, 1987, 1; Richard Hanley, "Russo Regrets Jane 'Should Be Executed' Remark," *Waterbury Republican*, April 24, 1988.

27. Klan members later complained that the anti-Fonda veterans turned against them after the *Waterbury Republican* publicized their involvement. See "Klan Says It Has Taken Part in Anti-Fonda Protests," *Waterbury Republican*, July 20, 1988.

28. Jack Goldberg, "Aldermen Reject Anti-Fonda Stand," *Waterbury Republican*, April 26, 1988, 1.

29. "Poll Shows Support for Fonda Film," *Waterbury Republican*, January 15, 1988, A13; ibid.

30. Jane Fonda, interview with Barbara Walters, *ABC News 20/20*, June 17, 1988; Michael Rapoport and Clark Johnson, "Veterans Anxious to See Interview," *Waterbury Republican*, June 17, 1988.

31. Dominic Bencivenga, "Fonda Meets Viet Vets in Naugatuck," *Waterbury Republican*, June 19, 1988. On the astonishingly common motif of crazed Vietnam veterans, see Jerry Lembcke, *The Spitting Image: Myth, Memory, and the Legacy of Vietnam* (New York: New York University Press, 1998), 101–26, 157–58.

32. Bill Leukhardt, "Vets Say Fonda Apology Not Convincing Enough," *Waterbury Republican*, June 18, 1988.

33. Burke, *Camp All-American, Hanoi Jane, and the High-and-Tight*, 179–80.

34. For a discussion of these movies, see Lembcke, *The Spitting Image*, 144–82.

35. *Los Angeles Times*, December 21, 1972; *New York Times*, December 27, 1972, 52.

36. For more of these stories, see Burke, *Camp All-American, Hanoi Jane, and the High-and-Tight*. Web searches regularly turn up vitriol about Fonda.

37. See Jeff Jacoby, "When Jane Fonda Spoke Out," *Boston Globe*, June 17, 1999; and Jonah Goldberg, "Plain Jane," *National Review*, July 27, 1999.

38. Telephone conversation with Jerry Lembcke, October 15, 2003. When he was released, Benge appeared on *ABC Evening News* on April 3, 1973, and claimed that, when Fonda came to Hanoi in 1972, a North Vietnamese official had confided in him that they were suspicious of Fonda and thought that she might be a CIA agent.

39. See, for example, Bruce Herschensohn, "When Night Fell in Indochina," http://www.nixonlibrary.org/Vietnam_Article.shtml. Herschensohn also falsely claimed, on the Nixon Library Web site, to be an "Academy Award–winning documentary filmmaker." The claim was removed in December 2004, after the Nixon Library was contacted about it. Herschensohn did work for the Motion Pictures and Television division of the U.S. Information Agency in 1969, when the agency received an Oscar in the Short Documentary category for *Czechoslovakia, 1968*.

40. See, for example, Henry Mark Holzer and Erika Holzer, *"Aid and Comfort": Jane Fonda in North Vietnam* (Jefferson, NC: McFarland & Company), 75n34, 75nn36–37, 91nn2–4, 91nn6–7, 91n9, 91n11.The Holzers use their attacks on Fonda to offer a ringing defense of the conduct of the war in Vietnam, asserting that bombing dikes is an acceptable way for the United States to wage war. In a touch of irony, Henry Holzer, who condemns the Vietnamese for mistreating American POWs, defends torture when the United States does it. "We can handle Mohammad with kid gloves, or we can jolt him with jumper cables," Holzer wrote after September 11, 2001. Holzer says that "torture, of whatever kind and no matter how brutal, in defense of human rights and legitimate self-preservation, is not only not immoral, it is a moral imperative." See Henry Mark Holzer, "Should the U.S. Torture al-Qaida Prisoners? Yes: National Security, Saving Lives Outweigh All Other Concerns," *Columbus Dispatch*, March 15, 2003. Henry Holzer has also written *The*

Layman's Guide to Tax Evasion and advocates a constitutional amendment "to eliminate government's power over the monetary system."

41. See, for example, Mary Hershberger, "Mobilizing Women, Anticipating Abolition: The Struggle Against Indian Removal in the 1830s," *Journal of American History* (June 1999): 15–40; Kathryn Kish Sklar and Helen Baker, "How Did Women Peace Activists Respond to 'Red Scare' Attacks During the 1920s?," in *Women and Social Movements in the United States, 1775–2001*, http://womhist.binghamton.edu.

42. Johanna Neuman, "Lessons of 'Hanoi Jane' Leads Antiwar Forces to Shift Strategy," *Los Angeles Times*, March 19, 2003. A *New York Times* article on March 2, 2003, just before the U.S. invasion of Iraq, urged celebrities to remain silent, asserting that when Jane Fonda spoke out against the war in Vietnam and traveled to Hanoi, she "deeply offended even those who opposed the war." The record does not support this and one reader wrote in to say that "actually, many of us in the 1970s were fortified by her outspokenness against the war in Vietnam." See Rick Lyman, "Celebrities Become Pundits at Their Own Risk," Week in Review, *New York Times*, March 2, 2003; and Wendy Perron, "Jane Fonda's Voice," Letters to the Editor, *New York Times*, March 9, 2003.

43. Fred Lawrence Guiles, *Jane Fonda: The Actress in Her Time* (New York: Doubleday & Company, 1982), 187.

44. See Ann Oldenburg, "When Stars Speak, Do We Listen?," *USA Today*, February 9, 2005.

45. See, for example, *St. Louis Globe-Democrat*, October 17, 1972, 5A.

46. Emmett Watson, "News," *Seattle Post-Intelligencer*, January 10, 1975.

47. See Robert McNamara with Brian VanDeMark, *In Retrospect: The Tragedy and Lessons of Vietnam* (New York: Random House, 1995), xvi.

INDEX